CZECHOSLOVAKIA
AT THE CROSSROADS
OF EUROPEAN HISTORY

CZECHOSLOVAKIA AT THE CROSSROADS OF EUROPEAN HISTORY

JAROSLAV KREJČÍ

Professor Emeritus, University of Lancaster

I B TAURIS & CO LTD
Publishers
London · New York

Published in 1990 by
I B Tauris & Co Ltd
110 Gloucester Avenue
London NW1 8JA

175 Fifth Avenue
New York
NY 10010

In the United States distributed by
St Martin's Press
175 Fifth Avenue
New York
NY 10010

In Canada distributed by
McClelland & Stewart
481 University Avenue
Suite 900
Toronto
Ontario M5G 2E9

In all other countries distributed by
I B Tauris & Co Ltd, London

British Library Cataloguing in Publication Data
Krejčí, Jaroslav
    Czechoslovakia at the crossroads of European history.
    1. Czechoslovakia. Political events, history
    T. Title
    943.7

ISBN 1-85043-194-9

Printed and bound in Great Britain by
Redwood Press Limited, Melksham, Wiltshire

To those who brought us the promise of a new freedom

Contents

Preface   ix
Acknowledgements   xiii

1   Embracing Christianity
    West or East? Focus on Moravia   1
    Closer or looser links? Focus on Bohemia   8

2   From the periphery to the core
    Between pope and emperor. Fiefs and estates   15
    In the Gothic sunshine. The hidden rifts   22

3   Reforming Christianity
    The Chalice versus the Cross. The path of
        revolution   32
    The Chalice side by side with the Cross. The
        warring estates   51

4   Failure to sustain the impetus
    Impulses from abroad. North or south?   64
    The ban on pluralism. Escape to baroque   84

5   Rebirth of national consciousness
    New breezes from the West. The school of
        adolescence   93
    The stops and starts ahead. Land and
        language   105

6   From ethnic to political nation
    School for parliamentarianism. National or
        class consciousness?   118
    Trying out democracy. A nation state or state
        of nationalities?   137

7   In the frontline again
    Between Swastika and Red Star. Disturbing
        the balance   156
    East or West? The new rebirth   172
    Miracle of the 'velvet revolution'   195

Summary   203

Chronology and Map   209
Notes   213
Select Bibliography   236
Index   247

Preface

This is not a conventional history book. It is rather an account of the course of events which mark the crucial points in the development of two closely related nations, the Czechs and the Slovaks, from the time when they made their first appearance in history up to the present day. This development is viewed from the vantage point of changing ideas and confrontations which followed these changes; the latter highlight turning points in Czech and Slovak history. These issues often merely reflected the development of European civilization at large, but sometimes the Czechs themselves took the initiative and the outcome was a bitter conflict. Whether imported or homemade, however, such problems and confrontations always cut across national boundaries.

Three times in their history the Czechs stood in the forefront of a conflagration stretching far beyond their borders; their country became the place of opposition against mightier forces in their surroundings. In 1420 the Hussite Czechs challenged the Roman Church and the Roman Empire with their Reform Manifesto (the Four Articles of Prague) and withstood the assaults of several crusades; the confrontation resulted in a compromise. In 1618, the Protestant Bohemian estates revolted against their Catholic king and thus unleashed the Thirty Years War in Europe; this led to their eventual defeat. In 1938 the Czechs, this time in participation with the Slovaks, after having faithfully held their island of pluralism and democracy against the fascist and semifascist tide in the neighbouring countries, sacrificed themselves only to postpone World War II by one year; the result was that they were squeezed between two great expansive powers (Nazi Germany and Soviet Russia) with ideologies and ways of life totally alien to the Western European traditions of which, until then, Czechoslovakia had been a part. Whilst in the sequence of these turning points the military involvement of the Czechs decreased, the resulting conflagration grew ever larger, both in scope and intensity.

Meanwhile the Czechs experienced, whether as a result of their defiance in 1618 or of their lack of defiance in 1938, two periods of submission marked by little glory but much suffering. Until November 1989, the Czechs and Slovaks were experiencing a new period of submission as a result of World War II and the communist *coup d'état* in 1948. They attempted to emancipate themselves from it in 1968 but the result was a military assault by Big Brother, equipped with unprecedented striking power, and the enforced return to submission. As the playwright, Václav Havel – one of those who have refused to submit – put it, people in that situation live their life 'outside history'; they cannot participate in it and what they learn about it is a concocted Orwellian-type picture.

Yet the Czechs proved not only to be daring challengers but also enduring survivors. After all the ruptures and periods of gloom in their history, they always rediscovered their more glorious past and managed to re-establish a dynamic link with it. The events of the end of 1989 have shown this most dramatically.

Their next of kin, the Slovaks, were given little opportunity to play a conspicuous role in European history. Their first common venture with the Czechs, or, to put it more accurately, the common venture of their respective forefathers, in the Great Moravian realm broke down more than a thousand years earlier. From then until 1918, the Slovaks were incorporated into the multiethnic Hungarian kingdom. In the nineteenth century, however, its dominant nationality, the Magyars, wanted to turn that kingdom into the Magyar nation state. Yet World War I put an end to that prospect and opened a new chapter in Slovak history – the cohabitation with the Czechs in a common state, the Czechoslovak Republic. Further development was partly affected by the problems resulting from that cohabitation.

Despite renewed attempts, after 1968, on the part of the communist establishment to convert the Czechs and Slovaks to the Marxist-Leninist creed, their endeavour completely failed. Without any experience of their liberal, democratic past, the young generation proved emphatically that it prefers the values of a free society based on human rights to a totalitarian society based on coercion. The nationwide protest of late November 1989, that was started by the students and which eventually united all generations and social groups of the population, was an unmistakable witness of the rebirth of the nation. Whatever may yet happen in the short run, 'the move into history again' is irreversible.

The aim of this book is to give a synoptic view of the predicament of the two related nations. The focus on changes and conflicts of ideas is intended to make more sense of the sequence of events than a general narrative could provide. Also the ubiquitous struggle for power and wealth tended to be articulated in the form of some kind of ideology.

The conflicting ideologies were sometimes more, sometimes less, outspoken. In the short run, their focus shifted according to the particular circumstances; in the long run, their tenor depended on the spirit of the epoch. At the time when Christianity dominated all intellectual and cultural life, secular considerations played second fiddle in the world of ideas. This, however does not mean that ideological stances on secular matters had less impact on the real course of events. On the contrary, they often won the upper hand: the more lofty religious principles were bound to serve as a pretext for worldly interests.

Our narrative takes into account all issues that entered the forefront of public affairs in the country, irrespective of whether they were cultural, political or economic in nature: it follows the headlines of history.

Acknowledgements

The author, who was born in 1916 in Moravia, close to the Slovak border, lived for the first fifty years of the Czechoslovak Republic (1918–68) in that country, most of the time in Prague. The dramatic events of that epoch left a deep imprint on his mind and feelings. What has been going on in Czechoslovakia since he left the country in 1968 is for him a matter of grave concern. It has never occurred to him that the present could be understood without reference to the past; the passions of the latter often re-emerge in a new, more or less distorted form. This book is also intended to elucidate this tendency in the two nations' history.

In writing this book the author received a great deal of help. Most of it came from his wife whose unwavering assistance and relentless questioning and consultation during all stages of the work in progress was essential for the completion of the book. The author is also very much indebted to his old friend and colleague Professor Zdeněk R. Dittrich of the University of Utrecht; he kindly read the whole manuscript and made most valuable comments and suggestions. Needless to say, responsibility for whatever has been written rests entirely with the author. Furthermore the author would like to extend his gratitude to Dr Philip Payne and Mr Alan Airth of the University of Lancaster for having read and edited the manuscript with great care and understanding. Mr Zdeněk Mastník from London was most helpful in supplying books which were not obtainable elsewhere. The assistance of the University Library at Lancaster University (its inter-library loan service headed by Miss T. J. Goodman) deserves special recognition. Special thanks are due to Miss Patricia Kitchen for her exemplary typing.

The author is happy to acknowledge the contribution which the Leverhulme Fellowship made towards the writing of this book.

1

Embracing Christianity

West or East? Focus on Moravia

Like so many other peoples in Europe, the Czechs emerged as a nation from the *Völkerwanderung*, the great migration of peoples which started towards the close of the fourth century AD, reached its peak in the fifth, and petered out by the close of the tenth. Although there is little certainty about the timing and direction of their migratory movements, it is generally assumed that the Slavs, who later became known as the Czechs and Slovaks, arrived in their present homelands from the east, probably from what is now Belorussia and western Ukraine. This happened in the course of the sixth century AD, i.e., at the time when the Germanic tribes had already invaded and destroyed the West Roman Empire.

   The arrival of the Slavic tribes in the territory of present-day Czechoslovakia went unnoticed by the European annalists until the time when the Frankish Empire began to expand into the area towards the close of the eighth century.[1] The first Slavs in what is now Czechoslovakia, Slavs whose name and organized polity is reported in the Eastern Frankish chronicles, were the Moravians.[2] Settling in the middle of the country around the river Morava, a tributary of the Danube from the north, the Moravians were probably the first to get in touch with what was then the civilized part of Europe: the ancient Roman provinces to the south of the

Danube which at that time were already the bulwarks of the developing Christian civilization. At that time Christianity still had the potential to unite Western and Eastern Europe in one civilization.

Thus the Moravians were the first to respond to the foreign challenge which came to them from three different quarters of Christendom: from the Eastern Frankish Empire with its main ecclesiastical outpost in the archbishopric of Salzburg and bishoprics of Passau and Regensburg; from the Holy See in Rome with its intermediary in the Patriarchate in Aquileia; and from the Byzantine Empire with its emperor and patriarch in Constantinople.

Although in religious terms the issue was between the Latin liturgy, on the one hand, and the Slavic liturgy on the other, in political terms it was a three-cornered contest. The Bavarian and other German clergy were primarily interested in extending their jurisdiction into the Slavic lands; they took the Latin rite and liturgy for granted. The papacy wanted to preserve and strengthen its leading position in all Christian lands and, in order to win over opponents, was ready, in certain circumstances, to make minor concessions. The Patriarch of Constantinople wanted to be considered as the equal of the pope and as such to be the guardian of orthodoxy which, in his view, was being menaced by innovations introduced in the Latin Church. The acceptance of the liturgy in languages other than the three canonic languages (Hebrew, Greek and Latin) was a bargaining point for the Byzantine Church. The Byzantine emperor was also jealous of his Frankish competitor's position as the secular head of the Christian world; yet the Islamic pressure from the south did not allow him much room for manoeuvre. This was the general scene for a major confrontation.

Missionaries from the West were the first to set foot in the Moravian and adjacent Slavic lands. The Frankish-Moravian alliance against the Avars, which in AD 796 led to the destruction of their khaganate in Pannonia, created a favourable climate for the spread of Christianity from that quarter.[3] Missionaries were coming not only from Germany but also from Italy, Ireland and Scotland. The Hiberno-Scottish seem to have been amongst the first.[4] Many were able to speak the Slavic language (in those days less differentiated than at the present time) for which they created the necessary ecclesiastical terminology which was translated, so it seems, mainly from old High German.

The old pagan habits were, however, slow to disappear. As we shall see later with respect to subsequent developments, the struggle with paganism lasted for several centuries before Christian beliefs and practices were wholeheartedly embraced by the population. Thus, under the aforementioned three-cornered contest, for which trustworthy historiographic evidence is available, there was yet another, less reported but in its substance much graver contest, namely between Christianity and paganism, a contest which concerned the basic attitudes to life and rules of interpersonal behaviour; in short, it was an ideological contest *par excellence*.

The elimination of Avar danger was a boost for what then became Great Moravia, a term first used in a Byzantine document.[5] Reopening of commercial routes to the south improved the economic position of Moravians and their first known ruler, Mojmír, was able to expand his domains. But the absence of the Avar danger also offered the Franks more opportunity to interfere in Moravian affairs; the interference was made easier by the fact that the clergy in Moravia was under the jurisdiction of the Bavarian episcopate; Mojmír's successor, Rostislav, decided to build up his own ecclesiastical hierarchy. When Rome was not willing to comply with his wishes, Rostislav asked for a bishop in Constantinople (AD 862). As the controversy between the Patriarch Photius and the Holy See concerning the ritual and dogmatic differences between Constantinople and Rome was not yet in full swing, the Emperor Michael III hesitated to send a high-ranking Church dignitary to Moravia; instead he dispatched two learned men, who were brothers, with excellent knowledge of Slavic language: the philosopher and diplomat Constantine (better known under his later monastic name Cyrillus) and the abbot Methodius, experienced in law and administration.

The main task of the two brothers was the education of the Moravian clergy. They came with a ready-made elaborated script suited to the Slavic languages, known as 'Glagolitsa' ('Cyrillic' is the name for another variant of the Slavic script that began to be used in Bulgaria) which, however, they had to modify slightly on the spot. It seems that the two 'apostles', as they were later sometimes hailed, acknowledged that Christianity in Moravia was of the Western type, but they maintained that Moravians deserved the liturgy, and indeed the whole Bible, in their own language. The ruler of Pannonia, Kocel, who had earlier become a vassal of the Eastern Frankish emperor, also favoured the educational work of the two brothers from Macedonia.

The Holy See became apprehensive and summoned the two brothers to Rome. Pope Hadrian II was quick to grasp the opportunity to kill two birds with one stone: first, by sanctioning the Slavic liturgy, to win the advantage in the contest with his rival in Constantinople (the sanctioning was formally proclaimed in the bull 'Gloria in Excelsis Deo' of 869); secondly, in establishing an episcopal hierarchy in the Danubian basin, to subject that area to direct supervision by the Holy See, without the intermediary of the Bavarian episcopate who were too much under the political influence of the Eastern Frankish emperors. The opportunity to do this was offered by the metropolitan see in Syrmium (in present-day Vojvodina), vacant from the time of Avar's rule. Since Constantine-Cyrillus, who had been envisaged for that post had died in the meantime, it was Methodius who was consecrated Archbishop of Syrmium in 869.

The resounding victory of the Slavic orientation in the Moravian Church, however, was a *casus belli* within the Western camp and eventually also within Moravia itself, where the Bavarian clergy had already become firmly established. Rostislav's nephew, Svatopluk, deserted Rostislav and recognized Frankish sovereignty. In the struggle between the two Moravians, Svatopluk captured Rostislav and extradited him to the Franks. They were quick to exploit the situation and occupied Moravia. At that time Archbishop Methodius was also captured by the Bishop of Passau and imprisoned in a Bavarian monastery. In response, a great uprising broke out in Moravia. The situation for the Franks became so grave that Svatopluk, who meanwhile had been arrested by his Frankish masters, was entrusted with the leadership of the campaign against the revolting Moravians; but once he came to Moravia, he changed sides, won the struggle and, in 871, became the uncontested ruler of Great Moravia.

While Svatopluk satisfied his personal ambition, the three-cornered contest between the institutionalized interests went on unabated. In 873, at the intercession of Pope John VIII, a compromise was reached and Methodius was released from prison; but the Slavic liturgy was banned by the same pontiff. However, the struggle between the supporters of the two liturgies continued. In 879, Svatopluk asked the pope for help in resolving the issue. Methodius was again summoned to Rome; the result was a compromise formally proclaimed in the bull 'Industriae Tuae' of 880, a compromise which contained the seed of even greater discord.

On the one hand, Methodius' theological stance was found unexceptional and he was confirmed as archbishop (this time of Moravia and not of Syrmium) and the Slavic liturgy was again condoned. But, on the other hand, the gospel was first to be read in Latin and only then in translation; furthermore, a staunch supporter of the Latin liturgy, an ethnic German called Wiching, was consecrated Bishop of Nitra, whilst Svatopluk and his dignitaries were entitled to attend services according to the Latin rite. Thus, in fact, a dual ecclesiastical power was established in Great Moravia. As Wiching could count on the support of the court, he in fact became the head of what may be described as the Latin faction in the Moravian Church. In a way, this compromise foreshadowed a similar compromise which, 554 years later, the Council of Basle struck with the Hussite reformers in Bohemia. We shall return to this in due course.

Constantine (Cyrillus) and Methodius undertook a heavy burden of civilizing work. In many respects they waged an uphill struggle. The penal code with the help of which Methodius tried to promote law, order and justice in Svatopluk's realm has been appreciated as a masterpiece of Christian legislation. The Byzantine paradigm, the *Ecloga*, renowned for its cruelty, acquired in Constantine's translation and adaptation a substantially humanized form. The stress on higher ethical standards, especially in the upper strata of society, however, was a political liability for Methodius. The Latin clergy showed more understanding for human weaknesses, especially in sexual relationships, and therefore found more support among influential people.[6]

Disappointed with the lack of papal protection against the obstructions of the lenient clergy and against the intrigues of his suffragan Wiching (the papal bull 'Pastoralis Sollicitudinis' of 881 contained only a soothing message), Methodius accepted the invitation to Constantinople, where Photius, after an enforced break of almost ten years, was then in the second term of his patriarchal office. Methodius' visit to Constantinople brought the full endorsement of the Slavic liturgy. It seems that Methodius also conformed to Photius' position in the only dogmatic question which divided the Byzantine from the Roman Church: the rejection of the words *filioque* (words meaning that the Holy Ghost is not only from the Father but also from the Son), added to the Nicene Creed at a regional synod in Visigothic Spain and widely accepted in the Latin Church.

After his return, Methodius undertook a fatal step which toppled the frustrating compromise; he excommunicated his Latin opponent, Wiching, and his followers, and cursed them as heretics. But this step could be effective only as long as Methodius was alive. Approximately a year after his death (in 885) Pope Stephen VI rehabilitated Wiching, helped him to his former post, and in addition banned the Slavic liturgy. Svatopluk, in his turn, expelled the Slavic clergy and thus deprived the Slavic liturgy of those who practised it; the expellees found refuge amongst the Bulgarians who at that time had a common frontier with Svatopluk's domain.

The fate of the Slavic liturgy was finally sealed by a new migratory wave of nomadic peoples from the Asian steppes – the Magyars – who at the beginning of the tenth century invaded and occupied Pannonia and thus separated the Moravian from the Bulgarian settlements. Any contact between the Moravian and Bulgarian Churches was interrupted. Furthermore, the Great Moravian realm itself fell victim to the assault of the Magyars during the first half of the tenth century.[7]

Thus the life of the first political and cultural formation in Czech and Slovak history came to an abrupt end. The contest for cultural orientation, which marked the second part of the history of Great Moravia, was part of a wider confrontation. Both sides in it, the Latins as well as the Byzantines, hesitated for a long time before they took the decisive step towards definite schism; this occurred only three centuries later, in 1054, and even after that attempts were made to bring about reconciliation. The involvement of Great Moravia took place in a particularly acute stage in the unfolding conflict, in fact at the height of its first round. This was perhaps the reason why popes were so cautious and so willing to strike a compromise in matters which would not impinge upon their claims for primacy in the whole of Christendom. If the Holy See eventually abandoned its policy of compromise, it was to a large extent because the Moravian ruler himself opted for the West.

The two main axes alongside which the Czechs, and to a large extent the Slovaks also, were to cope with further challenges of a more than domestic dimension were, on the one hand, Roman Catholicism with its canonic law, Latin rites and liturgy stretching all over Western Europe, and on the other hand, contact both friendly and bellicose with successive political formations of the Germanic nation which claimed leadership in that part of Europe.

Closer or looser links? Focus on Bohemia

The destruction of Moravian power which in the last quarter of the ninth century comprised most of what is now Czechoslovakia (not only present Moravia and western Slovakia but also the whole of Bohemia acknowledged Svatopluk's sovereignty) brought to an end the prospect of the development of one Slavic nation in that area. The centre of gravity of political integration shifted to the west, to Bohemia. The territory which is now Slovakia (at that time occasionally referred to as 'Lower Moravia') was incorporated by the beginning of the eleventh century into the newly formed and newly Christianized Hungarian kingdom. Known as Upper Hungary, or simply Upper Land, Slovakia then continued to be part of the Hungarian kingdom until 1918, when modern Czechoslovakia was created.

The territory which remained formed the homeland for the Czech nation; this continued to be divided by geographic conditions into two lands with close political links: Moravia, in the basin of the river Morava which flows to the Danube and thus to the Black Sea, and Bohemia, whose rivers flow to the Elbe and thus to the North Sea. Intermittently the Bohemian rulers raised claims on yet another land with neat geographical demarcations, namely, Silesia, where the river Odra with its tributaries flows to the Baltic Sea. Silesia was inhabited by the Slavic tribes who later – except where they were absorbed by Germanic immigrants – acquired either a Polish or, in the uppermost section of the Odra basin (which for the greater part of its history was attached to Moravia), a Czech national consciousness.

This was the geographic scenario in which the ethnic Czechs, identified by a common language, developed their political framework. Of the three geographic units, only Bohemia and Moravia (the latter reduced in size by comparison with the earlier period) were welded together, for the larger part of their history, by a dynastic link which eventually acquired the character of an unwritten constitution. Moravia (with a population about half the size of Bohemia) was the junior partner, a domain for lateral branches or the Crown princes of the Bohemian dynasty. Silesia, split into a host of principalities, depended more often than not on Polish rulers in the earlier phase of her history. From the mid-fourteenth century it was attached to the Bohemian Crown, but in the mid-eighteenth century its greater part was lost to Prussia. After World War I, Poland acquired a small part of it; as a result of World War II, the remaining Prussian part of Silesia, purged of most of its German population, was returned to Poland. Thus two areas of East-Central Europe, Silesia and Slovakia, experienced a millenial cycle: the former has been reincorporated into Poland, the latter reunited with the Czechs.

But it is not our intention to discuss the geopolitical history of the lands which eventually became present-day Czechoslovakia. As we saw above, the focus is on the position of the Czechs and Slovaks within the wider context of European history in general, and on the involvement of these two ethnic groups in the turning-points of European civilization in particular.[8]

The Moravian story was the first venture of the as yet undifferentiated Czechs and Slovaks, a venture which exceeded their parochial orbit; the ancestors of these nations became implicated in an international confrontation. With respect to what was to happen later, this involvement was to have still graver consequences. As time went by, the Greek Orthodox, ethnically Graeco-Slavic East, differed from the Latin, Romance-Germanic West not only in the type of Christianity it practised but also, much more pertinently, in a different configuration of cultural, political and economic attitudes and arrangements of social life. With the turn of the first millenium of the Christian era, the existence of two Christian civilizations within the geographic confines of Europe began to acquire more distinct features; but it was only with the consequences of the Latin Crusaders' assault on Constantinople and with the Tartar occupation of the Ukraine in the thirteenth century that the two related Christian civilizations took different courses of socio-cultural development.[9]

The memory of the two saints and brothers, Constantine (Cyrillus) and Methodius, however, was spared the consequences of the schism. They are revered in both Churches. Cyrillus did not live long enough to see the worst, but Methodius, who survived him by sixteen years, passed away at the time when passions were already running high. Given his record he was, to borrow Dittrich's words, 'the last mighty personality of the not yet divided ecumene'. The present Pope, John Paul I, rightly appreciated Methodius' place between the Christian East and West, when he made of the tradition initiated by the two brothers one of the cornerstones of his ecumenical policy.

When the Moravian leaders opted for what was to become the Western version of European Christianity, they made a decision of cardinal importance. Similarly, like the Poles to the north and the Slovenes and Croats to the south, the Czechs and Slovaks were incorporated into the Latin

Christian civilization. They became member nations of a socio-cultural configuration which, in contrast to its Eastern Greek and Russian counterparts, showed a much greater willingness to change, a much greater readiness to undergo transformation and to embark on untrodden paths. With their decision, the Moravian forefathers of the Czechs and Slovaks opted for a more dynamic course of history than would have been the case if they had followed the Byzantine example.

The transfer of the centre of gravity in political development from Moravia to Bohemia increased the relevance of the proximity to Germany for the further development of the Czech nation. For the Czechs there was less scope for choice; this fact was reflected in the diminishing interest of the pope in Czech matters. Great Moravia, for example, had got her archbishopric with one suffragan in 880, whereas Bohemia was to wait for her bishopric until 973 and for her archbishopric until 1344. Moravia, which had lost her metropolitan see with the collapse of her empire, is reported to have had a bishop, probably with a missionary role, a few years after the bishopric had been founded in Prague. The regular bishopric in Moravia was founded in the city of Olomouc in 1063. Although this comparison says nothing about the respective quality of religious life, the facts show the difference in the political importance of the two Czech states on an international scale.

Once the issue between Eastern and Western Christianity had been resolved and the Czechs of Bohemia had taken the lead, it was the struggle with paganism – still widespread – which became the main preoccupation of both the ecclesiastical and secular leadership. The Slavic liturgy seems to have coexisted for many years with the Latin liturgy, though the former was always less prominent and gradually diminished. (It is supposed to have come to Bohemia with Duke Bořivoj, the Přemyslid, who, according to one, albeit doubtful, source, was baptized by Methodius

on his visit to Moravia *c.* 880).[10] The issue was not between
these two versions of Christian practice but between Christianity in general, on the one hand, and pagan tradition on
the other.

Almost two centuries passed before pagan habits were
eliminated from Czech society. Their perseverance was
manifested in several ways. Documents mention especially
the reluctance to conform to Church marriage and burial
and also the frequency of murder and slaughter in resolving
the tribal and inter-family feuds as evidence of the pagan
traditions.[11] In this respect, however, we have to bear in
mind that, as in other parts of Europe, the civilizing process
was very slow and that the clergy themselves often behaved,
and resolved feuds, in a way incompatible with the canonic
law. On the whole, however, as elsewhere in Europe, it was
the Church which represented the main civilizing agent in
terms of establishing a more humanitarian and refined way
of life.

The encounter between Christianity and paganism was
resolved in two ways. Either the pagan rulers received baptism of their own accord and the folk were supposed to follow suit, or they yielded to force of arms. The Czech rulers,
both in Moravia and Bohemia, chose the former way; they
soon became anxious to join those who were spreading
Christianity by the sword. Thus the Czechs and Slovaks
spared themselves much bloodshed and suffering; above all
they avoided the prospect of extermination, the fate which
was met by the Polabic Slavs and the Baltic Pruz.

This does not mean, however, that weapons were idle in
the Czech lands: there the struggle between advancing
Christianity and receding paganism was not always a
straightforward one. The main feud was between those
whom we might term the 'zealots' and the reluctant or lukewarm converts. The former were more likely to make friends
abroad and also to accept the suzerainty of the German
kings over the Bohemian duke. The lukewarm converts

favoured Christianity as far as it helped them in their aspirations to power; as rulers by the grace of God, supported by the teaching and administrative skill of the loyal clergy, their position *vis-à-vis* their subjects was considerably strengthened. Otherwise, however, they were keen to preserve their customary freedom of action irrespective of what the Church required of them; also, they did not welcome foreign tutelage.[12]

The wife of the first Christian ruler of Bohemia, Ludmila, and her grandson Wenceslas (the good King Wenceslas of the English carol) were the most prominent zealots who fell victim to assassination by their next of kin. Wenceslas (in Czech Václav the Saint) was murdered by his own brother Boleslav, and his courtiers, too, were slaughtered (the precise date has been a matter of dispute; recent opinion favours the year 935).[13] What followed was a protracted war between Boleslav (Boleslav I, the Cruel) and the German King (later Roman Emperor) Otto I. Its outcome was Boleslav's recognition in 950 of the German king's suzerainty and acceptance of the duty to pay him a tribute.

Boleslav II (the Pious) preferred to reduce his dependence on the German king through ecclesiastical organization. In 973 he succeeded in obtaining a bishopric in Prague; by the same act, as a special favour, Bohemia was withdrawn from the jurisdiction of the Bavarian Metropolitan (whose proximity made it easier to interfere in her matters) and was subordinated to the geographically distant archbishopric in Mainz.

The first Bishop of Prague was, like the members of the ruling German dynasty, from Saxony; the second was the learned Adalbert (Vojtěch in Czech). Adalbert was a member of a noble Bohemian family, the Slavnikids, whose prestige was second only to that of the ruling Přemyslid dynasty. Because of rivalry between the two clans, he was *persona non grata* at the Přemyslid court in Prague but, being a personal friend of Otto I (Roman Emperor from 962), was somewhat protected by the Emperor's influence at court. Adalbert's missionary zeal, however, led him to spend more time abroad than in his diocese. When Boleslav II eventually decided to settle his accounts with the Slavnikids and exploited the absence of their foremost fighters by slaughtering their clan *en masse* in 995, Adalbert was out of the country.[14] His martyrdom came when preaching the gospel to the pagan Pruz.

The martyrs, Duchess Ludmila, Duke Wenceslas and Bishop Adalbert (Vojtěch) became the first Czech native saints.[15] In that sense they may be considered the heroes of the winning side in the less conspicuous ideological confrontation between Christianity and pagan tradition on Czech soil. They joined Constantine (Cyrillus) and Methodius the saints of the earlier, more explicit ideological encounter which, as the fate of the main actors indicates, did not take such a brutish form.

In Czech iconography, St Cyrillus and St Methodius are venerated as the Slavic apostles in general and as Moravia's patrons in particular. St Wenceslas became patron of Bohemia, protector of the whole Czech nation. Irrespective of what he really stood for (it seems that he was a rather cosmopolitan and pacifist type of Christian) tradition made of St Wenceslas a dedicated patriot whose help was solicited in any national difficulty; with prayers for his intercession on their lips the Czechs took up arms, whether for war or revolution. As so often in history, the legend overcame the reality. But did not the native saint who, by his early canonization and widespread popularity, helped the Czechs to be received as equals in the family of Christian nations, deserve such embellishment?

2

From the periphery to the core

Between pope and emperor. Fiefs and estates

Once the Czechs definitely entered the orbit of Latin Christian civilization they became part of its life. Although at first the Czechs' participation was only peripheral, their intimate relationship with what for several centuries was to become the key political power in Western Europe, the Holy Roman Empire, gradually pulled them into its internal conflicts. It was, above all, its contest with the other power, the papacy, which because of its spiritual dimension and wider territorial coverage was still more formidable, that gave the Czech partnership in Western European history a more than merely parochial dimension. The pull was so strong that, eventually, after four centuries of expansion, Bohemia entered the forefront of Western European development.

On their march from the periphery to the core of Western European civilization the Czechs became increasingly involved in the main ideological issues which shook its inner life. However, at that time, the Czechs merely took sides or, since they were themselves divided, were pulled into the whirlpool of confrontations; they did not take their own stand nor did they move to the front of the stage. Often needs and interests, personal quests for power, wealth and glory, overshadowed other considerations. We have to bear in mind that, at that time, there was no demarcation

between private and public sphere in matters of government and ownership, and that the number of people
involved in such matters was very limited.

In the tenth century AD, when the Czechs contributed
their first martyrs to the Christian hagiography, there was
throughout Europe little scope for a quiet life in Christian
virtues. On the one hand, Western Europe suffered a threefold shock of foreign invasion: the Muslim Saracens from
the south, the Vikings from the north and the Magyars from
the east. This was a challenge that had to be met with
intensified missionary activity, which eventually brought
positive results at least with the Scandinavians and the
Magyars.

Nevertheless, there was a feeling that Christian representatives and Christian institutions were not living and
functioning as they should. One of the causes was the inadequate education and commitment of the clergy. Another
was the over-dependence of the clergy on secular rulers and
landowners who, in return for their endowments of
churches, arrogated to themselves the right to appoint the
clergy and to share their emoluments. Realization of the
failure of the Christian and Christianized authorities to live
according to the principles of their religion provoked a
widespread desire for moral reform. Its birthplace was the
Romance/German borderland stretching from the Cham-
pagne to the lower valley of the Rhône, with the most
renowned centre in the Burgundian monastery of Cluny
which, from c. 950 to 1050, provided the impetus for a
ramified and widespread monastic movement of religious
purification.

The reformers maintained that in order to keep the
Church aloof from moral decay it should be as far as possible freed from entanglement with the secular authorities.
The clear-cut separation of the spiritual from the temporal
power was to be accompanied by full emancipation, the
complete independence of the former from the latter. This

at least was the theory, but in a situation where many churches were built as private endowments and, at the same time, the temporal administration was largely manned by ecclesiastics, often in the highest ranks of the hierarchy, the separation of the spheres and the emancipation of the Church was a difficult task indeed.

The front which eventually crystallized was not clear-cut. For personal reasons, many Church dignitaries aligned themselves with their lay bosses or partners, while many temporal nobles joined the camp of reform. The contest eventually resulted in the struggle between the emperor and the pope which has become known as the investiture con-test, i.e., the contest for the right to appoint or elect Church dignitaries and to provide them with the appropriate endowments. Although the first round of this contest ended with a compromise in 1212 (the Concordat of Worms) and its second round ended in the mid-thirteenth century with the collapse of the lay contestant in the struggle, the Staufen dynasty, the basic contradiction never died out in the public life of Western Europe. With varying degrees of intensity and in different conceptualizations, the coexist-ence of the two powers, or to use the expression of that time, of the 'two swords', the spiritual and the temporal, remained an intriguing, but at the same time also stimulat-ing, feature of European history until modern times.

For the Duke of Bohemia, the struggle for the investiture provided an opportunity to exact favourable conditions in his relationship with the Empire, more advantageous than could have resulted from the not infrequent military con-frontations between him and the German/Roman king and emperor who began to assume, at least in some respects, the position of his feudal suzerain. We shall touch upon this point later. The emperor was ready to reward with favours any timely and effective help he received. On three occa-sions Bohemian assistance was rewarded with promotion of the Duke of Bohemia to the rank of a king, a status shared

by nobody else in the German part of the Empire at that
time. The first promotion occurred in 1085, when the King/
Emperor Henry IV bestowed the royal title on the Bohemian
Duke Vratislav II, albeit only as a personal privilege. The
second elevation to the dignity of a king, this time as
a hereditary promotion, was awarded by Frederic I,
Barbarossa, to Vladislav II in 1158. But in the confusion
after Vladislav's resignation and later death (1173 and 1174
respectively) the royal title fell into disuse. Only the third
elevation to royal status, awarded to Přemysl Otakar I by
the Golden Bull of Frederic II in 1212 during his desperate
fight with Pope Innocent III, had lasting consequences.
(The subsequent establishment of primogeniture in the
inheritance of kingship instead of seniority in the wider
Přemyslid family was particularly helpful in this connection.) At the same time Frederic II awarded the Bohemian
king the title of the 'Highest Cup-bearer' which implied the
right to be one of the electors of the king/emperor.

Significantly, it was only at this time that the direct consequences of the investiture contest reached the outlying
countries. In 1215, on his return from the Lateran Council,
where the reform policy of the Church had been outlined in
the most uncompromising form, Andrew, Bishop of Prague,
who until then had been a faithful servant of the king, challenged the status quo. The ensuing bitter struggle ended in
1221 with a massive exemption of the Church from the jurisdiction of temporal authorities. The Bishop of Prague
ceased to be appointed by the king and from then on he was
to be elected by the episcopal chapter. In addition to this,
the laity's interference in other ecclesiastical appointments
and participation in proceeds from tithes was either abolished or reduced. Bishops' subjects were exempted from
taxation of land, the corvée, and also, in part, from secular
jurisdiction. Jurisdiction in marital matters was ceded completely to the Church.

The Church/State relationship was, however, not the only

issue at stake. No less important was the formation of lay institutions of the realm which, up to that time, had not yet taken on firm contours. Perhaps we may best describe the original type of polity as a *patrimonium* of the king or duke, a *patrimonium* which, to some extent and in various ways, was shared by the nobility.[1]

If we look more closely at the social structure of the Middle Ages we can discern several elements and lines of development. First, there were the residues of the past: the surviving remnants of the Roman times. Their main stronghold, albeit in greatly modified form, was the Roman Catholic Church. Its hierarchical organization and legal concepts were the main agents of systematic organization in the often turbulent and confusing circumstances of social life. The other remnants of antiquity were the cities which, especially in Italy and some other Romance areas, continued to uphold elements of urban culture. They represented scattered islands of more intensely integrated societies. On the other hand, there were many vital residues of the Germanic, Celtic and Slavic tribes which, as a response to Christianization, only gradually began to forge their own type of organization.

The organizing process moved on two lines: one may be described as 'contractual', which led to feudal relations, and the other as 'associational', which brought together people of equal status who then began to act as one established order or estate of peers. Social orders as institutionalized tiers of social stratification had appeared already at the time of the Roman Empire; in those conditions, however, they could not achieve the level of self-assertion and autonomy which was reached with the estates in Western Europe during the age of Christianity. Here the orders mostly developed from new, endogenous roots. A prototype of the feudal relationship also can be traced to the Roman age: the peasant colonate which in some respects paved the way for the medieval and later forms of bondage. But the classic feudal relationship, in the upper tier of society, emerged as a response to the repeated collapse of central authority under the impact of various waves of *Völkerwanderung* and, above all, under the blows of foreign invasions in the ninth and tenth centuries (the so-called Dark Ages). The more or less contractual nature of Western European feudalism bears witness to the enormous difficulties in bringing greater order and discipline into a society which was dominated by unruly warriors.

To Bohemia and Moravia feudal organization came from the West, from the Frankish and later German/Roman Empire. As such they affected mainly the external relations of Bohemia and, only to a small extent, the relation of the ruler with his nobility and to some extent also with Church dignitaries. Most important was the relationship of Bohemia with other lands of the Bohemian Crown – the Bohemian fiefs, such as Moravia (for the most time divided in three fiefs, the margravate, with its seat in Brno, the bishopric with its seat in Olomouc and the Moravian part of Silesia, the Duchy of Opava), various principalities in Silesia, and the more or less temporarily acquired fiefs in neighbouring areas. As earlier under the dukes, Bohemia herself continued to be viewed as a fief of the German/Roman king; royal succession in Bohemia was hereditary in the Přemyslid family. But the King of Bohemia was, in this respect, in a stronger position than the duke used to be; by the bull of 1212 he also became one of the seven electors of the German/Roman king.[2]

However, within the country, the feudal law did not make as much headway as did the associational line of development, especially in the uppermost tier of society. By the mid-thirteenth century three lay estates crystallized: upper nobility (the barons), lower nobility (the gentry) and royal boroughs. We shall examine this development in subsequent chapters. On the other hand, in the lower tiers of society, namely the country folk who in the Bohemian lands, as in most parts of Europe, did not constitute an estate of free-men, contractual relationships similar to those in the upper tier began to spread as well.

This happened as a result of the massive peasant immigration from West Germany and the Low Countries in the course of the eleventh, twelfth and thirteenth centuries. In contrast to older custom with these settlers, a new, regulated type of peasant holding appeared in the Czech lands. It was known as *emphyteusis* or holding according to the German (or Dutch or Flemish) law or 'pre-emption' (sometimes called 'hereditary') law. According to this 'law' the landlord who preserved his 'direct ownership' (*dominium directum*) ceded, in return for a sum of money as pre-emption (*arha*), the inheritable right to use the land (*dominium utile*). It was a kind of tenancy with the right to sell the tenure, with the consent of the direct owner, to someone else. The tenant was required to pay a rent, as a rule in money (the use of money increased with the development of cities), but often also in work (corvée). Gradually, with the growth of a money economy, many of the old holdings of the native population were also adapted to the new law. Thus the traditional type of bondage gave way to a much looser form of dependence.

As the medieval annalists had little interest in economic matters, and legal documents are scarce and inconsistent in terminology, it is difficult to assess with any reasonable certainty the real situation – the effective social status of peasantry in the earliest period of Czech history. What apparently mattered for them most was, first, the extent of payments to landlords whether in kind, work, or money; second, personal security which was endangered not only by foreign but also by domestic civil wars (nobility of all ranks used to settle their mutual accounts at the expense of their subjects); the right to free movement came a poor third. Bondage, as we are able to deduce from documents of that epoch, seems to have been primarily a matter of circumstances (being a farmer, belonging to the village community, and last but not least, it was simply the custom) rather than any explicit law.[3] As will be shown, bondage by law was introduced into the Bohemian lands much later.

In the Gothic sunshine. The hidden rifts

Altogether five Přemyslids enjoyed the royal status acquired in 1212. Ninety-four years after the Golden Bull in which the inheritable kingship was bestowed by Emperor Frederic II on Přemysl Otakar I, the last male Přemyslid, the young Wenceslas III, who had reigned for only one year, was assassinated when he was about to start a campaign to re-establish his father's claim to the Polish Crown.

Before that happened, the Přemyslids tried in several ways to enlarge their hereditary domains. They were quite well positioned for the kind of power game in which wars, weddings, and bribes were the main avenues of success. New settlers, extended cultivated area, rising towns, enlarged production of crafts, growing commerce and, last but not least, the opening up of rich silver deposits, increased the bargaining and striking power of the King of Bohemia.

Yet the growing political aspirations of the higher aristocracy hampered the Přemyslids' progress. In 1247, the rebellious barons were able to win over to their side the Crown Prince (Přemsyl Otakar II) against his father, the King (Wenceslas I); in the years 1276–8 they helped to bring down Přemysl Otakar himself. The expansionist attempts were directed first mainly towards the south, to the Austrian lands, and then to the east where the Silesian principalities and eventually the whole of Poland were at stake; attempts were also made on the Crown of Hungary. The expansion to the south was checked (first by diplomatic and then by military means) by the German/Roman King Rudolf Habsburg; he was the first to bring that princely family from obscurity to the stage of history where they were later to flourish until the early twentieth century. Nor was the expansion to the east particularly successful; as far as Silesia was concerned, its main phase was yet to come.

What from our point of view is more important, however, is the definite formation of estates (orders) which from then on for about four hundred years were to constitute an additional dualism to that of Church and State: namely the dualism of royalty and country. The latter contrast also led to the clash of concepts, which in various forms and intensity occurred in all Western European countries. In essence it was the strife between two concepts of polity: patrimonial monarchy versus polity of estates, a strife in which personal interests and ideological justification were inseparably intertwined. In Bohemia, the important step towards unfolding this duel was made in the 1250s when the nobles began to run the supreme court of the land which was authorized to adjudicate all issues concerning the nobility. In fact this development created a triple judiciary because it added one more avenue of the law to the royal and ecclesiastical jurisdiction.

From then on the king had to beware two institutionalized powers beside his own. Not only the Church but also the magnates created a legitimate sphere for their interests. When Wenceslas II (1288–1304) wanted to provide his prosperous country with higher education on the line of the universities in the Romance countries, the barons wrecked the project. They realized that it was legal studies in Italy and France which provided ambitious monarchs with arguments and expertise for a more centralized rule. The ideological battle between the legists supporting the claims of secular monarchs for unlimited sovereignty, on the one hand, and the theologians claiming the supremacy for the pope, on the other hand, which was in full swing in the thirteenth century, made the Czech barons apprehensive.

In such a situation the king's strength was based increas-

ingly on the royal boroughs. Above all the capital Prague
and the silver mining town of Kutná Hora represented particular economic strength. That the boroughs themselves
had to enforce law and order in their precincts, as was
explicitly postulated in Wenceslas II's Charter of 1285, led
them to develop their own institutions for upholding the
economic order and enforcing the law. Thus, as the Czech
historian/sociologist Jan Slavík pointed out, the urban institutions created a model for the later development of
monarchical administration, a model in which the principle
of common wealth rather than private or group interest
began to assert itself.[4]

This process, however, took time, and in the wealthiest
cities there was scope for at least some burghers to attempt
to take part in the power game of aristocracy. The following
episode may illustrate both this point and another impend-
ing issue of that time. In 1309, in the unsettled situation
after the death of the last Přemyslid three years earlier, the
richest families of the commercial patriciate in Prague and
Kutná Hora, wanting to acquire the status of nobility, took
some hostages from among the nobles; their intention was
that the nobles' daughters should marry their own sons. But
as soon as the hostages were released the whole concession
was revoked, the patricians (who had quarrelled amongst
themselves in the meantime) were defeated and had to
leave the country. As they were of German origin and
employed German mercenaries, the struggle acquired an
inter-ethnic flavour which was promptly echoed by the anti-
German riots of the Czech population in the capital. Thus,
the Czech-German antagonism which until then had been
the subject of occasional polemics or pamphlets, became an
issue of urgent concern.

In 1310 the Bohemian magnates, in their quest for a pres-
tigious but weak monarchy, undertook a bold step. They
negotiated with the Emperor Henry VII of Luxembourg the
enfeoffment of his son John with the Bohemian Crown.

John of Luxembourg did not disappoint their expectations. He confirmed the barons' hereditary rights to their possessions (the idea that they were fiefs of the king was increasingly becoming a fiction), accepted their conditions on taxes, and then set out on an adventurous life of a king errant spending most of his time on campaigns abroad. There he died while helping the French King Phillip VI against his English rival Edward III in the battle at Crécy in 1346.

But John's son, Charles, was of quite different mettle. Being a diligent and effective administrator and a strong-willed pragmatist he began to look after the lands of his inheritance as soon as his chivalrous father, as *rex otiosus*, entrusted him with their regency: Moravia in 1334 and the whole kingdom in 1337. Married to a French princess and enjoying a good and friendly relationship with Pope Clement VI (his former tutor in Paris) Charles was at an advantage at the Holy See which was then in Avignon and completely dominated by the French. Thus in 1344 the Prague bishopric was elevated to archbishopric and a new bishopric was founded in East Bohemia. The year 1346 brought a quick succession of events. In July, Charles was elected, as Charles IV, the German/Roman king. In August, he took over the Bohemian Crown from his dead father. In January 1347, Pope Clement VI consented to the foundation of a fully fledged university in Prague, the first university beyond the Alps and the Rhine. In April 1348, Charles founded and endowed this university; it was to cater for four nations: the Czechs, the Poles, the Saxons and the Bavarians. This time the magnates did not dare to offer opposition. At the same time, Charles founded the New City of Prague; this more than doubled the extent of the city which became a twofold capital: for Bohemia and for the Empire.

Intense cultural activity unfolded; the golden era of Gothic in the Bohemian lands was set in train. The French impulse was felt particularly powerfully; Gothic architectural monuments and Gothic arts are still an impressive visual reminder of the Czech accession to the core of Western European culture. With this cultural blossoming came economic growth. Public order and royal preference for *laissez-faire* bolstered domestic and international commerce. Measures were taken to make the transit trade routes run through Bohemia and Moravia. Both these countries, especially Bohemia, were also less affected by the great epidemic ('Black Death') of 1348–50 than other West European countries, a fact which significantly contributed to their relative weight in the European context.

Charles's reign was also the golden age for the Church, if not (to the same extent) for Christian piety. Especially impressive were the number of Church institutions and the splendour of their appearance; in religious life there was apparently more exuberance than genuine piety. The latter often found refuge in popular heresies to which, however, the Church authorities showed no mercy; Charles gave the Inquisition his full support. The first archbishop, Ernest of Pardubice, was aware of the disadvantages of the Church basking in wealth and glory: he took measures to supervise the conduct of clergy whose life was to be freed from worldly influences as far as possible; towards the end of his career he invited to Prague, with the king's consent, the popular puritanical preacher, Conrad Waldhauser from Austria.

However, the many commitments which now involved Prague in European politics (and Charles IV often needed to bestow Church benefices on men for diplomatic rather than religious reasons) did not leave enough scope for ethical concern. Charles IV himself seems to have been mainly concerned with the devotional aspects of religiousity. Apart from building churches, he was renowned as a passionate collector of relics which he then allocated to various churches in Bohemia and Moravia and thus promoted the splendour and also the financial side-effects of their cult. There can be little doubt that Charles IV was a profoundly Christian believer (he also composed various homilies); but his twofold royal vocation required of him much diplomatic skill and manoeuvring which could not be overly burdened with moral scruples. But who has ever combined sainthood with great statesmanship? It is sufficient to say that Charles was not an impetuous, insensitive man as were so many of his peers. Preferring negotiations to wars and knowing how to exploit the issues of economic competition and commercial rivalry, he was also fortunate to be in a position to negotiate for himself four advantageous marriages (his three earlier marriages ended with the natural deaths of each wife); each marriage brought him a new territory or pacification of a former foe.

Charles's prudence was also the main reason why he decided to undertake the coronation journey only in 1355; he dragged out the decision for so long despite many exhortations from those who wanted a strong personality to bring order to Italy where disorder was chronic. Neither the passionate plea of Cola di Rienzi nor the flowery encouragement of Petrarch, nor indeed the pragmatic proposition of Venice could speed up his journey to Rome. Charles was well aware of the disaster which had beset his predecessors on similar occasions when they dared to enter, even with a strong military force (any other manner was out of the question), unruly and bitterly divided Italy. When Charles eventually decided to go to Rome, it was after long and tedious diplomatic preparations but nevertheless with a considerable army. Having received the crown from the pope's legate (in the circumstances the pope's continuous presence in Avignon seemed to be unavoidable) he immediately returned home; a fact which only exposed him to bitter reproaches from Italian patriots dreaming about the renaissance of Roman imperial power; but he also excited some hostile reactions on the part of his former friends. The Italian Renaissance was a rich source of inspiration in philosophy, arts and ways of life; in this respect the Renaissance was rather too successful; it undermined the religious morality of quite a few Church dignitaries. There was, however, no place in it for a revival of the imperial glory of Rome.[5]

Charles could well forget about Italy. His transalpine domains created enough problems. In Germany more order was badly needed with respect to the succession of the kings/emperors designate. After long and tedious negotiations Charles succeeded in codifying election rules (the Golden Bull of 1356). For the Czechs, two points were of particular relevance: the position of electors (the King of Bohemia was one of them) was strengthened and as 'pillars of the Empire' they were directed to be conversant with, in addition to Latin, the Italian and Czech languages.

The codification programme in Bohemia was more ambitious. The whole complex of power within the kingdom was to be regulated and the position of the king reaffirmed. Yet the draft of the Maiestas Carolina was resolutely rejected by the barons. Charles had explicitly to renounce the whole project and to confirm the validity of established custom. He managed to put through only a few, more or less theoretical, decrees dealing with the juridical protection of the subject population.

Charles was more successful in strengthening the links between the lateral lands (Moravia and especially the newly acquired Silesia and Lusatia) and the Bohemian Crown, and in securing the German Crown for his oldest son, the future King of Bohemia, Wenceslas IV (1378–1419). The other successions also proceeded according to Charles's testament: all of the four sons (by various wives) who survived him were well provided for (the dynastic acquisitions in Germany, such as Brandenburg and other wedding arrangements, proved most useful in this respect), but none of them was able to cope with the situation which then developed.

Above all, the state of affairs in the Empire proved beyond the powers of Wenceslas, who lacked the determination, the skill and the patience of his father. Wenceslas gave up the coronation journey to Rome, entrusted the care of Italy to his energetic cousin Jobst, the Margrave of Moravia, and eventually, in 1400, saw himself deposed as the German king; it was fully ten years later that this position was recovered for his half-brother Sigismund who was then already Margrave of Brandenburg, and thus one of the electors, and, in addition, the King of Hungary.

What was to happen in Bohemia proved even worse for Wenceslas IV. The king's preference for lower nobility (with whom he felt more at ease in his wordly pleasures) alienated the magnates. There was also much litigious ground with the archbishop into whose field of jurisdiction the king liked to intrude.[6] On two occasions a group of the barons, with the help of two members of the dynasty, Jobst and Sigismund respectively, took the king into captivity and forced him to change domestic policy.

However, the feuding of the king (with the magnates on the one hand, and with the archbishop, the ascetic John of Jenstein on the other), was eventually overshadowed by cracks in the very structure of society as a whole. The undercurrent of discontent with the state of the society in general and of the Church in particular proved to be more dangerous than the old rivalries. Although attempts were made to improve the moral standard of Church representatives (the archbishops Ernest of Pardubice and then John of Jenstein made significant efforts to this effect) the distress was too great for them to contain. Its roots were in the structure of the Church itself.

The Luxembourg dynasty ascended the Bohemian throne at the time when the claim of the pope to supremacy in Latin Christendom reached its climax. The most dramatic expression of this claim, embodied in Boniface VIII's papal bull Unam Sanctam of 1302, evoked an uproar. In 1306 Pope

Clement V had to declare it invalid in France and three years later he himself had to move to Avignon which he then made his seat instead of Rome. Clement V was the pope with whom Emperor Charles IV entered into a multifaceted and intriguing relationship of give and take. The Czech historian, Josef Šusta, in a succinct analysis of the complex situation, described this cooperation as a 'condominate of the Crown and the Holy See over ecclesiastical life'.[7] The contemporary English humanist William Ockham, in his turn, branded Charles a 'popish king'.[8]

There were many causes for discontent. The most intriguing was the distribution of ecclesiastical offices. Too often they were awarded on the basis of political considerations, family ties or bribes. Nepotism and simony were widely held as the main vices of the Church administration. Accumulation of prebends and the absenteeism of those in charge was also bitterly criticized.

One of the causes of the moral crisis was seen in the transfer of the Holy See to Avignon. But it was not only the pressure of the French king and of the French cardinals which kept the pope in Avignon. Rome was in those days so riven by internal feuds and bloody strife that the attempt of Pope Gregory XI to return there had to be abandoned. When eventually in 1378 (the year of Charles IV's death) the majority of cardinals who gathered in Rome elected as pope an Italian bishop willing to stay in the Holy City, the Roman mob, ignorant of the favourable vote which had already been taken, invaded the conclave in order to enforce the decision. The French cardinals used this event as a pretext for declaring the election invalid and elected another pope who then returned to Avignon.

This was the start of the great schism of dual papacy which was to last until 1415. Now it was up to the secular rulers to decide whom they wanted to have as the legitimate pope. France, Spain, southern Italy and Scotland opted for Avignon, others supported Rome. Wenceslas IV followed his father's preference and put the weight of the Empire behind Rome. No wonder that the Roman pope was then careful not to upset Wenceslas by supporting the Archbishop of Prague against royal encroachments.

With the schism the situation worsened enormously. The quest for reform took various lines. Within the Church there was a call for a general council to take over the leading position in the Church. Outside the Church, various heretic movements known already from earlier times found a new justification for turning their back on the official Church. On both sides, within and without the Church, there was a quest for more piety, a piety often marked with mysticism and asceticism. In the midst of all these streams, supporters of the lay power could now argue with good reason that the pope had forfeited his claim to supremacy and that the temporal authorities had to intervene.

Although theoretical supporters of this idea cropped up in many countries, the greatest headway in this direction was made in two of them: England and Bohemia. The contact between these two countries became closer when, in 1381, the English King Richard II married Anna, a daughter of Emperor Charles IV. Tradition has it that Anna of Bohemia brought to England the use of pins and Central European fashions. The young Czechs who came to study in Oxford brought back something much less innocent: the books of John Wyclif.

3

Reforming Christianity

The Chalice versus the Cross. The path of revolution

The contact with England brought to Bohemia ideas which found fertile ground there. Yet there was a significant difference between the intellectual atmosphere in the two countries. In Bohemia the quest for rectification of the Church was pursued more by the moralists/preachers than by the scholars as was the case in England. The spiritual climate in Bohemia showed more affinity with that in the Netherlands, from where – parallel to the contact established by the Luxembourg dynasty – some Beghards and Beguines and other pieist features of the *Devotio Moderna* made themselves at home in the Bohemian lands. But whichever path had been chosen, those who trod it did not escape the apprehensive watch of the Church authorities. Conrad Waldhauser had to justify the zeal with which he censured the clergy; his fiery and dauntless successor Jan Milič of Kroměříž had to travel to Avignon to defend himself against the accusation of heresy. Although he cleared himself of the charge, his pupils continued to be harassed by the domestic Church authorities.

Scholars who did not preach or write in the Czech language were also not safe from the Church's suspicions. The most prominent of them, Matthew of Janov, was no less critical of the Church than Milič; like him, Matthew was convinced that the Church had become dominated by the

Antichrist whose reign has been foretold as preceding the second glorious coming of Christ. Although Matthew did not avoid the temptation to identify the Antichrist with one particular person in the Church (Pope Clement VI in Avignon) he eventually looked for the Antichrist in the complex of all abuses and vices in the contemporary Church. Matthew looked for the gist of Christ's message and criterion of truth in the Bible and not in any personal authority. Like Milič, Matthew saw the most effective remedy for all kinds of shortcomings in frequent attendance of good sermons and daily acceptance of Holy Communion.

It would be out of place to mention in this context all those who took part in the ramified reform movement before its main personality and martyr, John Hus, appeared on the stage. One name only has to be added, Thomas of Štítné, a country layman who, in close contact with the reformers in Prague, started to systematically cultivate philosophy and theology in the Czech language. There were many more who joined him in this venture but only with John Hus did the use of the Czech language become widespread in discussing religious issues.

John Hus was a typical product of his epoch: a genuine believer, a dedicated preacher and moralist; he did not hesitate to stand up for his convictions against any authority. His concern was primarily with the ethical rebirth of Church life and only secondarily did he become involved in theological arguments. In this respect he was strongly influenced by Wyclif but did not adopt his views unreservedly. In the turbulent circumstances he sometimes used Wyclif's arguments for their moral implications without pondering too much their theological pitfalls.[1]

There were many theological and philosophical issues which were then hotly debated among the scholars, but three interconnected theses can be considered the crux of the matter: first, that the true Church is not a visible institution with pope, bishops, monks, parsons, etc., but rather an invisible entity comprised of all those, past, present and future, who were predestined for salvation, including the predestined laity but excluding the 'foreknown' for damnation clergymen; second, that the final arbiter in all religious issues is the Bible; third, that nobody in a state of mortal sin has true lordship over other creatures according to God.

Although, in theory, the principle of 'no lordship in mortal sin' was applied both to ecclesiastical and to secular authorities, its theological nature and the circumstances in which it was proclaimed were a greater threat to the power of the Church than to that of temporal rulers. Strangely enough, the latter were even supposed to discipline the unworthy clergy.

To these three basically theoretical but in fact inflammable theses was added a fourth which was at the same time of practical and symbolic value: the request to dispense the Holy Communion in both kinds (bread and wine) to everybody, and not only to the clergy. The instigator, Jacobellus de Misa (Jakoubek of Stříbro) also included children amongst those entitled to participate in this dispensation.

From the outset, the struggle became a very complex one. Several practical issues were intertwined; frequent changes of sides and position made it still more complicated. The basic positions were as follows: what the king wanted primarily was calm; then he wished to recover that earlier constitutional prerogative which strengthened his stance *vis-à-vis* the Church authorities, who were themselves bitterly divided. From the Pisan Council in 1409 which intended to end the papal schism there were in fact three incumbents for the office of pope; it was up to the ecclesiastical and lay authorities in individual countries to make a choice; thus there was scope for additional conflicts.

The main preoccupation of the Archbishop of Prague, however, was the waning discipline in the Church. In principle he favoured moral reform but reprobated any widespread critisism of clerical abuses. He was also concerned

with heresy and apart from its suppression outside the
Church, was sensitive to accusations of weakness with
regard to the spread of Wyclif's ideas.

The university dons were divided on various lines. First
there was a philosophical dispute between the 'nominalists'
and 'realists', concerning the understanding of general concepts, the 'universalia'. Nominalists maintained that they
have no substantial reality in themselves but are merely
names invented to describe particular phenomena, whereas
realists maintained that 'universalia' do indeed have objec-
tive reality. Then there was a division between those who
favoured and those who did not favour reform. Apart from
that there was a growing rivalry between the Germans and
the Czechs who in comparison with the three other nations
in the university administration were in a minority. (It is also
worth noting that the Polish students were mostly German-
speaking Silesians.) The intertwining of these rivalries
assumed the following shape: German masters – with a few
notable exceptions – joined the nominalist camp led by the
University of Paris, whilst most Czech masters opted for the
realist school, whose main protagonists were in the University
of Oxford. For the nominalists the Church was compounded
of its visible representatives. For them the misbehaviour of
individual representatives did not invalidate the institution.
For the realists the spread of unholy practices cast a
shadow on the institutions themselves. Therefore, the realists looked instead to the Bible as the infallible source of
religious authority.[2]

Thus it may be inferred that wherever the realists dominated higher education, there was scope for a reform movement which went beyond mere moralization and became
concerned with institutional alternatives. The doctrine that
dignitaries in mortal sin forfeited their *dominium* was a logi-
cal consequence of their stance. Here the theoretical issue
touched the hard core of everyday life: sacraments administered by evil priests put the salvation of laymen into jeop-

ardy. Such a state of affairs could not be tolerated but, as Church representatives were not in a position to help, reform had to be carried out with the help of the wielders of secular power. Yet, the interest of the secular authorities lay elsewhere and only occasionally coincided with those of the reformers as the feud between the king and archbishop illustrates.

King Wenceslas favoured the Pisan Council against the stance of the Archbishop of Prague, who supported the acting pope in Rome. As this was a question of ecclesiastical law, it was brought to the university, where the German nominalist majority decided against the king. This provided a welcome opportunity for the Czech, realist, minority led by Hus to persuade the king to change the statutes of the university: in January 1409, by the Decree of Kutná Hora, the king granted three votes to the Bohemian nation against one to be held by the three foreign nations (considered from then on as one Teutonic nation). Thus the Czech reformers acquired an influential institution for their cause. When subsequently the Curia condemned the seventeen writings by Wyclif as heretical, this verdict was contested by the university, where John Hus became the main link with the popular movement.

As long as the Archbishop of Prague continued in his alliance to the Roman pope, and the king acknowledged the pope elected in Pisa, the archbishop's measures against the Wyclifites were ineffective. Only when the archbishop switched sides and acknowledged the pope-elect in Pisa could he take effective measures against John Hus. In 1411, Hus was anathematized by the Pisan pope. To make things still worse, John Hus decided to condemn as immoral and sacrilegious the sale of indulgences, the proceeds of which were to finance the war of the Pisan pope against the supporters of the Roman pope; as the king was to participate in the proceeds of these sales, Hus could not hope for his support.

The situation became increasingly acute. The Pisan pope reaffirmed the anathema against Hus, who then left Prague and spent two years under the protection of his friends from the lower nobility. The reform party hardened its stance. Jacobellus de Misa (Jakoubek of Stříbro), who was a university master and more radical than Hus in those days, declared the pope to be the Antichrist and, towards the end of 1414, started to serve, in defiance of the explicit disapproval of the Curia, the Holy Communion in both ways (*sub utraque specie*; hence the reformers were also called *Utraquists*). The Eucharist in both kinds became a symbol of the equality of laymen with the clergy before God.

In contrast to the English, the Czechs possessed all the ingredients necessary for turning the word into flesh: indignation over the Church's betrayal of its Christian mission, practical suggestions as to who should see to improvements, and finally the belief that reform was the sacred duty of the whole nation which, by virtue of its stance, became a sort of Chosen People.

The linkage of these three elements of Czech reform was epitomized in the sensible interpretation by Hus and his associates of the doctrine of dominion. For them the sacraments were valid to the recipient, even if administered by an evil priest, but the administration of the sacraments was to the evil priest's damnation. Thus no feeling of insecurity could ensue. Furthermore, religion had to be more understandable for the believer. Therefore, the vernacular was to be used more extensively, and eventually the rediscovered source of supreme authority in the Church, the Holy Writ, was to be translated. The simplification and standardization of Czech orthography undertaken by John Hus effectively helped to further this purpose. An extraordinary spread of literacy in fifteenth-century Bohemia and Moravia was testified by foreign observers.

The extent of the Czech nation as a chosen, even sacrosanct, community was demarcated by another reform theologian, Jerome of Prague, as follows: 'from the king to the knight, from the knight to the squire, from the squire to the peasant; from the archbishop to the canon, from the canon to the lowliest priest; from the mayor of the town to the councillor and the burgher, from the burgher to the lowliest worker'.[3] Thus, in the religious context, the unity of the nation was conceived in much broader terms than in the political context, where the differentiation of social status according to the estates was taken for granted.

Meanwhile a new Council was summoned to Constance with the aim of abolishing the threefold schism, reforming the Church, and dealing with the heretical teachings. John Hus, who always demanded a public hearing, accepted Sigismund's warrant of safe conduct and went to Constance. There, however, he was arrested and, in the teeth of protests both from the Czechs present in Constance and from others who sent letters from Bohemia, was condemned for holding the Wyclifite heresies and burnt at the stake (July 1415). Thus the reform movement got its martyr, soon to be venerated by his followers as a saint. From then on, the movement which had earlier been largely known as Wyclifite, was styled either Hussite, after its saint, or Utraquists or Calixtins, after its symbol.

(Those who did not want to join the reform were known in contemporary Bohemia as *sub una*, in Czech '*pod jednou*'. Later historiography styled them often simply as Catholics. This term, however, implies that the Utraquists were not Catholics which, as further development has shown, cannot be sustained. Therefore I am using here the term Romanists; the Catholic-Protestant dichotomy appeared only a century later.)

Shocked by the Council's disregard for, and contempt of, Czech feelings, 58 barons and 391 members of the lower nobility convened a meeting and sent a letter to the Council protesting against Hus's condemnation. By way of response, the Council indicted all who signed the protest and burnt at the stake yet another reformer, Jerome of Prague. The University of Prague promptly declared Hus and Jerome innocent of heresy, but in 1416 the Council retaliated by suspending the activity of the university. In August 1417, while a large chiliastic movement was spreading through the country the Hussite priesthood began to work on the common programme of reform.

As the king did not want to oppose the Council's decision, he put pressure on the royal boroughs and, albeit less effectively, on the nobility. In response to royal pressure, the Hussite nobility started to disregard the ecclesiastical prescription controlling the filling of offices and took care to provide their churches with Utraquist priests.[4] In Prague, all but four of the churches were returned to the Romanists on the king's orders. The king appointed new city councillors, all Romanists, and forbade all processions. On 22 July 1419, however, a procession led by a Hussite radical, John Želivský, violently turned a Romanist church mass into a Utraquist one, and then went to the town hall to demand the freeing of the Hussite prisoners. When their request was not granted, they stormed the town hall and threw the councillors out of the windows – the so-called first defenestration of Prague. When the king received the news of the event he suffered a series of strokes and died; being childless, he was succeeded by his half-brother, Sigismund, whose accession was, for many people, unpopular.

In the country the Hussite movement held power over several institutions without whose consent Sigismund could not take possession of his heritage. At first it seemed that the Hussite nobility, the university and the councillors of the city of Prague would yield to Sigismund's double game of appeasing and menacing tactics, but as soon as he had shown his true intentions, namely to suppress the Hussites by force (the pope declared a crusade at his instigation), the mood changed and the opposition stiffened. Those Romanists who still remained in Prague had to leave the city and their property was confiscated. They were mainly Germans, of whom only a few became Utraquists. Meanwhile the radical Hussites, hard-pressed in their towns and assembly places, founded a new town of their own in southern Bohemia named after the biblical mountain, Tabor. Another Hussite faction established its camp on the mountain called Horeb in eastern Bohemia. The royal borough Hradec Králové became their main urban centre.

As soon as the reformists established their solid bases, disagreements and divisions began to appear amongst them. Nevertheless a common programme was hammered out and eventually condensed into four articles, the so-called Four Articles of Prague, which in the final version of October 1420, read:

> 1. That the Word of God shall be freely and without hindrance proclaimed and preached by Christian priests in the kingdom of Bohemia.
> 2. That the Holy Sacrament of the body and blood of Christ under the two kinds of bread and wine shall be freely administered to all true Christians who are not excluded from communion by mortal sin.
> 3. That since many priests and monks hold many earthly possessions against Christ's command and to the disadvantage of their spiritual office and also of the temporal lords, such priests shall be deprived of this illegal power and shall live exemplary lives according to the Holy Scripture, in following the way of Christ and the Apostles.
> 4. That all mortal sins, and especially those that are public, as also other disorders contrary to the divine law, shall be prohibited and punished by those whose office it is so that the evil and false repute of this country may be removed and the well-being of the kingdom and of the Bohemian nation may be promoted.[5]

Within this common programme several factions with various degrees of postulated change crystallized. They were known according to their geographical power base which to a large extent also reflected their social background. The moderates acted under the label of the Prague Party, which in itself was quite a broad Church. It was represented by several noble families, most university masters and some gentry, but its main stronghold was in the Old Town of Prague (after it became converted into the Czech city) and in some other royal boroughs which acknowledged Prague's leadership. The majority in the New Town of Prague inclined to the radical view; this often resulted in internal conflicts.

The radicals themselves had two centres: one in Tabor, the other in Horeb; their followers were mainly peasants, burghers and gentry. In its original form, Tabor was a settlement of those who were largely imbued with the adventist spirit; a kind of consumer communism was practised, but this was soon abandoned, apparently when the prophecies of the Day of Wrath passed unfulfilled and a more realistic approach had to be adopted. In religious matters, however, Tabor continued to be more radical, although it ceased to be a haven for overtly heretical teachings.[6] The Horebites took up a position between that of Tabor and that of Prague.

The main differences between individual factions were religious; the key issue was the Eucharist and religious rites. The most moderate Hussites were satisfied with serving the Holy Communion in both kinds and in all other matters conformed to the Roman Church. The bulk of the Prague Party was more resolute in trying to implement the Four Articles of Prague in practice; what was most conspicuous was their desire for a simplification or the rites, and, at least initially, their dispensation of the Eucharist to children.

The Taborites abondoned the solemn rites altogether and denied quite a few orthodox beliefs, such as the belief in purgatory, and the belief in the efficacy of consecrations, of auricular confession, or the intercession of saints, etc.

With regard to the Eucharist they did not stick firmly to the orthodox doctrine of transubstantiation, but were more inclined to follow Wyclif's doctrine of remanence. They saw themselves as the Primitive Church reincarnate, as an autonomous section of the Church Militant. They were not inhibited by the desire to preserve unity with the universal Catholic Church, and elected their own bishop, Nicholas of Pelhřimov, in a noncanonical way. The Horebites followed a similar path but in a less conspicuous fashion.

Only the most extreme radicals who were not aligned with any of the other parties did not hesitate to outrage the Romanists and the Hussites alike by their open heresies, the most apparent of which was the denial of the presence of Christ's blood and body in the Eucharist. This heresy, characteristic of the so-called Pikharts, who were to be found all over Europe, went so far that even the Taborites could not accept it. The leading Pikhart theologian, Martin Húska, was eventually burned at the stake, after attempts by the chief Horebite priest, Ambrose, to convert him had failed. As the Holy Communion in both kinds became the main common symbol of all the Hussites, they were highly sensitive to any dilution of its sacramental value.

The extremists created only one compact community known as Adamites; imbued with the heresy of 'Free Spirit' (endemic throughout the whole of Western Europe), they had seceded from Tabor and established themselves in a nearby fortress, where they practised their licentious lifestyle and from where they undertook raids upon the surrounding countryside until they were annihilated by the Taborite forces. In contrast to the Adamites, there were gentle, pacifist radicals represented by the outstanding thinker, Peter Chelčický, who left a permanent impact on the Czech Reformation.

Religious differences made individual factions easily distinguishable from one another. Although individuals might fluctuate and the political positions of individual factions might change, the doctrinal demarcation remained pretty distinct throughout the whole revolutionary period.

To ascertain the political meanings reflected in these religious differences, it is necessary to observe the actual behaviour of the different factions. On the whole, those factions which deviated from Catholic doctrine in matters of rites only stuck to the idea of unity with the universal Church, and were not particularly interested in political or socio-economic changes. Moral regeneration would, in their view, heal all wounds. However, alongside the acceptance of the general social framework, there was a strong endeavour on the part of certain individuals to improve their legal and/ or economic position within the estate structure of the society. The Third Article of Prague provided a welcome moral justification for the confiscation of the Church's property (which before the revolution was about one third of the land in Bohemia), a lure which not even the Romanists could resist. In fact, only about one third of the barons joined the Hussite camp; here they sided mainly with its most moderate faction which, in principle, favoured a compromise with the Church and the king.

As the strength of all Hussite parties resided to a large extent in the royal boroughs, they were naturally interested in the promotion of their status in the country's diet and government. This, indeed, did happen. The weight of royal boroughs in general, and of Prague in particular, in the estate diet increased enormously.[7] Furthermore, the prestige of the leading boroughs, such as Prague, Tabor and Hradec Králové, was enhanced by their virtual sovereignty in religious matters. The priesthood of each party seated there decided, sometimes with the participation of laity, what should be believed, or rather how religion should be practised, within its sphere of power. Although politically less independent than, for example, Italian cities such as Florence, Venice and Genoa, in the period 1420–36, their ideological sovereignty far surpassed anything in contemporary Europe. In this respect, these Czech cities foreshadowed Zurich, Geneva and other cities of the Protestant Reformation.

In national policy the radicals were against any compromise with Sigismund, but in principle did not object to a king from another dynasty, provided he adhered to the Four Articles of Prague. As it turned out, another Sigismund, Sigismund Korybut, a prince related to the Jagiellon dynasty of Poland-Lithuania, became a serious candidate for the Bohemian throne.

However, considering the situation in the country as a whole we must bear in mind the imperfect position of what we would nowadays call the state. Each lord was master in his domain, and if he was strong enough in men, weapons and fortified castles, he could defy any external power. At a time of civil war each baron, each squire, and – when royal power was vacant – even each royal borough, could choose their political allegiance according to their own will. The conquest of a fortified castle or walled city was a difficult matter, and most warfare was waged at the expense of the peasantry. No wonder that the country was regionally divided between individual parties, often in perplexing enclaves without continuous borders. However, most of eastern and central Bohemia was Hussite, whereas in the west the Romanist domains prevailed. The south and the north were almost equally divided between the two camps. In Moravia the Hussites were in a minority.

Under these circumstances there was wide scope for fighting even amongst the Hussites themselves. One of the bloodiest battles of the whole period was fought in 1424 between the Prague Party and the Taborite army under the command of their formidable leader John Žižka, in which the latter was victorious. There were virtually no stable alliances or battle fronts between the parties. Negotiations with Sigismund of Luxembourg were attempted whilst factional Hussite groups occasionally concluded regional truces with the Romanists which allowed them to join their infighting. In such cases the 'holy war' – as it was seen by the radicals – looked more like the traditional feudal skirmishing.

When, however, menace came from abroad, the Hussite factions stood together; on such occasions the fight became for them a truly holy war. Apart from repeated attacks by Sigismund's Hungarian armies and occasional attacks from other neighbours, between 1421 and 1431 five crusades were launched by the combined forces of the Empire and papacy against the Hussites. All were utterly defeated.

In my opinion, there were several reasons why, in contrast to all other crusades undertaken against heretics or pagans in Europe, the crusades against Hussite Bohemia were an abysmal failure. Firstly, morale on both sides was totally different: on the one hand there were the dedicated warriors of God, defending their faith and country against foreign invasion; on the other hand was a hotchpotch of soldiery not particularly imbued by missionary zeal or martial virtues – their quality did not match their numbers. Secondly, there was a new military technique and tighter discipline on the side of the Hussites. More ample use of artillery and above all movable fortresses of heavy wooden wagons which, placed in good strategic positions such as hills, were virtually unconquerable by traditional mounted assaults. Last but not least, it was the cooperation of people of all estates of the realm: the military expertise of the gentry (John Žižka being the most notorious), combined with the technical know-how and economic strength of the boroughs, was matched by dedicated volunteers from the peasantry.[8]

Victories over the invading armies contrasted with inconclusive situations at home; in order to speed up the end of the war the radicals expanded their military campaigns abroad. The raids to the neighbouring countries were accompanied with propaganda letters and pamphlets, which in some instances found an echo amongst the malcontents.

Yet in spite of a negligible effect in terms of conversions, the nuisance value of the Hussite raids was big enough to bring the Church authorities to look for a political instead of a military solution.

The Hussites were not the only problem facing the Church authorities. A whole range of issues were to be resolved by the Council summoned in 1431 to Basle. The issue of who was to lead the Church, the pope or the Council, was still pending; the Council eventually took several steps which were not to the pope's liking. One was to put the Hussite question on the agenda and consequently invite their delegation to Basle.

Most Hussites were genuinely interested in reconciliation with the Roman Church. As their deviations from the acknowledged religious standard were of a ritual rather than of a dogmatic nature, they considered themselves good, even better, Catholics than the others. As their maximal requirement, they wanted the Church to accept their view, which they claimed to be based on the Scriptures and the practice of the Early (Primitive) Church only, whereas the Roman Church was blamed for having introduced many 'adnovations'. These, however, were considered by the Curia to be superior and more dignified than the practice of the Primitive Church. By way of a compromise, the Hussites would content themselves with an agreement according to which Hussite practice would be recognized as legitimate and as generally applicable throughout the kingdom of Bohemia. They did not want to create a schismatic Church, but an acknowledged branch of the universal Catholic Church.

Negotiations started in April 1429, but the Hussites' request to obtain a public hearing from the Council was the main obstacle to agreement. Meanwhile, the last attempt was made to curb the military power of the Hussites. The fifth crusade (1431), in which perhaps the largest number of crusaders, recruited from all over Europe, took part, failed ignominiously.

Only then did the Council get ready to accept the Hussite demand for a public hearing. In the preliminary talks between the Hussites and the envoys of the Council in Cheb (Eger) in May 1432, it was agreed that both sides should accept the Bible and the practice of the Early Church as the criteria for discussion. Thus (and this is significant for similar situations elsewhere), where a reformer – John Hus – failed, the revolutionaries succeeded.

During the negotiations, or rather disputations, in Basle, a delegation of the Council visited Prague; they realized that there were essential differences within the Hussite camp, and entered into closer contact with the Hussite moderates. This faction was becoming increasingly concerned by the continuation of the war, which badly affected both the economy and cultural intercourse with other countries. Another worrying factor was the worsening of discipline in the armies of the military brotherhoods, where mercenaries began to appear increasingly side by side with the dedicated warriors of God.

All these developments led to a reversal of fronts and alliances. The Hussites split right in the middle. The radicals failed to tilt the balance to their favour and the Prague Party made an alliance with the domestic Romanists. In such a constellation the latter did not need any support from abroad; on the contrary, such aid might only have damaged their cause.

The new coalition was numerically stronger. In military technique there was no significant difference – all the Hussite innovations were used on both sides – and neither does there seem to have been too much difference in spirit. In the Battle of Lipany, on 30 May 1434, the united Taborite and Horebite armies were utterly defeated.

As the military power of the radicals was eliminated, it was possible for the Hussite moderates to make a deal with the Council in Basle on the basis of a compromise interpretation of the Four Articles of Prague. The form agreed – the so-called Compacts of Basle – was a diluted form of their original version. The Articles about freedom of preaching and the punishment of mortal sin were accepted in a general way, but with a more precise definition of those who should have the right to preach (i.e., only ordained persons) and of the authorities who should be entitled to proceed against sinners. The Article against the worldly dominion of the Church was in the Compacts worded in a way which made it impossible to use it as a justification for further confiscations of Church property. Oddly enough, the most difficult agreement was that concerning the communion from the chalice to the laity. As Heymann points out, this type of communion never became an issue between the Roman and Greek Orthodox Churches, but here, within the Czech context, it had a deep political connotation. It was a symbol of equality between the laity and clergy and also a symbol of Czech specificity which the universalistic spirit of Latin Christian Europe was not ready to accept. Nevertheless the representatives of the Council (but, unfortunately for the Hussite case, without the approval of the pope) agreed 'that the chalice be given to those men and women who were used to it and expressly demanded it as long as they otherwise lived in the favour and ritual of Christ and the Sacred Church'.[9]

In that form the Compacts of Basle were finally signed in a common diet of the Bohemian and Moravian estates, which took place in July 1436, in the Moravian city of Jihlava. This act made manifest the formal reconciliation of the Hussites with their Romanist counterparts, as far as they were represented by the Council of Basle, and with Sigismund of Luxembourg as the legitimate King of Bohemia.

In 1435 the Hussites, i.e., the Prague Party, who acted then on behalf of the whole movement, elected their own archbishop, John Rokycana, and, after the signature of the Compacts, wanted him to be appointed according to canonic law by the pope. But, not approving of the Compacts, the pope did not appoint the Utraquist candidate; even amongst the representatives of the Council there were many who had serious reservations concerning the validity of the Compacts. In their view, the peculiarities of the Bohemian Church should be tolerated only as long as was absolutely necessary, i.e., as long as there were people able to defend them by force of arms. Thus the upholding of the compromise became a delicate power game.

As soon as Sigismund installed himself in Prague, he attempted a complete restoration of the *ancien régime*. In Prague, only the most moderate of the moderates were tolerated, which meant, for example, that John Rokycana had to find refuge with his Bohemian supporters. The pressure continued after the death of Sigismund in 1437, who had not had long to enjoy the throne that had taken so much to recapture. From then on, for many years, there was virtually no royal power in the country. In principle, there were two serious candidates for the Bohemian throne, one from the Austrian Habsburgs (Albrecht) and the other from the Polish Jagiellon dynasty (Kazimír). But the premature death of the former in 1439, and the irresolute action of the latter, left the matter unresolved. The nobles on both sides were not interested in the re-establishment of a strong royal power: they preferred the precarious, indecisive balance of power whereby order in the kingdom was upheld by regional truces, the so-called *Landfrieden*, agreed by the local barons, knights and royal boroughs.

The consolidation had to come from the moderate Hussites, who were apparently the strongest faction numerically, and dominated the East Bohemian *Landfrieden*. From 1444, George of Poděbrady became their leader; he possessed a considerable talent for combining diplomacy and force. Having about a third of Bohemia solidly behind him, he could embark on a well-prepared campaign for the unification and pacification of the country. In 1448 he took the city of Prague by force – incurring only minimal casualties. In 1449 the Romanist nobility united in a counter-league (the League of Strakonice), but they did not dare to take up arms. In 1452 most of them attended a diet which elected George governor of the kingdom for two years. Soon after that, Tabor surrendered to George's military expedition, which put an end to its political and religious sovereignty.

In 1453 Ladislas the Posthumous, the thirteen-year-old son of Albrecht the Habsburg, was crowned as the Bohemian king but, in 1457, amidst preparations for his wedding with a French princess, he died. This time, however, the Bohemian estates did not look abroad for a suitable candidate. There had been too many disappointments with candidates from abroad; they preferred the comparative stability achieved by George of Poděbrady. In March 1458, they elected him King of Bohemia. The Moravian estates accepted the election later in the same year.

As far as the Czech situation was concerned, the revolution was over, and issues other than religious ones came to dominate political divisions. If the religious issues nevertheless remained on the cards, it was because of the papal Curia which was not willing to recognize even so moderate a deviation from the uniform ritual standard as communion from the chalice for everybody. It may be worth noting that it took five hundred years before the Roman Curia could condone this practice of the Primitive Church – its legitimacy was recognized by the Second Vatican Council (1962–4).

The end of the revolution, however, was not the end of Czech reform, despite the political consolidation's adherence to the Compacts of Basle, which provided too tight a framework to accommodate the concept of Utraquism. In 1457, in an East Bohemian village, a small community picked up Chelčický's tradition and constituted itself as the Unity of Brethren (*Unitas Fratrum*). What had begun as a primitive Christian revival developed into a most articulate, autonomous denomination of the Czech Reformation.

The Chalice side by side with the Cross. The warring estates

After the more or less contemporary struggles on the one hand between the Slavic and the Latin liturgies and, on the other hand, between Christianity in general and hidden Pagan tradition, the confrontation between the chalice and the cross was the second period of religious, or essentially ideological, contest in Czech history. All the other conflicts on Czech ground until then, such as the investiture contest or the chronic antagonism between the king and the estates, were primarily struggles for power, struggles between institutions which adhered to the same religious formation. Their ideological differences concerned the division of power, not the principles of faith or forms of worship. These power issues were not specific to the Czechs; they were a part of the Western European situation in general. On the other hand, issues of faith and worship which caused the Czechs so much trouble were limited to a particular area of Europe. The controversy between the Slavic and Latin liturgy concerned only the southern Slavs and the people of the area which is today Czechoslovakia. The chalice in the fifteenth century was an exclusively Czech matter and symbol. Why was this?

The advance from the periphery to the core of Latin Christian civilization was an achievement of all Bohemians and Moravians, both of the Czech and German tongues. Also, the call for reform was not limited to the Czechs. Nor must we forget the mighty intellectual impulse from England. It was Wyclif's ideas which in Hussitism transformed a moral into a theological issue. And some German masters at the University of Prague were even more radical than the Czech ones.[10] But when the theological issue percolated down to the grass roots of society, only the Czechs became involved. There were, however, enough of them who rejected the appeal of reform and opposed the Hussites tooth and nail. As so often in history, the radicals carried the day and enforced a compromise with their foes, only to be swept from the stage by a coalition of moderates on both sides.

The Compacts of Basle led to a stalemate. Each side interpreted the agreement differently. The Utraquists saw in the Compacts the legal basis for continuation of their specific practices; confirmed by the supreme authority in the Church they could not be considered as heretical. Consequently, the Utraquists saw themselves as orthodox Catholics. Most Romanists in Bohemia and Moravia found this stance acceptable. As a result, the Catholic Church in Bohemia operated in two branches, each headed by its own Consistory, whilst the seat of archbishop was vacant. In Moravia the Romanists followed the Bishop of Olomouc, whereas the Utraquists conformed with their Consistory in Prague. George of Poděbrady who had proved his impartiality already as regent, won recognition as a king in all domains of the Crown. With the exception of Breslau (capital of Silesia), even the staunchest Romanist German cities acknowledged him as their lawful sovereign.

The Holy See, however, saw in the Compacts of Basle a temporary arrangement, allowing the Eucharist in both kinds for laymen only to those who practised them when the Compacts were agreed. Everybody else was expected to conform to the Holy Communion in one kind (*sub una specie*). As no other deviations were condoned in the Compacts, it was expected that the special status of the Utraquists in Bohemia would phase out during the second generation.

Furthermore, we have to bear in mind that the conflict between the Hussites and the Roman Church occurred against the background of two simultaneous contests within Latin Christian civilization at large. There was, as we have seen, continuous rivalry between the ecclesiastical and lay authorities, rivalry in which the lay side received welcome ideological support from the jurists inspired by the revived interest in Roman law. In addition, the disarray in the Church caused by the papal schism resuscitated the time-honoured concept of an ecumenical council as the supreme body in the Church. This can be seen as a parallel of the struggle within the lay camp so that the relation of papal autocracy to episcopal republic resembled that of royal autocracy to aristocratic republic. Whereas the struggle within the lay power structure remained in most countries more or less inconclusive, the analogous issue within the Church ended with the victory of the pope.

From the time of the ecumenical councils in the first eight hundred years or so of Christian history, there were only two ecumenical councils of the West which managed to emancipate themselves from papal sovereignty: the Council of Constance (1414–18), which, having sentenced John Hus and Jerome of Prague to death as heretics, provoked the Hussite revolution, and the Council of Basle (1431–49), which helped to bring the revolution to an end by concluding an agreement with the Hussites. However, the Council of Constance also finished with the papal schism. Following an appalling start in Basle, Pope Eugen IV was able eventually to re-establish his firm leadership of the Church. Leaning on the puritanical vogue in contemporary monasticism (known as observantism, meaning strict observation of the monastic rules), and trying hard to heal the rift between the Latin and Greek Churches, he showed more imagination and skill than his opponents. As the temporal rulers began to see that negotiation with the pope alone was more expedient than with the sporadic congregations of clerics, so the pope used the opportunity to deal with the rulers in order to outflank the supporters of the Council. In a series of concordats, several secular rulers were able to obtain, without reformation, a significant extension of their jurisdiction in matters formerly claimed by the Curia to be its own, exclusive, prerogative. On the other hand, to reassert his autocratic claims within the Church the pope did not hesitate to use the most formidable weapon in his canonical armoury. In the bull 'Execrabilis' of 1459, Pope Pius II forbade appeals to councils against papal verdicts and branded such appeals as heretical; anyone who attempted to appeal was declared *ipso facto* excommunicated. The concept of heresy was stretched beyond its theological limits.

Wishing to remain within the Church, the Hussites anxiously observed the apostolic succession. Although they elected their moderate leading theologian, John Rokycana, archbishop, they required the pope for his confirmation. As this was not forthcoming, Rokycana did not dare to ordain priests. The situation was resolved in a way which was by no means edifying for the Utraquist establishment. Candidates for priesthood travelled to Italy, where, under the pretext of conversion, they obtained ordination. In the pope's country clergy were evidently less scrupulous than elsewhere. Also, poor priests from linguistically related Poland occasionally came and settled down as Utraquist parsons. Administering the chalice to laymen was, for them, a lesser evil than the squalor in their home country. Only later, against the pope's will, two Italian titular bishops, apparently led by conviction, came to Bohemia (the first in 1482, the second in 1504) in order to help the Utraquist Church to maintain its union with the Catholic Church.[11]

In such a situation any initiative for moving ahead rested with the king. In Czech historiography, George of Poděbrady looms high in the list of kings. Usually he appears as second to Charles IV. With respect to the more complicated situation and the heavy odds he had to cope with, however, he deserves, in my opinion, not less but rather more appreciation. Charles's situation was much easier: there was no ideological barrier between him as emperor and king and on the other hand the pope. Only in his involvement in Italian matters was he confronted with a particular ideological flavour of the Renaissance. On the other hand, George represented a dissident version of Catholicism which the pope wanted to suppress as quickly as possible, but which George was not willing to abandon. His hands were bound by a sincere adherence to the Compacts which implied a twofold, mutually incompatible, loyalty: on the one hand to the Utraquist people with its cherished tradition reaching back to John Hus, and on the other hand to the Roman Catholic Church with the pope at its head, the same pope whose cooperation George needed in order to safeguard the legitimacy of his own position as the King of Bohemia and elector in Germany.

In order to appease the pope, George went as far as he could, perhaps even a bit further. According to the rules set up by Charles IV, episcopal assistance was needed for his coronation as king, but none such was available locally at the time of his election: in Prague, as a result of papal policy, the seat was vacant; in Olomouc (Moravia) the incumbent bishop was not yet nominated, and the Bishop of Breslau (Silesia) was vehemently hostile towards what he considered to be a heretic king. George arranged with his son-in-law, Mathias Corvinus, King of Hungary, to send two of his bishops; but they needed some assurance that the king was not a heretic. George could confirm this in good faith, by oath, but although this approach was, in principle, defensible, it nevertheless presented practical difficulties. The oath implied obedience to the pope who saw in it the promise of submission. The fact that the oath was not made in public but kept secret was understood in Rome to be merely a tactical and temporary expedient.

As George wished to retain the Utraquist variant of Catholicism, a tedious manoeuvring between the two positions ensued. The Holy See, under three successive popes and supported by many high-ranking clerics, worked assiduously, though with varying degrees of intensity, to bring George to submission. On the other hand, George could rely on the prevalent mood amongst secular rulers who were increasingly wary of clerical interference in their own domain; he also was aided by several prominent jurists from Germany, Italy and France who joined his service.[12]

Apart from the Curia, George's main enemy was the capital city of Silesia, Breslau (now Wroclaw); and the King of Hungary, following the death of his wife (George's daughter), went over to his father-in-law's enemies. In Germany, however, many secular princes were quite sympathetic to him (George with his four sons and two daughters was able to conclude quite a few advantageous marriages), as was the Polish king. The Curia had to try hard to win support for confrontation, which, given George's intransigence, was inevitable. There was much manoeuvring on both sides, manoeuvres in which other issues became intertwined. For many, the Ottoman advance in the Balkans and their menace of Hungary appeared more important. However, the Curia seemed more irritated by what it began to perceive as heresy in its own backyard.

Things came to a head when George asked for formal recognition of the Compacts by the pope. The pope answered by cancelling their validity. The king appealed to the Council of the Church (thus committing heresy); as a result he was excommunicated and all secular rulers were invited to a crusade. The epoch of crusades, however, was already over. Only Mathias Corvinus of Hungary, who had been promised the Bohemian Crown, helped the pope with a military might sufficient to match George's forces. Supported by those of George's subjects willing to obey the pope's summons, Mathias was able to score some victories. In Olomouc (Moravia), in the seat of a bishop who joined the campaign, Mathias was proclaimed King of Bohemia and yet, following his failure to conquer the country, the war continued to drag on.

Of general significance was the fact that the Czech Romanist barons did not start the war against their king as a religious issue but as a defence of estate prerogatives against the encroachment of the king (the very same stance taken later by Protestant nobility against the Catholic Habsburgs). George's main support was amongst the lesser nobility and royal boroughs. But even this division was inclined to fluctuate as changes of self-interest proceeded to divide old loyalties, whilst diplomatic activity continued throughout the hostilities.

As a last resort, George conceived the idea of securing the succession of the Bohemian Crown for a prince of a friendly dynasty in a powerful state. Although even this plan was not without obstacles, it worked: after George's death (in 1471), Vladislav, the son of the Polish King Kazimír, was elected King of Bohemia by Utraquists and Romanists alike. The resulting Polish–Hungarian conflict which followed (since Mathias refused to relinquish his claims to the Bohemian Crown) was eventually settled by a compromise in which Bohemia was left to Vladislav and the other lands of the Bohemian Crown to Mathias. Vladislav, however, was entitled to redeem them for the sum of 400,000 ducats. Following the death of Mathias without issue in 1490 Vladislav was elected King of Hungary so that Moravia, Silesia and Lusatia were reunited with Bohemia without any payment.

In that respect the succession of the Jagiellon dynasty was a fortunate solution for the Czechs. Otherwise, however, the situation was equivocal. Within the European context, Poland represented the type of state in which the division of power between king and nobility was tilted towards the latter. Apart from that, Vladislav was not energetic and consistent enough to assert himself against opposition. Being king of two countries, each with particular problems, he was in no position to rule effectively in either. The considerable weakening of royal authority, which started in the Hussite wars and which George of Poděbrady was able to restore only in part, continued further. Thus, although an affectionate Romanist, the king helped the Utraquists to survive. Irrespective of whom the king appointed to the chief positions in the realm (and he preferred Romanists), the

Utraquist nobles and royal boroughs maintained their own regional religious independence. Attempts by the radical Romanists (with the king's connivance) to split Utraquist ranks failed, and the anti-Calixtin agitation of the Romanist monks evoked a riotous reaction in Prague.

Both sides came to the conclusion that the status quo could not be changed by force. Weary of religious bickering and aware of the growing urgency of other issues, the two religious parties resolved to make peace. It happened at the Conference of Kutná Hora in 1485.

The two parties reaffirmed the Compacts as one of the basic laws of the land and accepted the existing division of parishes and churches whilst all polemics and aggressive sermons were to stop. The free choice of either form of Holy Communion was extended from members of the higher estates to their peasant subjects. The contract was to last for thirty-one years, i.e., to 1516, but by 1512 it had been extended in perpetuity. No one could have foreseen that soon a more vigorous reformation from abroad would upset the balance on which the agreement of Kutná Hora was based.

Ideally the peace agreement between the Romanists and Utraquists can be seen as a sign of maturity, a symbol of religious tolerance; but it can also be surmised that the two parties opted for a peaceful solution because they became more lukewarm in their religious feelings. The growing spirit of Renaissance, which affected the Romanists more than the Utraquists, mollified their intransigence, with worldly matters beginning to attract more immediate attention. Indeed, it was in this direction that the weight of controversy and conflict lay towards the end of the fifteenth century.

In the calmer atmosphere between religious parties the diverging interests of estates provoked an open conflict already heightened by economic change which compounded traditional rivalries. In contrast to the overall growth in population and production in the late Přemyslid epoch, towards

the end of the fifteenth century complaints were voiced concerning the disappearance of many villages and the decline
of cultivated areas.[13] The scarcity of labour in agriculture
was also widely felt and foreign trade suffered because of
disruption in commercial routes.

The confiscation of Church property, the Crown's mort-
gage of fixed assets and the disappearance of many yeoman
on mercenary service abroad, led to a concentration of
landed property in the hands of aristocratic families. Deval-
uation of the currency (stopped only temporarily towards
the end of George's reign) and the resulting inflation made
cash rents unpopular with the landlords so they increased
the amount of work (the corvée) required from the peasants
and began to farm on their own account (the so-called
'dominical' at the expense of the 'rustical') concentrating on
sheep breeding, brewing and introducing fish-pond cultivation.

Yet despite the structural changes in the economy (in
some areas peasants were evicted from their holdings) it
was the scarcity of agricultural labour that prevailed, being
aggravated by the migration to towns. The nobles sought to
reverse this trend by legal measures which, like many others,
failed to be fully effective, but nevertheless brought about
significant change in the social status of the peasant population. They inaugurated the epoch which has been dubbed
the 'second bondage'.[14] (A similar development took place
in all countries to the east of the river Elbe, that is in the
area which after 1945 became part of the Soviet bloc.)

Under these circumstances, the upper estates, three in
Bohemia (barons, knights and boroughs) and four in Moravia
(where the clerical estate was not abolished by the Hussite
revolution), got a strong economic impetus for their traditional rivalry. The main issues can be summarized as follows: from the middle of the fourteenth century through the
Hussite wars the political power of the royal boroughs substantially increased. Cities, especially Prague and Kutná

Hora, acquired a considerable number of villages whose ownership was duly entered in the landed-estates registers which the aristocracy considered their own privileged preserve. On the other hand, noblemen acquired property in the cities but resented their consequent subjection to city law. The economic interests of the cities were also challenged by the expanding production of crafts on the estates of the nobility. The hottest debate concerned the rights of brewing within a mile of the city walls which had always been a privilege of the boroughs. Wanting to curb the strength of the cities, the nobles also tended to reduce their representation at the estate diet, or at least to limit their voting rights to matters directly concerning them.

As long as the rivalry between the estates was overshadowed by religious strife, the knights, who were solidly Hussite, tended to side with the royal boroughs who were also substantially Utraquist. (The upper nobility, as we have seen, was predominantly Romanist.) Once the religious truce was concluded in 1485, however, the economic interests of the lower nobility pushed them towards alignment with the barons. The king, being both personally and institutionally weak, tended to accede to a stronger pressure which came from the nobles rather than the burghers. Several legislative acts were passed in favour of the nobles.

It is a good illustration of the changed power relationship in the realm that it was now the nobles and not the king who were interested in codification; now they could resolve all pending issues in their favour. What a contrast to the situation in the middle of the fourteenth century when Charles IV's Code was marred by the barons!

At the turn of the sixteenth century, it was not the king but the royal boroughs who, in Bohemia, could stem the tide of the barons' power. The boroughs utterly rejected the project of codification already sanctioned by the king. In the absence of any central authority which could have enforced the law, a civil war seemed inevitable. But the economic and military strength of the cities made the prospects of victory for their foes most unlikely and eventually both sides preferred to attempt a compromise which ultimately resulted in an agreement known as the St Wenceslas treaty (1517). Of its detailed clauses the following points show the nature of the compromise agreed upon: the cities gave up their brewing and crafts monopoly within a mile of their precincts; but they preserved the right to participate in the diets and to acquire registered landed estates. Also a sensible demarcation of jurisdiction between the cities and the countryside was negotiated.

Although this compromise too, like that between the religious factions, was not always duly observed, it nevertheless brought more peace to the Bohemian lands. However, the failure to consider some sections of society remained a flaw in both these agreements. The treaty of 1485 did not include the Unity of Brethren whose separation from the Catholic Church was considered as proof of heresy by Utraquists and Romanists alike; in 1508 a royal decree declared a ban on them. Only the fact that there was no central authority which might have enforced the decree helped the Brethren. Being law-abiding and hard-working people their presence was considered an asset in quite a few estates. As time went on some Utraquist noblemen even converted to their faith. The peace agreement of 1517 between the estates was even less comprehensive. As a matter of principle, peasants were not party to, but objects of, regulations imposed upon them by the king and the higher estates. In a way the compromise was achieved at their expense. Their choice of habitat, although already limited by circumstances of vocation, was further reduced by legal measures, and their burden, mainly in the amount of work performed for their landlords, increased. Towards the end of the fifteenth century, several peasant revolts were recorded in the annals.

With these qualifications, the Czechs entered the sixteenth century with reasonably high expectations; the danger of civil war was averted and a particular blend of religious and political pluralism offered an adequate framework for further developments of national culture. The literary cultivation of the Czech language which had begun in the thirteenth century and gathered momentum in the late fourteenth century not only produced some outstanding works of art but the growing literacy prompted by interest in religious issues also gave it a wide currency. Czech was the third modern European language (after French and Italian) into which the whole Bible was translated. In 1489 at Kutná Hora it appeared in print richly decorated with Gothic paintings. (The first printed book in the Czech language, however, was neither the Bible nor any other religious writing, but a Renaissance topic, the 'Chronicles of Troy', printed in 1468 or a few years later in the Romanist city of Plzeň.)[15]

The Czechization of the boroughs, caused mainly by immigration from the countryside but partly by expulsion of those Germans who opposed Utraquism, was an important factor in the promotion of written Czech for administrative purposes. Finally, and this was a point of prestige, the military might of the Hussites, reaffirmed by the prowess of George's armies and, less gloriously, by wandering units of mercenaries, extended the use of the Czech language beyond its home country.[16] Quite a few Czech terms relating to weapons and military technique were taken over by German and other languages.

The outside world did not allow the Czechs to rest on their laurels: the year 1517, when the warring Bohemian estates made their peace, was also the year when Martin Luther nailed his 95 theses to the gates of the Wittenberg chapel, thus starting the second, more powerful, round of Reformation. Two years earlier, in 1515, an extraordinary contract between the Jagiellon and Habsburg monarchs was concluded: Vladislav's daughter Anna was betrothed either to the widowed Emperor Maximilian I, who was then fifty-six, or to one of his grandsons. This event was to have long-lasting consequences for the Czech nation.

Last but not least, while this was going on in Central Europe, the epoch-making transoceanic discoveries of the Portuguese and Spaniards shifted the centre of economic and political gravity in Europe towards the shores of the Atlantic. The Czechs stayed put within the old core of the Latin Christian civilization; exhausted by their reforming zeal and wasting their remaining energies in overlapping rivalries, they were poorly equipped for the challenge which was to meet them in the near future. The existence of their rudimentary religious pluralism and the vigour of their boroughs may be seen as pointers to a hopeful future for the Czechs. However, the traditional divisions caused by religion and politics were to be complicated by Europe's new geopolitical setting; it required more imagination, broadmindedness, discipline and skill from them than they were able to show in the series of crises which was to meet them in the next hundred years.

4

Failure to sustain the impetus

Impulses from abroad. North or south?

In the sixteenth century religious Reformation became a pan-European issue. This might have led the Czechs out of their cultural isolation which had resulted from their independent interpretation of Christian tradition; but in fact the wider Reformation created a more difficult situation for them. The vigour with which the German and then the Swiss Reformation challenged the established Church soon provoked a similarly vigorous response from revitalized Catholicism. Czech society matured to a comparative tolerance brought about by the bitterness of religious wars and the softening influence of the Renaissance, but this was gradually upset by the spread of increasing tensions from abroad. Thus also in Bohemia and Moravia the mood became radicalized, although the live and let live attitude only slowly gave way to new enmities.

Luther's ideas spread with astonishing speed amongst the German-speaking population in all lands of the Bohemian Crown and also amongst the German settlers in Hungary; from there it made many converts amongst the Slovaks. Amongst the Czechs, Lutheranism found a sympathetic response with many Utraquists; Luther's explicit praise of John Hus (voiced especially at the great public religious disputation in 1520 in Leipzig), established a connection between the two Reformations. The fact that Luther went much further than the Hussites, and severed his link with the Roman Church altogether, encouraged many of them to move ahead in that direction. For the Brethren, who had abandoned all links with the official Church from the outset, Luther's Reformation brought a confirmation of their stance. On the other hand, Luther's radical rival Thomas Münzer (the later builder of a revolutionary community at Münster in Westphalia), who in 1521 visited Prague where he hoped to find kindred souls, returned utterly disappointed. The right time to come to Prague for that purpose had been a hundred years earlier.

Eventually, it was not Münzer's Anabaptism but Zwingli's and Calvin's teaching which constituted the more effective radical wing of the Reformation. From the 1540s Calvinism spread not only along the Rhine valley to Germany, the Netherlands and overseas to Scotland and westwards to France, but also to Central Europe up to its most eastern confines in Poland, in Hungary and above all in Transylvania. In the Bohemian lands it found a sympathetic response from the Brethren who, although influenced by some of its tenets, preserved in principle their separate doctrine and organization.

Meanwhile, the political scenery of the Bohemian lands experienced a significant change. On the surface it seemed merely a change of dynasties. In fact, it was the beginning of a new era in Czech history.

In 1521 the fall of Belgrade opened the Hungarian plains to the Turkish advance. But the Hungarian aristocracy cared more for their own interests and privileges than for their king who had thus to defend the country with inadequate forces. Nor was help forthcoming from other Christian rulers. In 1526 at Mohacs in southern Hungary the young King Louis I, the Jagiello, not only lost the battle but also his life. Within fifteen years virtually all the Hungarian lowland, i.e., that part of the kingdom which was inhabited by the Magyars, became a province of the Ottman Empire. Of

Hungary proper, apart from a narrow strip of land along the Austrian border, only the mainly Slovak-inhabited north (the Upper Land) remained a part of the Latin Christian world. Transylvania in the east managed to preserve virtual independence as a tributary state of the Ottoman Empire.

The death of the childless Louis Jagiello left the Bohemian throne without an heir. According to the Habsburg-Jagiello agreement of 1515 it was eventually Ferdinand Habsburg, the younger son of Emperor Maximilian, the Archduke of Austria, who married Anna, the daughter of Vladislav, King of Bohemia. The Bohemian estates, who had not been consulted on the agreement, claimed their right to freely elect their future king, even though they lacked interest in any other candidate. Ferdinand, scenting a favourable wind, complied and all the twenty-four electors nominated by the three Bohemian estates gave him their vote. Later, in 1526, Ferdinand was also elected King of Hungary by a part of the Hungarian nobility; the other part elected the Duke of Transylvania as king. The resulting conflict gave the Turks further opportunity to intervene.

Leaving aside the motives for the Hungarian decision, we may ask ourselves, as many have before, why it was that Romanists and Utraquists alike, (many of them Lutherans) voted for an incumbent whose personal record and family background were calculated to make the electors suspicious? As Archduke of Austria (from 1522) Ferdinand showed a remarkable determination in suppressing the autonomy of the boroughs, in containing the rights of nobility and in stopping the Lutheran Reformation from spreading. His older brother, Charles, from 1516 as King of Spain and from 1519, as Charles V, King of Germany, showed in his Spanish domains even more resolve in pursuing a similar policy; only in Germany, where the king was a titular rather than effective head of the realm, did Charles fail to make progress in this respect. In Germany the struggle for autocracy could be more effectively pursued by local dukes and princes (lay and ecclesiastical).

As the combined power of Charles and Ferdinand became menacing (their domains embraced about a quarter of Western Europe and immense overseas possessions into the bargain), their neighbours, including the pope, became apprehensive. Against the Habsburg on the German throne Pope Leo X supported the candidature of the French king; he did his best to persuade the three ecclesiastical electors to cast their votes for him. However, the moneys of the Fuggers, the wealthiest commercial house in Europe, with whom the Habsburgs had mutually advantageous dealings, carried more weight with the prelates than did the pope. (Louis, King of Bohemia, faithfully observing the agreement of 1515, needed no bribe to vote for Charles.) Although the pope graciously accepted the effective vote, it was only in 1530 that Charles V achieved the coronation as emperor in Rome.

Pope Clement VII also preferred an alternative candidate to the Habsburg for the Bohemian throne and the very lack of his support for Ferdinand proved a recommendation to the Utraquists. The fact that Ferdinand was the wealthiest candidate and thus in the best position to help repay the enormous royal debt accumulated during the Jagiellon rule was also viewed as a great asset by all Bohemian estates irrespective of religion. As far as the autocratic policy of the Habsburgs was concerned, the Bohemian estates apparently trusted their own strength to protect their privileges. Before the coronation, the estates forced Ferdinand, under the menace of withdrawing their vote, to confirm in writing his allegiance to the law of the land, i.e., to promise to observe the privileges of the estates including the Compacts of Basle.

It has also been maintained that when casting their vote the Bohemian estates were concerned with the danger of the advancing Turks in the Danubian basin and wanted to create a strong bulwark against them. Such reasoning was more likely in Hungary and even there it was not shared by all the interested parties. The preoccupation with internal matters, however, does not show that the Bohemian estates were overly concerned with what was going on in Hungary. The Turkish danger seems to have played a more significant role with the Moravian estates, who were closer to the scene of military operations, and this difference between them and their Bohemian counterparts was deepened by yet another divergence of opinion. The Moravian estates, like the estates of other lateral lands, were not consulted about the election of the king who ultimately became their sovereign; the Bohemian estates considered this decision their own prerogative. As a response to this haughty stance, Moravia and the other lateral lands accepted Ferdinand as king on the strength of his marriage with Anna Jagiello. Although this may look like a merely juridical quibble, it exemplified that lack of unity which continued to jeopardize any joint action of the estates on behalf of the Czech nation as a whole.

In 1526, after two earlier short-lived trials, the Habsburgs acceded to the Bohemian throne and reigned for the next 392 years, a similar duration to their rule throughout the majority, if not the whole, of Hungary. The stage was set for a grandiose project of welding together three groupings of countries, the Austrian, the Bohemian and the Hungarian. Ruled from Austrian Vienna, the societies of these countries were to be integrated politically and ideologically.

The task with which the Habsburgs were preoccupied in the first two centuries of their rule was as follows: monarchic autocracy was to contain the oligarchy of the estates. Pluralism was to be abolished, or at least reduced to the minimum in its two most sensitive areas: the structure of political power and the field of religious beliefs and practices.

This was a daunting proposition and not all the Habsburgs on the Austrian, Bohemian and Hungarian thrones were keen to participate in its implementation. Many of them felt satisfied with the *modus vivendi* already existing with the estates, some even sympathized with the Reformation. But a sense of dynastic duty brought them into line; their vacillation merely gave temporary comfort to their opponents, a respite in the run towards the final goal. The vanguard of reinvigorated Catholicism, the Jesuit order, and the court of Madrid, forbade any prolonged deviation from the path assigned to both Spanish and Austrian branches of the House of Habsburg.

In Bohemia and Moravia it was the whole cultural and political orientation of the Czech nation which was at stake. In contrast to the king whose objectives were coherent, the estates were divided not only by their interests as estates *per se* but also by their religion, in which respect the situation was becoming more complicated than under the Jagiellons.

The traditional Utraquism was losing momentum. Only three points distinguished it from the official Church. The choice of Eucharist for laymen, the use of the Czech language at Mass and the commemoration of John Hus's death as a Church holiday. The Hussites split into those who looked for *rapprochement* with the Roman Church (the so-called 'old Utraquists') and those who wanted their establishment to adopt Lutheranism with its more radical marks of separate identity: the Bible as the only source of theological reasoning, justification by faith alone, abolition of priestly celibacy, of monasticism and also of quite a few sacraments. The struggle between the old and new Utraquists for the domination of their Consistory gave the king the opportunity to intervene on behalf of the former.

Meanwhile Luther's Reformation in Germany was followed in Switzerland and France by an even more radical deviation from Catholic orthodoxy; Zwingli and Calvin did not hesitate to reject the belief in the real presence of Christ's body and blood in the Eucharist and established their separate religious organizations more on republican than episcopal foundations: the apostolic succession for priesthood was abandoned in the Lutheran and Calvinist wings of Protestantism alike. In the mid-sixteenth century Calvin's teaching began to exert a strong influence on the Unity of Brethren.

The new religious issues failed to mitigate the ongoing struggle between the autocratic and polycratic tendencies. On the contrary, religious divisions provided the old rivalries with a new vigour. On the other hand, dynastic interests cut across the dividing lines based on religion. European politics began to look like a two-tier kaleidoscope, in which the traditional personal feuds and estate wars were overlaid and interwoven with the ideological strifes of two or three religious concepts. The perennial struggle for power, wealth and prestige often acquired ideological connotations.

Gradually a new geopolitical division of Western Europe began to crystallize. Broadly speaking, the Protestant north stood against the Catholic south. The demarcation was by no means clear-cut. For more than a hundred years the border between these two versions of what was until then Latin Christianity was in flux; even after its stabilization numerous and sizeable enclaves remained on both sides. But the difference was clearly visible: it was not only a matter of religion, i.e., of faith and style of worship, but could also be perceived in the art, working habits and general style of life. We may say, with tongue in cheek, that the more mundane and introvert north clashed with the more emotional and exuberant south. In each of these parts of Europe the bequest of the Renaissance took on a different flavour.[1]

Bohemia and Moravia became the frontline countries in that division. In the sixteenth century the north exerted a stronger influence and the German-speaking population of all Bohemian lands largely turned to the Lutheran Reformation; most of the Czech Utraquists followed suit and even the Brethren let themselves be influenced. Catholics

remained in a minority; especially in Bohemia where their
numbers dwindled considerably, perhaps to as little as 10
per cent of the population. The division of power between
the king and the estates, a division which gave the latter a
wide range of virtual independence, facilitated this development.

The development of this division in neighbouring Germany
gave Ferdinand his first opportunity of extending royal
power at the expense of at least one estate, the boroughs. In
this respect Ferdinand followed the pattern of the Habsburg
policy of confrontation: his own with regard to the Austrian
cities, especially Vienna, and his brother's more vigorous
approach in Spain and the Low Countries. In Bohemia the
issue was delicate, and its overtones were to have a radical
influence on further development, so much so that the
events involved must be recounted in some detail.

In 1546 the conflict between Emperor Charles V and his
supporters in the Catholic League, and the imperial estates
of the Protestant Union of Schmalkalden led by John
Friedrich, Elector of Saxony, culminated in war. Hard
pressed by the Schmalkalden armies, Charles asked his
brother Ferdinand for help; lacking money for sufficient
mercenaries himself, Ferdinand turned to the Bohemian
estates with a request for the dispatch of their home guard
to Germany. This demand put the Bohemian estates in an
awkward position. The Protestant estates knew that the
army would be used against their co-religionists; but the
case was not presented to them as a religious issue, a view
supported by the fact that some Protestant princes of Saxony
(rivals within the elector's own family) sided with the
emperor. The Bohemian estates, irrespective of religion,
could unite on the constitutional position that the home
guard was not designed for an engagement beyond the border. Nevertheless the Bohemian estates reluctantly summoned the levies, but kept them idling within the kingdom.
As the situation for the emperor continued to deteriorate,

Ferdinand risked a constitutional conflict, summoning the home guard himself to operate beyond the border. This was viewed as an infringement upon the rights of the land, so that the estate diet was summoned in contravention of the royal prohibition and agreed to press the king for more decentralization and lower taxation. For the campaign the king had to satisfy himself with small contingents sent by some Catholic barons and by three boroughs ruled by Catholic councillors.

Meanwhile, the situation on the battlefield changed and it was the Elector of Saxony who asked his co-religionists in Bohemia to help him against the emperor. This, however, would have been outright high treason, which the nobles sought to avoid, although there were some who spoke for taking such a risk. (Only an insignificant contingent provided some help to the elector who temporarily occupied a silver mining town in Bohemia close to the Saxon border.) Indecision proved to be the worst possible option for the Bohemian estates since it not only offended the king but failed to help his foe. In 1547 the elector was defeated and was made prisoner. The king could now take his revenge.

A good strategist and tactician, and aware of the limits of his real power, Ferdinand proceeded gradually, trying to isolate individual opponents and their groups; he focused his retribution on the boroughs, while offering the nobility an easy escape. Although a part of the nobility was still inclined to resist and the walled and well-armed cities like Prague could withstand a military intervention, the councillors were frightened and hoped for pardon while submitting themselves to royal mercy. Other boroughs followed the example of Prague. However, this submission did not bring mercy but instead a devastating punishment. In a series of decrees dealing with individual rebellious cities separately (altogether twenty-eight of them, the three Catholic boroughs which had helped the king being spared), Ferdinand required first the extradition of all their weaponry; then he confiscated all their landed property outside the city walls and imposed heavy fines (hostages from the foremost burghers' families were taken until the payments were made). Following this, all the statutes granting the boroughs autonomy were withdrawn and royal officials were put in charge. Having thus assured himself that the boroughs would not vote against him at the diets, he graciously granted them the right to participate in their proceedings.

In contrast to the summary treatment dealt out to the boroughs, only individual noblemen (sixteen barons and nineteen knights) were to taste the king's wrath. All were punished by confiscation, total or partial, of property, and two knights were executed along with two prominent burghers of Prague.

Although the issue between the king and the estates was presented on both sides as a purely constitutional matter, the religious implication was obvious. The king exploited his victory by increasing pressure on the religious front: not only generally against the Protestants in the boroughs which were now completely under his command, but more particularly against the Brethren who were not protected by the Compacts and whose members were believed to be ringleaders in the plot against the king. The old, obsolete edict against the Brethren of 1508, passed by King Vladislav, was reinvigorated and applied to the property confiscated from the nobles, and the bishop of the Unity of Brethren was convicted on a charge of conspiracy and put in gaol. Only the lack of Catholic missionaries prevented the king from making recatholization effective.

The main effect of the first confrontation between the Habsburgs and the Bohemian estates was the elimination of the royal boroughs from further contest. Politically and economically their significance was reduced to a minimum. The contrast to the situation thirty years earlier, when the boroughs were able to withstand the combined pressure of the aristocracy and the king, is striking. From 1547 on, it was the nobility who provided the only counter-weight to royal power and the protection of the Reformation rested wholly on their shoulders.

Without going into further detail, we may ask why the Bohemian boroughs, having played the leading role during the Hussite wars and thereafter preserving a respectable place in the power structure of the realm, were so easily out-manoeuvred and deprived of their significance? In brief, there were three reasons, economic, demographic and psychological. The increasing competition of entrepreneurial activity on the part of the aristocracy deprived them of a substantial share of the domestic market. Decreasing immigration from the villages, combined with insufficient reproduction among urban dwellers, caused a population decline in many boroughs. Last but not least, they lacked the dedication necessary to mount a successful defence of their cause.

Ferdinand's inability to translate his victory over the estates into religious conversions led the king to invite the Jesuits in as missionaries. The first of them came to Prague in 1556; later they opened their own college there and between 1556 and 1597 two more Jesuit colleges were founded in Moravia and four more in Bohemia. It was a more tedious task to fill the Prague archbishopric (the seat was vacant from 1421); initially Ferdinand linked this issue with the recognition of the Compacts by the pope, a move which would help to bring the old Utraquists into the bosom of the Catholic Church. The Curia, however, did not see this point. Eventually, an archbishop was appointed in 1561 but only one element of the Compacts, albeit the most important concerning the choice of Eucharist for laymen, was granted to Germany and the archbishopric of Prague in 1564. (Bohemia apparently was not to be treated as a special case.) But all this was too little and too late.

Meanwhile in 1562, the king imposed his own nominees on the Utraquist Consistory against vigorous protest from the now thoroughly Lutheran nobility. In 1563 the Council of Trent which from 1545 had been drawing up principles of Catholic reinvigoration or 'Catholic Reformation' concluded its work. Papal autocracy was strengthened and discipline in the Church was tightened. Reconciliation with the Roman Church, desired by humanists throughout Europe, was now regarded by the neo-Utraquists as out of the question.

With Ferdinand's death in 1564, the situation changed in favour of the Protestants. The new King Maximilian (as Emperor Maximilian II) acceded to the throne as a Lutheran sympathizer; it seems that in his heart he was an enlightened and ecumenical Christian without any denominational bias. Before he took his post however, he had to promise the mighty Habsburg clan that he would do nothing to harm the Catholic cause. Furthermore, he consented to send his four sons to be educated at the Spanish court. Thus it was merely a respite from intolerance which could be expected for the duration of his reign.

The Protestants attempted to use the new situation for the acquisition of legal status for their religion; this would give them complete independence from the Roman Church. In 1567 the Bohemian estates requested, amongst other things, that the king exclude the Compacts of Basle from the statute books of the realm and not press for their approbation by the pope. This meagre compromise, concluded at the Council of Basle, could provide no ground for subsequent religious differentiation. In 1572 the neo-Utraquists withdrew from the Utraquist Consistory because the king arrogated to himself the nomination of members who were old Utraquists hostile to Lutheran innovations.

The request to grant religious freedom was voiced by the estates in all Maximilian's domains, but for the Czechs in Bohemia and Moravia the situation was complicated by the separate existence of the royally banned Unity of Brethren. The Bohemian estates found an opportunity to press their demands in 1575 when the king asked the diet for an additional levy for a campaign against the Turks in Hungary and for the acceptance of his oldest son Rudolph as the future king. The estates made their approval dependent upon granting tolerance to non-Catholics. The king tried to exploit the division between the Lutherans and the Brethren; but the two factions realized the necessity of a united front and, under pressure from laymen, their theologians eventually agreed a common creed known as the Bohemian Confession. In comparison with other parts of Europe, where Lutherans and Calvinists were unable to find a common language and often pursued contradictory policies, the agreement between the Bohemian Lutherans and the Brethren was a remarkable achievement. Although the Brethren kept their separate organization, it was the common policy that mattered.

Subsequent negotiations with the king were more difficult, but eventually a compromise, excluding the royal boroughs which were not supposed to follow a different religion from the king, was achieved. Maximilian gave his royal consent to the existence of a Protestant establishment, and as a *quid pro quo*, received the levy and acceptance of Rudolph as his successor; the latter also had to express his consent. Officially, however, nothing was committed to writing. The king let the Protestant leaders know that under the circumstances he was unable to offer more, and assured the representatives of the Catholic Church that the whole exercise was merely a tactical manoeuvre. The estates were left to write their own account which was then deposited in the archives of the land. Thus nothing was in fact resolved.

Under Maximilian's successor, Rudolph, as Emperor Rudolph II (1576–1611), the struggle between Protestantism and Catholicism became more acute. Educated in Madrid, Rudolph began his rule with a determination to strengthen his authority and promote recatholization. But later his unsettled mind turned to his hobbies of astronomy, alchemy and art collecting; his autocratic temper prevented him

from being influenced in a more radical direction by the
most ardent Catholics. Only in 1599 were their representatives appointed to all important offices in the kingdom and
similar practices introduced into royal boroughs. Non-
Catholics on royal estates were ordered to convert to
Catholicism.

Despite various pressures, religious pluralism, nurtured
by the spirit of the Renaissance and Humanism, continued
to flourish, and Czech culture blossomed with it. Protestants and Catholics alike entertained lively contacts with
their co-religionists abroad, the Lutheran, Calvinist and
Catholic centres of culture and education. Young noblemen
often studied abroad. Although the University of Prague
failed to recover fully from the loss of contact with other
universities during the Hussite period, secondary education
in schools run by the Unity of Brethren and later also by the
Jesuits was nevertheless very good. The influence of the
Renaissance and of Humanism was felt in *belles-lettres*,
architecture, visual art and the whole style of life of the
upper classes. Czech literature attained its zenith in the
new Czech translation of the Bible, the so-called Kralice
Bible, which was elaborated and published with an extensive commentary during the years 1579–94.

Czech culture also profited from the temporary transfer
of the imperial court from Vienna to Prague (1583–1612)
which, thanks to Rudolph, became an international centre
of culture for over two decades. At Rudolph's court the
most renowned astronomers and artists together with the
less glorious alchemists enjoyed generous support. Prague
acquired a certain cosmopolitan flavour nourished by the
multiethnic nature of the Reformation and Counter-Reformation, whilst the importance of religion excluded any lan-
guage-based nationalism. This was in marked contrast to
the Hussite period, during which the use of Czech spread
into many German-dominated towns, for during this era the
percentage of German speakers again increased.

However, neither science nor a deeper understanding of Christ's message was capable of challenging bellicose bigotry; indeed, differences of faith gave the unending wars of kings and estates an ideological dimension. In the overall context, the most remarkable event was the revolution against Spanish rule which occurred in the Netherlands. Failure of the Spanish army, the finest in Europe at that time, to suppress the rebellious Dutch showed how effective could be the blend of a Calvinist ideology imbued with religious self-righteousness and tinged with nationalism, when supported by urban self-assertiveness. It has to be pointed out that, apart from Switzerland, only in the Netherlands had the Reformation become almost exclusively a matter of the third estate. Elsewhere its most effective support came either from royalty or aristocracy.

Dramatic events in other countries, such as the massacre of the Protestant leaders in Paris and other French cities in 1572, the subsequent establishment of a Huguenot state within the kingdom of France, and the unsuccessful Spanish attempt to curb Protestant England in 1588, all excited interest in Bohemia. The young aristocrats educated abroad often returned home radicalized in their partisan attitudes. The Habsburg royal courts in Austria and Spain pressed for a faster and more resolute pace of recatholization.

Discord in the Austrian lineage of the Habsburg family between Rudolph and his younger brother Matthias, however, produced a setback for this policy. The successful uprising of the Hungarian estates in 1604 forced Rudolph to a peace in which he granted the Hungarian estates a free choice of religion and equality between Protestants and Catholics, with the result that some radical Catholics also became discontented with Rudolph's rule in Bohemia and Austria. Matthias used this opportunity to push his succession to the throne, concluding an agreement with the confederation of Hungarian, Austrian and Moravian estates to the effect that they would help him to the throne in return for his consideration of their religious demands. The Bohemian estates were also invited to join the coalition but they saw better prospects in forcing concessions from the embattled Rudolph. Thus, divided, the Czechs began their fight for religious freedom. The Bohemians put their money on Rudolph, the Moravians on Matthias, and as long as the issue between them remained in abeyance, the division did no harm. In 1608 Matthias reconfirmed the traditional religious freedoms to the Moravian estates, including the royal boroughs,[2] and even granted them the right of armed resistance in their defence.

In Bohemia Rudolph offered stronger resistance and even dissolved the determined and recalcitrant diet, arguing that national law was founded on the Catholic and Utraquist creed. It was only the military mobilization by the estates, and the support they received from Silesia and the confederation headed by Matthias, which brought Rudolph to capitulation. On the 9 July 1609 he signed the Charter, the main parts of which can be summarized as follows: religious freedom was granted to all persons of *'sub utraque'* (the more pertinent label 'the Bohemian Confession' was avoided in the final edition); Protestant estates obtained the right to elect their 'defensors' (a kind of tribune) and to supervise the University of Prague. At the same time, the leaders of the Protestant and Catholic estates concluded an agreement, which was then incorporated into the statutes of the land, that allowed for the concrete implementation of Rudolph's Charter in detail.

Against the background of the political climate in Europe at large, the interdenominational peace in the Bohemian lands (Silesia obtained a similar charter) was a remarkable achievement. The tradition of religious tolerance which marked Czech society from the 1480s was not yet dead and the estates were able to exploit an extraordinary coincidence of events to bring it to a new fruition. Also remarkable was the extension of religious freedom from the privileged estates to all citizens. Although not necessarily always observed in practice, this was nevertheless a clear rejection of the principle *cuius regio eius religio* (whose the region, his the religion) valid in neighbouring Germany.

The Catholic radicals, however, did not give up. In agreement with Rudolph, the archduke and bishop, Leopold of Passau (another Habsburg) ordered mercenaries to launch a raid on Prague in the hope that this might help Rudolph revoke his Charter. The attempt not only failed but also sealed Rudolph's fate. The Curia and the Spanish court took Matthias's side; Rudolph was forced to abdicate and Matthias became king and emperor in 1611.

Nevertheless the idea of religious peace in Bohemian lands within a bitterly divided Europe proved to be a dream. The situation in Western Europe was becoming increasingly complicated; tensions became more acute and alliances more volatile. Both the Protestant and Catholic camps were divided. The Protestants were split between the Lutheran faction, based on northern and eastern Germany with Saxony as the leading power on the one hand, and the Calvinist faction based on countries on the Rhine such as the Netherlands and the Palatinate on the other. The Catholic camp was divided on purely political lines: the formidable force of the combined Spanish and Austrian Habsburgs, at that time supported by the Curia, was opposed for most of the time by France, Savoy and Venice. Thus the Calvinist faction led in Germany by the Elector of Palatinate, often found common ground with the anti-Habsburg forces. In this context it also has to be stressed that the Calvinists considered it lawful to revolt against an oppressive ruler. On the other hand the Lutherans preferred to stick to Luther's principle that a revolt against a legitimate power was a sin; thus it happened, for instance, that the Elector of Saxony used this argument whenever it suited him to support the Habsburgs against his Calvinist rival, the Elector of Palatinate. Moreover – *les extrêmes se touchant* – some Jesuits began to condone the assassination of a tyrant (naturally a Protestant or crypto-Protestant) as a lawful act.

Each side jealously watched the other and looked for the opportunity to expand its domains. Matthias abandoned his earlier flirtation with the Protestants; when he transferred his imperial seat again to Vienna, he left in Bohemia a government composed of radical Catholics. Despite this and the increasing tension of the international situation, the estates of the Bohemian lands preferred to do nothing. In 1617 they accepted Ferdinand of Styria, a cousin of the childless Matthias, as his successor, although his previous record in purging Styria of all non-Catholics was decidedly ominous.

Only one act which appeared as a direct infringement of Rudolph's Charter by the ecclesiastical authorities brought the Protestant estates to action. The *casus belli* was the destruction of two Protestant churches built by private collection from abroad, on the ecclesiastical estates in north Bohemia, both, incidentally, in the German-speaking area. The legal question was complicated but neither side wanted to resort to arbitration as envisaged in Rudolph's Charter. The radical Protestant barons were keen to settle their accounts with the radical Catholic barons who, as members of the Bohemian government, showed more zeal for recatholization than the ecclesiastics and the king.[3]

The Protestant defensors summoned their estates who voiced a strong protest but were rebuked by the king. Once again they met in contravention of royal decree and accused certain members of the government of a traitorous infringement of Rudolph's Charter. Only two of the three alleged culprits were in Prague at the time; they were charged, found guilty and, together with their clerk, thrown out of the window. This incident, which took place on 23 May 1618, was the so-called second defenestration of Prague.

The defenestration was not intended to start a revolution. (All the three 'executed' survived and only one was hurt.) The estates hurried to send the king a message in which they assured him of their loyalty, blaming everything on two of his ministers who had been justly punished according to the Charter. But at the same time the elected directory (a kind of executive committee) of the estates sent messengers to all the other lands of the Bohemian Crown with requests for support and made similar approaches to other Protestant governments abroad. Ironically, the most effective help to the Bohemian estates from abroad (a contingent of mercenaries under an experienced general) was provded by the Catholic Duke of Savoy.

On the advice of his cautious counsellors the king showed a readiness to negotiate, admitting that Rudolph's Charter might have been violated. Neither side, however, was genuinely keen to negotiate although there was also no enthusiasm for war, but once the process of confrontation had started it could not be stopped and inevitably the pre-emptive military operations resulted in war.

Meanwhile the death of Matthias gave the Bohemian estates the opportunity to forget their acceptance of Ferdinand as the legitimate king and to claim the right to elect another. However, before they made their decision, the anti-Habsburg front widened as the Bohemians were joined by the Moravians following their successful coup against a government loyal to the king, and the Austrian estates soon followed suit.[4] (The Silesian estates had supported them from the start.) Thus virtually almost all Ferdinand's lands were involved in the war against him.

Since wars in those days were fought almost exlusively by mercenaries who cost far more than national servicemen, money was an indispensable requirement of success. The estates had been accustomed to collect taxes slowly and, unfortunately for the Protestant cause, the fact that they were now to use the money for their own benefit did nothing to change their habitual reluctance to pay. They were convinced that they were fighting on behalf of the whole Protestant camp, and so they considered themselves entitled to

ask for help from co-religionists abroad, but only the Netherlands helped with a significant subsidy. The Austrian
Habsburgs, on the other hand, had more sources of financial
aid at their disposal, the most generous of which were the
Spanish court and the Fuggers. In terms of men-at-arms,
Bavaria, with her staunchly Catholic duke, became the most
important ally of the Habsburgs.

In Germany, it was Friedrich of Palatinate, leader of the
Protestant Union, and a zealous Calvinist, who showed a
genuine interest in helping the Bohemian estates. Since
Friedrich was the son-in-law of James I of England, the
Bohemians hoped that the latter would not refuse help, but
the King of England was interested in marrying his son to a
Spanish princess and preferred to encourage negotiation.
Nevertheless the wishful thinking of Bohemian leaders led
them to offer the Bohemian crown to Friedrich of Palati-
nate, thus by-passing another possible candidate, John
George of Saxony, a dedicated Lutheran.

The new king proved to be a dubious asset to the Protestant cause. The alienation of the Elector of Saxony, who
then found it easier to strike a deal with the Habsburgs, was
not outweighed by the effective help of the Calvinist camp.
In Bohemia itself, Calvinist radicalism was manifested in an
iconoclastic 'reformation' of Prague cathedral and in personal changes in the royal domains, which ran counter to the
current mood of the country.

More important for the continuing struggle was the abandonment of the project to transform the Bohemian Crown
lands into a confederation of estate republics in which the
boroughs were supposed to regain some of their earlier
power and prestige. Although the aristocracy was in no
mood to share any real power with them it expected the
boroughs to take over the main burden in financing the war.
Significantly, no one thought of the peasants although they
bore the brunt of the ravages of war, plunder and slaughter
by mercenary armies, friends and foes alike. Only one baron

of Upper Austria showed enough wisdom and courage to suggest measures for improving the peasants' lot with the aim of involving them in a common cause.[5] But nobody listened.

The war unfolded as a chain of more or less incoherent campaigns with alternating fortunes. Following two years of extensive manoeuvres on the territories between Prague and Vienna, the imperial army, led by Maximilian of Bavaria, clashed with the Bohemian army on the White Mountain west of Prague on 8 November 1620. In a short, bloody battle, the Bohemians were defeated and the gates of the Bohemian capital opened to the victors. No attempt to defend the walled city was undertaken.

With the exception of a few boroughs helped by mercenaries under foreign command, all cities in Bohemia surrendered whilst the Moravians, whose contingent at the White Mountain showed particular bravery, also stopped fighting. The Silesians surrendered, after the Elector of Saxony (an ally of Ferdinand the Habsburg) guaranteed their religious and estates' liberties. The Lusatians surrendered directly to the Elector of Saxony. The estates of the Bohemian Crown ceased to be partners in the war which they had started and which, in a much wider European context, was to rage until 1648.

The ban on pluralism. Escape to baroque

Although the battle on the White Mountain was not the end of the war, it put an end to the pluralist framework of the Bohemian state. Irrespective of what happened later on the battlefields, the several reversals of fortunes which brought various parts of Bohemia and Moravia under occupation by the armies of the north (Danish, Saxon and Swedish – there was even a Saxon presence in Prague of half a year's duration), the House of Habsburg fully exploited the opportunity to resolve the pending issues of pluralism versus uniformity.

Religious pluralism was to be wholly abolished. Pluralism of estates was to be stripped of its substance.

Immediately after the success in Bohemia, measures for recatholization began to be discussed at the court in Vienna. At stake were the extent and the methods of Counter-Reformation. Should only the radical Protestant denominations, such as the Brethren and the Calvinists, be banned or should the ban also affect the Lutherans and even the old Utraquists? How fast should recatholization take place, how should the process be phased, and to what extent should force be used?

Significantly, the local hierarchy, the two successive archbishops of Prague, stood for a milder and slower procedure, whereas the foreign advisers, including the papal nuncio and Ferdinand's Jesuit confessors, pressed for a comprehensive and speedy solution. Concern for a good relationship with Saxony caused some hesitation with respect to the Lutheran clergy; but here, eventually, the application of the principle *cuius regio eius religio* on both sides of the border created the tacitly agreed basis of no tolerance in either country. The old Utraquists were included in the ban for a pragmatic reason: if they were to be left out, all the other Protestants would flock to them and thus religious dualism would be preserved, albeit in an attenuated form. As far as the use of force was concerned, no definite decision seems to have been taken, but the practice was contingent on local conditions and, as long as the war was not over, on the international situation.

Retribution started with twenty-seven Bohemian leaders of the uprising being sentenced for high treason and executed; many more were sentenced to death in absentia.[6] The property of all those sentenced was confiscated. Between 1621 and 1624 all non-Catholic clergy were banned from the country. The Eucharist for laymen of both kinds and all other old Utraquist practices were abolished.

The nobles themselves were deprived of religious freedom only in 1627; they were given the choice of either converting

to Catholicism or emigrating. Approximately one-fifth of the
nobles left the country. In Moravia similar measures were
taken somewhat later and usually with less vigour; in particular, no leaders of the uprising were executed. On the other
hand, confiscations of property were carried out on a large
scale. After 1627, the only non-Catholics who were allowed
to stay were the Jews. In comparison with Poland and Hungary they were not numerous in the lands of the Bohemian
Crown. Squeezed into their ghettos and heavily discrimi-
nated against, they survived, as elsewhere in Christian
Europe, until the epoch of the Enlightenment, outside the
framework of the political and cultural life of the country.

In addition to a final ban on the remaining Protestants in
the country, the constitution of the Bohemian lands was
also changed drastically: that of Bohemia in 1627 and that of
Moravia in 1628. The Bohemian Crown in the Habsburg
male lineage became hereditary; no formal acceptance of
succession by the estates was needed for the future. The
rights of the estates in the administration, judiciary and legislation were reduced to the minimum. The diet was allowed
to discuss only matters put on the agenda by the king. The
administration was concentrated in the Royal Bohemian
Court Chancellery and its officials were to be appointed by
the king. He also became entitled to grant foreigners the
right to settle in the country. Catholicism was declared the
exclusive religion of the realm and in official usage the German
language was granted equal status with the Czech.

The statutes of all the lands of the Bohemian Crown were
changed in a similar way. In Bohemia the clerical estate
which had been abolished during the Hussite wars was re-
established; in Moravia, where it had never ceased to exist,
it was promoted to the first rank. The representation of the
royal boroughs, however, was reduced to a mere token; in
the diet they were allocated only one vote.

It took two more decades, however, before the new
arrangements could become fully effective. After the victory

of imperial forces over the coalition of the Protestant princes led by the King of Denmark, which exposed the whole north of Germany to Counter-Reformation, Sweden, as the main protector of the Protestant cause entered the war in 1630. Her military might forced even the recalcitrant Saxony to join, albeit half-heartedly, the Protestant camp. With new hope, the Bohemian and Moravian exiles flocked to the Swedish colours. Yet the religious alignments did not become any more straightforward. The Elector of Saxony, despite being Lutheran like the Swedish king, pursued mainly his own territorial claims and obstructed the endeavours of the Bohemian exiles. France with her Catholic king and Cardinal Richelieu as prime minister, became the main financier of the Swedish campaign. When in 1635, after five years of brilliant successes, the Swedish armies suffered a defeat, France entered the war on the Swedish side. A few days later, Ferdinand II eliminated Saxony and most of the German states from the ranks of his foes by concluding a separate peace (Peace of Prague) with them; in this peace he ceded Lusatia to Saxony and granted freedom of Lutheran confession in Silesia. The ideological implications of the war were further weakened; in Bohemia and Moravia, however, they remained in full strength.

Before France became directly involved, Bohemians experienced yet another whim of fortune. In an atmosphere where religious fanaticism flourished intertwined with cynicism and a calculating self-interest, there was ample opportunity for unscrupulous condottieri to make enormous fortunes. The rise and fall of Albrecht of Wallenstein is a classic example. Of a baronial family, educated in the Unity of Brethren, Wallenstein converted to Catholicism, made a career in the imperial army, rising to the very top as 'Generalissimus', acquired vast estates and, as a duke, was promoted to the ranks of the empire's princes; but his ambition was not satisfied.

Having entered into secret, protracted negotiations with

the other side in the conflict, Wallenstein was offered the Bohemian crown, provided he changed sides. But Wallenstein lacked determination and several times missed the right moment for action. His gamble was readily unmasked. In 1634, Ferdinand's faithful officers murdered Wallenstein together with his associates. Thus not only was the dream of an ambitious upstart ended, but also the new hope of the Protestants in Bohemia was dashed. A new wave of confiscations of property further weakened the domestic aristocracy of Bohemia.[7]

From then on the fate of the Bohemian cause wholly depended on the goodwill of foreign powers which, however, pursued their own particular aims. Thus the compromise, sealed in the Peace of Westphalia of 1648, left the Protestant cause in Bohemia and Moravia out of the account. Only the reaffirmation of the Peace of Prague gave the Silesians the freedom of Lutheran confession. With the Saxon annexation of Lusatia confirmed, Bohemia and Moravia were abandoned to the mercy of their Habsburg masters.

Only after the peace was concluded could the Habsburg government embark on a more systematic implementation of its programme. According to the Jesuits' estimate, at the beginning of the 1650s more than two-thirds of the population of Bohemia and Moravia still adhered to the Protestant creed. Conversions were hampered by an inadequate number of Catholic clergy and administration. Therefore additional colleges and also bishoprics were founded.

With respect to the education of the clergy, frictions emerged between the Jesuits on the one hand and the Archbishop of Prague and other monastic orders on the other. The main bone of contention was the university (the Carolinum). The Jesuits wanted to get it under their power by means of a merger with their own college in Prague (the Clementinum). The struggle lasted until 1654 when a compromise was achieved in which the Jesuits got the upper hand.[8] The result was the Charles-Ferdinand University.

Missionary work was combined with administrative control and, where persuasion had not succeeded, with the use of force. Everybody was supposed to go to auricular confession once a year. Having fulfilled this duty he or she received a voucher which then had to be sent via the respective landlord to the secular authorities; as a means of checking this the ecclesiastical authorities had also to make their own accounts. In 1729 detailed instructions on heretic books and passages in otherwise unobjectionable books was published in Hradec Králové which, three hundred years earlier, had been one of the main strongholds of the Hussites. These instructions were entitled *Clavis haeresim claudens et aperiens* (the Key for recognition and uprooting of heresies). The author, a Jesuit named Konias, considered the majority of all Czech books on religion published between 1414 and 1620 to be dangerous and suspicious.[9]

Under the pressure of censorship and with a continuous outflow of people, Czech Protestant culture transferred its base abroad. It was mainly the Brethren who at that time produced outstanding works of literature which were then published in various places stretching from Holland through Germany and Poland to Hungary. One name in particular has to be stressed: that of Jan Amos Comenius, the last bishop of the Unity of Brethren, protagonist of modern didactic methods and pansophic compendia whose work acquired an international reputation. For some time he succeeded in basing his activity on Leszno in western Poland where, from the time of earlier persecutions, the Unity of Brethren had founded several settlements and won Polish converts also. Not only clergymen and authors in political matters (such as Pavel Stránský, author of *Respublica Bojema*, a comprehensive account of the historical background and political life in the Bohemian lands before the uprising), but also many artists had to develop their talents abroad.

At home it was not only Protestant writings but Czech literature in general which suffered a tremendous loss, with low levels of literacy effecting the demand for Czech books. Catholic missionary activity laid more stress on other media of communications, such as drama, music and, above all, visual art. Here lay the gist of the educational meaning of the Catholic baroque. Whether devised for the upper, aesthetically demanding strata, or for the more modest common folk, it embodied expression of drama or elation, thus offering a visual framework for ecstatic adoration or even mystical experience. The Virgin Mary became the focus of devotion; it was especially her cult which was to give the Counter-Reformation its gentle flavour but, at the same time, it provided a characteristic mark of Catholic orthodoxy, a mark which distinguished it ostentatiously from Protestant worship.

In 1729 Jan of Nepomuk, a victim of the capricious King Wenceslas IV by whom he had been martyred in 1393, was canonized as a symbol of revitalized Catholicism. This, however, was on the basis of a misleading account of his sainthood; in fact he was martyred and killed because he defended the rights of the Church against their usurpation by the secular power. The Archbishop of Prague complained vigorously to Rome on this matter. The legend, however, made Jan Nepomuk a martyr because he protected the secret of the queen's confession *vis-à-vis* her royal husband. The canonization was based on the legend as this took shape in Bohemia; thus the Curia in Rome, apparently unwittingly, avoided reference to an issue which was becoming topical again: encroachment on the part of the state upon the jurisdiction of the Church. This time, however, it was another ideological setting – the dawn of the Enlightenment – in which the monarchic state arrogated for itself more power whilst the church, needing the state's support, could not offer much resistance.

The triumphant advance of Catholicism and the manifest splendour of the baroque, however, was not matched by commensurate developments in other walks of life. Artistic blossoming contrasted painfully with the worsened status of the peasantry and with socio-economic retardation in comparison with other parts of Europe. Political consciousness on the part of the urban strata virtually disappeared. The gentry substantially declined both in numbers and in wealth. The aristocracy at large ceased to play an independent political role. Many of the warrior aristocracy tended to become court aristocracy and the court itself, with its permanent seat in Vienna, pursued its own interests more than ever. The Bohemian state ceased to be a subject of international policy, an actor in the political game of nations. nations.

In 1684 the Bohemian chancellor, Count Kinský, referred to the fact that in Bohemia at least one-third of the land still lay devastated as if it were common knowledge. According to the land register of 1682, over 22 per cent of the rustical (land in direct cultivation of the serfs) lay fallow.[10] The extent of the demographic decline (including emigration) has been estimated at between a quarter and a half of the total population. More recent authors tend to consider the lower figures as more probable. Not only villages but also many boroughs were ruined.

The lack of an adequate labour force led to a further tightening of bondage and to a substantial extension of the corvée. The bondsmen became wholly dependent on their landlords. It was a tacit *quid pro quo* between royalty and aristocracy: the reduction of the nobles' power *vis-à-vis* the king was compensated for by their extended dominion over their subjects. As the king declared many rights of the privileged estates forfeit because of their treacherous uprising, so the nobles, without any analagous cause, considered the traditional regulations and customs concerning the rights and duties of their subjects abolished, and took it upon themselves to impose new, arbitrary and more oppressive rules upon their subjects.[11] Grievances addressed to the authorities and ultimately to the king/emperor only brought some reprieve in exceptional circumstances; in most instances they were rejected. As a result, in the last quarter of the seventeenth century, a series of peasant revolts broke out in many parts of Bohemia and Moravia. Their savage repression did nothing to improve the situation.

The Czech historian, Josef Pekař, renowned for his Catholic sympathies, described the contrast between the heights and depths of society in Bohemia and Moravia after the Thirty Years War as follows:

> At a time when the official land registers abound in sad testimonies of the plight of the common men who because of inadequate yields and heavy levies flee from their petty holdings, in Prague (and also in the countryside) sumptuous baronial castles, churches, monasteries and splendid monumental cathedrals raise up their victorious cupolas in joyful exultation, the new Bohemia triumphantly addresses her thanksgivings to heaven, Bohemia of a few thousand, or even a few hundred people whose power and glory grows out of the ruins of hundreds of thousands.[12]

With respect to this situation one cannot but remember Max Weber's thesis of a twofold, contrasting, social function of religion. For those at the top, the splendour of the baroque appeared as a legitimation of their victorious cause. For those at the bottom, the elated devotional atmosphere of baroque piety was a salutary refuge, a compensation for the shortcomings abounding in other aspects of everyday life. By no means was this contrast a phenomenon unique to Czech history, nor for the particular period under discussion. But never in Czech history was the contrast expressed in such a drastic way.

5
Rebirth of national consciousness

New breezes from the West. The school of adolescence

After two centuries (1420–1620) abounding in religious strife and multifaceted cross-conflicts between the constitutional pillars of the political nation (king and estates), the Czechs and, to a large extent, their German-speaking cohabitants in Bohemia and Moravia, retreated into what may be described as a state of political hibernation which lasted for another two centuries. A substantial part of their élites had to emigrate. This did not affect the Czechs and Germans to the same extent. The ethnic Germans in Bohemia and Moravia who had joined the Czechs on their path towards heresy only after Luther led them in that direction were not a socio-cultural entity in their own right. Being a part of a wider linguistic community, they could emigrate to countries where their own language was spoken and their religion was practised. The continuity of German culture, whether Protestant or Catholic, was not interrupted; the border between the two versions of Christianity ran across Germany.

However, the only refuge with ethnically closely related people for the Czechs was in Upper Hungary, in present-day Slovakia. But this country was exposed to a recatholization drive similar to that in Bohemia and Moravia. Only the presence of Ottoman power in Hungary which lasted for 150 years prevented the Habsburg authorities from enforcing the Counter-Reformation as vigorously as in Bohemia and Moravia. Although the pro-Reformation Slovaks turned mainly to the Lutheran (the Augsburg) Confession (thus following the Germans settlers in their country), for literary and liturgical purposes they used biblical Czech, the language of the Kralice Bible. (Slovak as a separate literary language emerged only in the second quarter of the nineteenth century). It was from Slovakia, or from Hungary at large, that the remaining Czech Protestants later received moral and pastoral support.

The domestic environment in Bohemia and Moravia was not propitious for cultivation of the Czech language. After the Thirty Years War, almost 40 per cent of the Bohemian and Moravian nobility was composed of immigrant families.[1] Amongst them, as indeed in the cosmopolitan milieu of the Habsburg court, there were nobles of various ethnic origins such as Italians, Flemings, Walloons, Spaniards, etc. who preferred to use and cultivate Romance languages. Only later did German become the lingua franca of the administration and its use spread throughout all the upper middle strata of the Habsburg domains. Latin preserved its dominant role in the Catholic Church and in the traditional sectors of higher education. At court French was also widely used. Thus there was little need for high-quality Czech books.

A patriotic Jesuit, Bohuslav Balbín, interested in promoting the Czech language and the Czech national tradition with its loyally Catholic features, used Latin to express his views. Since there were apparently other reasons as well as this for Balbín being an odd man out in the Jesuit order, his pamphlet was published only in 1775, i.e., eighty-seven years after his death, and two years after the dissolution of the Jesuit order by the pope. Yet Balbín was not alone in his sentiments. Many native priests and also lay enthusiasts known as the 'patriots' were genuinely interested in promoting the Czech language.

At the turn of the eighteenth century the Czech-speakers in Bohemia and Moravia were mainly amongst the lowest strata of the population. The issue for the patriots was to forge a fully stratified, self-conscious nation again. Fortunately for them, that daunting task coincided with a fundamental change which affected the whole of Western European civilization; this occurred under the banner of two spiritual movements, the Enlightenment and Romanticism.

The Enlightenment produced a breakthrough, an opening towards rational, pragmatic reasoning and utilitarian values. With respect to culture, this meant free scientific questioning, better education, and classicism in artistic expression; with respect to society at large, it meant more concern for the common people with reforms introduced from above in order to improve their education and social status. In contrast to earlier social philosophies, that of the Enlightenment was, in principle, egalitarian, although it had a particular aristocratic wing and its practice was more often than not implemented by an absolutist government.

Romanticism was in many respects a response to the challenge of the Enlightenment. Dissatisfied with cold, dry rationality, people wanted to partake in some emotive experience which transcended the existence of the individual, squeezed mercilessly as it was within the narrow limits of time and space. But Romanticism not only meant a more sentimental disposition often aiming at some kind of personal transcendence, it also pointed out to a new rallying point, to a new idol. It was the new concept of nation, welding together all those who spoke the same language and shared a common culture and tradition. Given that the nation was placed at the very centre of the stage, any individual could find in it an ecstatic bond with eternity. As a frequently quoted motto put it: 'In children the nation lasts for ever.'

However, national consciousness based on language was not a new phenomenon in the Bohemian lands. In Czech literature it was occasionally voiced right from the early fourteenth century. The community of language played an important mobilizing role in the Hussite period of reform and revolution. But even then Czech national consciousness was overshadowed by religious concerns and loyalties. This was all the more the case at the time of the Reformation and Counter-Reformation. It was only with the coming of the nineteenth century that national consciousness based on language became the primary mark of differentiation within the population of the Bohemian lands.

Thus the Enlightenment and Romanticism, the two great intellectual movements which in one way or another affected the whole of Europe, opened a new path to self-assertion for the Czechs and Slovaks. With that perspective in mind, the Czechs eagerly and energetically began their march. The Slovaks quickly followed suit; but they met with many more obstacles.

In Czechoslovak history, the period from about the mid-eighteenth to the mid-nineteenth century is known as national revival. This means the re-establishment of Czech as a literary language and the recuperation of the national consciousness. The spirit of Romanticism was the godfather of these aspirations. The Enlightenment in its turn opened wider horizons for intellectual initiatives and reduced social barriers between individual estates. Thus the structure of the nation which, later on, was to re-enter the political arena, became significantly altered and its base was considerably extended.

The Habsburg Empire was pushed along the path of enlightened reform by its failures in wars. The difficulties started in 1740, when other European states refused to recognize Maria Theresa's succession to the Austrian throne which until then had been the prerogative of the male line only. Although Maria Theresa's father, Charles VI, had made the necessary legal provision concerning succession on the distaff side (the so-called Pragmatic Sanction of 1713), France, Bavaria and Prussia made objections and waged war against Maria Theresa. For almost two years the Franco-Bavarian armies occupied Prague, where a substantial part of the Bohemian aristocracy accepted Charles Albert, the Elector of Bavaria, as King of Bohemia. The Franco-Bavarian venture was short-lived. Prussia, however, made definite gains; after three successive wars (ending only in 1763), most of Silesia was ceded to Prussia for good.

Prussia's expansionist policy was accompanied by Protestant propaganda attempting to foster opposition against the Habsburgs in Bohemia and Moravia as well. Prussia also became the main refuge for religious dissidents. Emigration of secret Protestants to Prussia, combined with the emergence of new, more or less vacuous pietist heresies in the Bohemian lands, led to a new wave of persecution. But some felt that more positive measures had to be taken in order to match the influence and power of Prussia.

The reason for the Prussian and French military successes was seen to lie in better organization and in the unitary nature of the state. As in most of Western Europe, in these two countries the traditional concept of patrimonial monarchy sharing power with the institutions of privileged estates was on the wane. Instead, the state began to be conceived of as a corporate legal entity, as a juridical person in its own right; the monarch and the estates alike were supposed to be its servants. Servicing the state in its turn required educated personnel, a need which created a bureaucracy as a special stratum within society. In a way, the new concept of the state in the age of Enlightenment was a belated echo of the reception of Roman law. But the main practical motive lay in the urgent need for greater efficiency in international competition, a need which was rationalized by the spirit of Enlightenment.

Starting in 1748, the administration and judiciary of the

Austrian and Bohemian lands were gradually centralized. These lands together became officially known as 'Hereditary German Lands'; the term was used in contrast to the territories of the Hungarian Crown where the German-speakers were much less numerous. The fostering of German as the state language and the lingua franca in society was a matter of convenience; the motivation was rational rather than dictated by nationalistic feelings.

Other reforms were directed towards more and better education, improvement of the lot of the peasantry, and more religious tolerance. Except with respect to the last point, reform measures were already taken under Maria Theresa (1740–80). The issue of greater religious tolerance, despite the support of some enlightened clergy (most prominent was John Leopold Hay, Bishop of Hradec Králové), could be tackled only after her death when her son Joseph II (from 1765 her co-regent) became the sole ruler.

Yet even in the new social climate in Europe, the Toleration Edict passed by Joseph II in 1781 did not grant religious tolerance across the board. Only three non-Catholic creeds were admitted: the Augsburg Confession (The Lutherans), the Helvetic Confession (the Calvinists) and the Greek Orthodox Church. The Unity of Brethren and the Bohemian Confession were not included. The tolerated religions were allowed to organize a parish with a church and school in places with at least 100 families of the respective creed. The parish registers, however, were still to be kept by the Catholic parishes. The tolerated Churches were not allowed to display the customary public symbols of their existence such as church towers, bells, etc.; church entrances were not to open onto the street and the services had to be held behind closed doors. Furthermore, those who after 1782 wanted to join a tolerated Church had to undergo a six-week-long persuasion course by the Catholic authorities not to do so.[2] In civic matters, however, there was no discrimination against those who decided to join the tolerated Churches. Under these circumstances only about 2 per cent of the population of Bohemia and Moravia used the freedom given by the Edict. The scale of discrimination against Jews was also substantially reduced.[3]

Ironically, it was not the reformed Churches but the Catholic monarchy which, at least in the short run, posed serious danger to the Roman Church. Joseph II subordinated the Catholic Church to his rule to an extent which any German/ Roman emperor during the struggle for investiture would hardly have dreamt of. Royal assent was required for all public announcements of the Church authorities within the country; and their contacts with other countries were supervised. The state regulated the education of clergy and, for economic reasons, the number of Church holidays and sumptuous religious habits. Catholicism was to adapt itself to the austere spirit of the emperor. Monasteries which were not involved in social work were dissolved and their property sequestrated. As Chancellor V.A. Kaunits put it, 'everything that is of human and not divine measure in the Church is a matter for the Emperor'.

The other epoch-making edict of Joseph II, the Edict on Bondage, was even less comprehensive than that on religious toleration. Only personal bondage was abolished; peasants could marry freely and move to other places and occupations. However, they remained 'corvéable', though within limits imposed by other government decrees. They were allowed to buy themselves out of the corvée, but this liberty did not prove effective. Further, measures were taken to keep stocks of agricultural products for emergencies. The new land register of 1785–9 abolished the distinction between the dominical and the rustical; both holdings were then taxed at the same rate. By these measures the tax levied on the peasantry was supposed to be reduced by a quarter. Each farm would be able to retain about 70 per cent of its gross income for family consumption, production costs and community, school and church charges.

Joseph had his hands full in attempting to put his house in order. Unfortunately his fragile health allowed him only ten years of rule. His younger brother, Leopold II, who succeeded him in 1790, tried to consolidate the whole complex of reforms, but his early death in 1792 and, above all, the impact of the French Revolution once again drastically changed the social climate in the Habsburg domains.

When the French Revolution broke out, the Viennese court felt relieved; the power of France, that dangerous foe, seemed to be on the wane. But revolutionary France proved to be even stronger and, when Napoleon took control, there seemed to be no match for the French armies. Fortunately for the Habsburgs, Napoleon overplayed his hand and his empire collapsed within ten years of its creation. Yet, meanwhile, substantial changes occurred in the international position of the Habsburg realm. As a result of Napoleon's conquests, the last vestiges of the medieval Roman/German Empire were abolished. When in 1804 Napoleon declared himself Emperor of France, the Roman/German Emperor Francis II saw the writing on the wall and declared himself Emperor of Austria. Thus he killed two birds with one stone: first, he made a timely preparation for a new imperial title for himself (he was to renounce the old title of Roman/German Emperor two years later); second, his hereditary Alpine lands (great duchies, duchies, etc.) appeared under the common name Austria with a higher monarchic title than were his titles of King of Hungary and King of Bohemia. Furthermore, as emperor, the Habsburg ruler was in a better position than his Prussian rival to claim for his ambassador the presidency of the new German Confederation (*Bund*) founded in 1815, just before the Congress of Vienna closed its proceedings.

Although France was defeated on the field of battle and her political regime had to return in many respects to prerevolution status, revolutionary ideas remained alive. Indeed, the postulates of human rights, civil liberties, equality

before the law, and national unity became the most influential pointers to further development, not only in France but
in the whole of Europe and even beyond. Ideas of liberalism, equality and national solidarity appealed particularly
to the young, educated people who, according to circumstances, chose an appropriate programme from the, in practice not always mutually compatible, range of ideas. Some
preferred more liberty, some more equality, but both more
often than not were united with respect to national unity
and self-determination. In the German wars of liberation
and in the Italian Risorgimento the nationalistic bequest of
the French Revolution knocked at the door of the Habsburg
Empire.

The seeds of Czech national revival could now grow under
favourable conditions. Under a vigilant political regime,
concern with language and its multifaceted cultivation in art
was the safest outlet for patriotic activities. The situation
was not easy; the Habsburg regime was suspicious both of
liberal and egalitarian ideas. Catholic restoration was seen
as a salutary antidote to the heritage of the French Revolution and its spiritual parent, the Enlightenment.

Within Catholic restoration, however, Austrian and
Roman loyalties clashed. Furthermore, some Catholic
clergy considered the spirit of Enlightenment compatible
with their creed. (The most outstanding of them, the philosopher Bernard Bolzano, was banned in 1820 from the University Chair in Prague.) According to Emperor Francis's
guidelines for schools of all levels, 'pupils had to be taught
only such knowledge which would not disturb them in their
later work and would not make them unhappy.'[4]

Despite government efforts to the contrary, the spiritual
climate was becoming more liberal. The centralized,
bureaucratic government met with opposition from two different quarters. On the one hand, the aristocracy tried to
reassert its traditional power-sharing with the monarch. On
the other hand, the educated urban strata, the rising bour-

geoisie, began to use any opportunity to expand their cultural self-assertion. Novels, poetry, periodicals, theatre and indeed national balls became the most popular means of fostering national language and consciousness.

With respect to the more sophisticated cultural activities, especially the promotion of scientific knowledge, technology and historiography, there was some common ground between the aristocracy and the middle class. In different ways both were patriots. The patriotism of the aristocrats was related to their respective country; they saw themselves as Bohemians, Moravians, or Silesians, etc. The patriotism of the middle class was based on language, whether Czech or German. It was the German philosopher Johann Gottfried Herder who gave the most convincing exposition of this bond of loyalty and source of enthusiasm.[5] But even for the Czech and German patriots there was for some time a common ground: liberal or democratic ideas. Nevertheless, both linguistic communities began to look for support beyond the border, the Germans to the vast hinterland of German-speakers, the Czechs, numerically much weaker, to other Slavic nations. In the first instance, the Czechs' natural allies were seen in those Slavs living within the Habsburg Empire, the Poles, the Croats and the Slovenes. But for many the most promising seemed to be the great power of Russia.

Significantly, the first great scholar-historian of the Czech nation, František Palacký (1798–1876) started his work as a historiographer of the Bohemian estates. A Protestant from East Moravia, educated at the Slovak Protestant schools in what was then neighbouring Hungary, Palacký was highly respected both by conservative Catholics and by liberal nationalists. His scholarship and diplomatic skill made him the Czech national leader for almost half a century. In his monumental *History of the Czech Nation in Bohemia and Moravia*, he rehabilitated the Hussite past, thus giving the patriotic movement an inspirational example of bygone glory.[6]

Political stimuli came largely from abroad with, in 1830, the July Revolution in Paris, and the great Polish uprising against Russian domination. The former strengthened liberal sentiments, the latter exposed the pitfalls of a Panslavic nationalism. Karel Havlíček, editor of the first Czech political journal and a prolific liberal writer, who had spent several years in Russia and greatly appreciated Russian popular culture, fully realized not only the unacceptable nature of the tsarist regime but also the impossibility of nationalism stretching beyond one language.

A special problem of linguistic demarcation emerged with respect to the Slovaks. Although they lived from 1526 under the same royal dynasty as the Czechs, their country was a part of the Hungarian kingdom which in many respects had developed differently. The official language of Hungary was Latin until 1848, otherwise, until the early 1840s, the local population used their own languages more or less without restriction; this meant that as well as the dominant nation, the Magyars, the other ethnic groups were able to foster their vernaculars. The Slovaks, as far as they were Protestants, used biblical Czech for their literary purposes, often mixed with elements of local dialects. The Catholics, having their liturgy in Latin, were less in need of a common vernacular; various dialects were used in writing. But in the 1770s they too began to look for a standardized literary language.[7]

The first scholarly step in this direction was undertaken by the Catholic priest Anton Bernolák (1762–1813); his literary Slovak was based on the west Slovak dialect. On the other hand, the Protestant Slovaks preferred to modernize biblical Czech, broadening its range and register with some local idioms. As national loyalties came to be more strongly felt than religious ones the need for a common modern Slovak became urgent on both sides of the religious divide. Eventually it was a Protestant, Ludovít Štúr (1815–56), with a circle of close co-workers, who in 1843 chose to elevate the dialect of central Slovakia to the Status of literary Slovak. For some time both Bernolák's and Štúr's versions coexisted, but eventually the language based on the central Slovak dialect became more acceptable for all Slovaks.

The standardization of Slovak occurred at the time when the Magyars began to enforce the use of their language throughout the whole Hungarian kingdom; Hungary as a whole was to be identified with the Magyar ethnic nation. There was to be no difference between being Magyar and Hungarian. Consequently, the imperial regulation of 1812, instructing local authorities to support the use of local vernaculars, was abolished. In 1844 the Hungarian diet declared Magyar to be the official language at all levels of education, the judiciary and the administration. Almost all Slovak national associations were banned.

In the Bohemian lands, the Czech language was not exposed to a similar pressure; it was the language of the Czech elementary schools and its use was permitted in contact with the lower levels of the administration and judiciary. The Czechs also had more freedom, namely to publish their writings and form national associations. One of them, with a definite political aim and thus more or less clandestine, emerged in 1844 and was called the 'Bohemian Repeal'. The label was taken from Ireland, from the Loyal National Repeal Association which sought the repeal of the legislative union of Ireland with Great Britain agreed in 1801. The aim of the Bohemian Repeal was similar: the emancipation of Bohemia and Moravia from the centralized power in Vienna. Characteristically for that time, the Bohemian Repeal included a small number of German-speakers; it was the liberal views which were the unifying factor. Some democratic, egalitarian ideas also, though in a less distinct form, cropped up on the fringes of the movement.[8] When, in February 1848, Paris gave the signal to move forward again, the men of the Bohemian Repeal were in the vanguard of those who took action.

The stops and starts ahead. Land and language

The turbulent events of 1848 created a new situation in the Bohemian lands. As so often before the impulse came from France. The February Revolution in Paris showed malcontents in other European countries that there was a way of giving effective voice to their grievances. The extent and depth of dissatisfaction was enormous.

Tensions were especially acute in two respects: first, as everywhere else, large strata of the population wanted to be enfranchised; the third estate, as the French Revolution of 1789 understood it, required not only economic but also political self-assertion. Second, and this was specific to the composite Habsburg Empire, its constituent parts and/or its nations demanded more rights. With respect to the Bohemian lands, the issue was twofold: on the one hand, the state right of the Bohemian Crown and, on the other hand, the rights of the Czech nation. In Europe east of the river Rhine, 'state' and 'nation' have become clearly differentiated concepts.[9]

In the mid-1850s about 4½ million people lived in Bohemia, over 2 million in Moravia and about a ½ million in Silesia. In Bohemia two-thirds spoke Czech and one-third German. In Moravia three-quarters were Czechs and the rest Germans. Silesia (i.e., that part which was left to Austria after 1763) was trilingual with German, Polish and Czech. Amongst the Slavic peoples of Silesia only a proportion had a definite Czech or Polish national consciousness. Many considered their Silesian dialect, which was a transitional vernacular between Czech and Polish, as their mother tongue; since many of them also spoke German, there was a degree of Silesian national consciousness which gave way only much later to a more clear-cut differentiation between the Czechs and Poles.

The German-speakers in the Bohemian lands found it convenient to be incorporated into the domains of the House of Habsburgs; it guaranteed them their ethnic identity and on top of that linked them to the nation which dominated the whole Empire. Where some Germans of the Bohemian lands disagreed with the court of Vienna, it was with respect to civic and political rights. Broadly speaking, the issue was between the Austro-German liberals on the one hand and Austro-German conservatives on the other. But this was a quarrel within one and the same ethno-linguistic, i.e., national family, and the divide cut across the German population in all lands of the Empire.

For the Czechs, the issue was much more complicated. They wanted to preserve the separate identity of their lands as autonomous units; at the same time, and this applied in particular to the Czechs of Bohemia, they wanted to re-assert the unity of the three lands under the Bohemian Crown (the crown of St Wenceslas). They thought that this complex, the Bohemian state, should enjoy equal status with the Crown lands of Hungary (the crown of St Stephen) and the Alpine lands (Austria proper). However, the Czechs also wanted to emancipate themselves from the German domination which affected most aspects of their life. The Czech-speakers desired equality with the Germans in all respects and wanted to be granted an adequate institutional framework for their cultural and political self-determination. They also wanted the Slovaks in Hungary to receive cultural and political autonomy.

Thus Czech politics pursued a dual aim: reconstitution of their historical state, which by its nature was bilingual and, within this state, national self-determination. It could be reasonably expected that, being in the majority, the Czechs would eventually attain the dominant position in that state. Understandably on that point the Czechs were to clash with the German minority; for the latter a united Austria was a much better alternative.

In the Bohemian lands, however, there was yet another understanding of national loyalty with respect to 'nation' in its earlier (originally medieval) sense, i.e., belonging to a particular country, irrespective of language or ethnic origin. Most aristocrats shared this view; their patriotism was country-based. As they favoured autonomy for their lands, they often made common cause with the Czech nationalists in their struggle for a Bohemian state.

The imperial government in Vienna was not keen on concessions to any of these demands. In its view, the Austrian state was to be centralized as far as possible. Liberal reforms of any kind smacked of the French Revolution and were to be utterly opposed. Therefore, neither Czech nor German liberals were to be allowed to propagate their views. And, so far as national identity was concerned, in the view of the government in Vienna there was sufficient opportunity for it to be practised among the lower echelons of society.

The news of the February Revolution in Paris came like a bolt from the blue. The population of Vienna reacted with riots. The government was caught off guard. That pillar of Austrian absolutism, Prince Metternich, resigned and his successor promised reforms and immediately loosened the screw. In Prague (two days before the riots in Vienna started) a great gathering summoned by the Bohemian Repeal took place in the St Wenceslas Baths. The result was a petition to the emperor demanding specifically: reassertion of the unity of the Bohemian state, equal rights with the Germans for the Czechs in public life, local self-government, freedom of the press, of assembly, of religious creeds, etc., and, last but not least, the abolition of the remnants of serfdom. The responsibility for the implementation of these demands was entrusted to the elected committee (later named the National Committee). At the beginning it contained both Czechs and Germans, roughly corresponding to their porportion in the population of Bohemia as a whole. But the Germans, being in a minority, resented a second-class role, and one by one withdrew from the

Committee, which within little more than two months became virtually a Czech body.[10]

Meanwhile, the 'Sudeten Germans' residing in Vienna, where the German nationalist movement was strongest, founded the League of Germans in Bohemia, Moravia and Silesia for the Preservation of their Nationality. The League opposed the unification of the Bohemian lands, equal status for the Czech and German languages in high schools, and demanded the incorporation of all Austrian and Bohemian lands into Greater Germany.[11]

Thus, on the Czech side, a revolutionary institution was created; but the situation in Prague was not ripe for a real revolution. Although the Czech liberals (the core of the National Committee) had many points in common with the liberals in Vienna, divergent ethnic interests prevented them from making common cause. The situation was further complicated by the fact that the liberals and democrats in Germany conceived of a plan to make of the Confederation of the German States (constituted in 1815 at the Congress of Vienna) a federal state. For that purpose they started to organize elections to the parliament in Frankfurt to which all members of the Confederation were invited. As the Bohemian lands were a part of what the Austrian authorities called the 'Hereditary German Lands', the Czechs were supposed to participate. The most prominent of them, František Palacký, was offered membership in the preparatory committee.

Palacký declined, however, pointing out that all traditional links between Bohemia and the German Empire were links between the monarchs and not between the nations. A link between nations would be a novelty; he had no mandate to accept such a link and did not personally agree with it. Palacký further pointed out that there were not only the Czechs but also other non-German nations in the Austrian state; as these were situated between the German and the Russian giants, the great Austrian state with its spine on the river Danube was the best guarantee of their national identity. In this reply, published as an open letter, Palacký outlined the basic political idea which was to orientate Czech policy for seventy years to come. In the Czech view, the Austrian state was to become a multinational federation.

Although the Viennese government did not like the Frankfurt project either, the mood in Vienna prevented it from declining the invitation. Reluctantly the Austrian government consented to call the elections. The turn-out was uneven. In Bohemia only the Germans went to the polls, the Czechs declared a boycott. In Moravia it was more country-based patriotism which caused a low turn-out.

Yet abstention could not be substituted for a programme. The Czechs had two ways in which to deal with the danger of German integration: they could cooperate with the conservatives who wanted to keep Austria out of the liberal, nationalistic tide; or they could cooperate with other Slavic nations within the Empire to give more weight to federalist claims. A Slavic Congress summoned to Prague for the beginning of June 1848 demonstrated the potential strength of the Slavic element in Austria. Although the demonstration turned out to be rather theoretical (the Congress dispersed when there was an uprising in Prague), it nevertheless provided the occasion for the German nationalists to intensify their propaganda.

Meanwhile the mood in Vienna became increasingly radical. After the riots towards the end of May, the city of Vienna was virtually ruled by a revolutionary 'Security Committee'. The emperor left the capital and ruled, as far as the situation allowed, from Innsbruck in the Tyrol. All problems were to be resolved by the Constituent Assembly, elected by direct vote of male persons over twenty-four years of age without any property census. This great leap forward, however, was made under the 'pressure of the street'. Forces on the side of the status quo were strong enough to buy time for a counter-attack.

The imperial government in Vienna was not its own master. It had to take into account the situation in the city, but it could not be sure what the emperor (a weakling) might eventually decide. He could fully rely on his army led by generals keen to suppress any revolutionary action when ordered to do so. One of these most loyal supporters of monarchical absolutism was Prince Windischgrätz, the commanding general in Bohemia. He knew that he could not expect any firm order from the emperor and thus began to act on his own, in outright defiance of the instructions of the Viennese government and also of the government representation in Prague. (The latter began to cooperate with the National Committee.) After the news of the Viennese riots (26–7 May), in order to forestall a worsening of the situation, Governor Thum appointed for Bohemia a 'Provisional Governing Council' of eight respected citizens, four of them Czechs and four Germans.[12] Windischgrätz, however, believed he knew better how to stop further steps towards the 'abyss'. By an ostentatious display of military presence in Prague (in contrast to Vienna from where the army had withdrawn) he stirred rather than quietened minds. The students and their radical allies were particularly aroused.

All demands for the withdrawal of the army were rejected; the students legion supported by young workers took up arms. Some German radicals also joined in. After three days of fighting in the streets, the army retreated from the greater part of the city; on the sixth day, following a heavy artillery bombardment, the rebels capitulated. However, it was not only the radicals who were defeated but also the liberals who did not take part in the uprising. The National Committee was dissolved and martial law stopped all political activities for more than a month.

For the Czech liberals the only arena for further development was now in the Constituent Assembly elected for the whole state (except for Hungary and the Italian provinces) and convened for the end of July 1848.[13] But this institution also proved to be a merely temporary arrangement.

However, the Germans in the Bohemian lands became more apprehensive. In August 1848 a congress of represent-atives from German cities, communes and constitutional clubs in Bohemia expressed a wish to abolish the historical lands and to create instead provinces demarcated according to the principle of ethnicity. They also demanded unifica-tion with Germany.

At the beginning of October a new broadly based uprising took place in Vienna. Only after heavy fighting was this sup-pressed by the combined forces of two imperial armies. At the same time the Hungarian dissent developed into a full-scale revolution which was only defeated ten months later with Russian help. Towards the end of November the Con-stituent Assembly moved from a still-troubled Vienna to Kroměříž in Moravia. But even there it could not finish its task; at the beginning of March 1849 the Assembly was dis-solved by the army, and a meagre semiabsolutist constitu-tion was decreed. Under a new emperor, the eighteen-year-old Franz Joseph I, who ruled from 2 December 1848, the return to monarchical absolutism set in.

Not all the work of the Constituent Assembly was frus-trated. One great, though long overdue, step forward, the abolition of the last remnants of serfdom and patrimonial relationships, was taken for good; the corvée was also abol-ished, except for the crofters and landless peasants, in exchange for compensation. According to the type of holdings, farmers had to pay one- to two-thirds of the calcu-lated asset value. The emancipation of the peasantry (at the time two-thirds of the population in Austrian and Bohemian lands) was the only great reform – one might say the one great revolutionary achievement – which survived the reac-tion after 1849. The Viennese court apparently learnt the lesson of France where a satisfied peasantry became the main support for the imperial regime.

Pacification of the peasantry was badly needed because

in the cities, especially the big ones, the revolutionary mood remained at a high pitch. In March 1849, Prague again became the site of secret preparations for a new strike.[14] When in May, in Dresden (in Saxony, not far from the Bohemian border), a real uprising broke out, the Austrian government took pre-emptive measures to avoid a revolt in Prague, and arrested the potential ringleaders, both Czech and German. In the subsequent trials which took place from 1850 to 1854, altogether 958 persons were found guilty, of whom only 51 got prison sentences and 28 were sentenced to death. All the latter sentences however were commuted to long-term prison sentences.[15] A hundred years later, a victorious 'revolution' (the communist *coup d'état* in Czechoslovakia) showed much less magnanimity towards its opponents.

The revolutionary events of 1848–9, however, also gave the government an opportunity to undertake quite a few reforms of a retrograde nature: an overall tightening of the administrative grip on the country. The development followed almost step by step the contemporary pattern in France. By the end of 1851 the emperor abolished the semiabsolutist constitution and with three decrees re-established full absolutist rule with the so-called Silvester Patents.

The neoabsolutism of the young Franz Joseph was not, however, a match for that of his illustrious predecessor Joseph II. In the epoch of Enlightenment, the monarch could well afford to make decisions concerning all his subjects, including the churchmen. After 1848 absolutism had to be bolstered by more powerful ideological support. Only the Church could offer something of the kind; the deal was obvious. All restrictions imposed upon the Catholic Church by the old absolutism, such as *placetum regium*, etc. were lifted. The liberated Church was taken into co-regency with the lay state. In was the alliance of the throne with the altar which characterized the 1850s in the Habsburg Empire. But

to be on the safe side the state also practised its own vigi-
lance. Policing of society become one of its most important
functions. The right to form associations was shifted
towards the economic field. Whilst political associations
were virtually forbidden, entrepreneurs were encouraged to
cooperate in various forms of commercial companies. This
was in fact a combination of political authoritarianism with
supervised economic liberalism. In such a climate Czech
political life was interrupted and cultural activities were
carried on in a very low key. In a way it was a new time of
darkness in Czech history.

Fortunately, the international situation did not permit a
permanent freeze in public life in the Habsburg monarchy.
The young emperor, keen to pursue a vigorous great-power
policy, overestimated the striking power of his armies and
also his financial resources. Two lost wars in seven years
were the result. Each of them brought Austria territorial
losses and, moreover, constitutional reforms. In 1859, Austria
was defeated by the alliance of France and the Sardinian
kingdom and had to cede Lombardy to the nascent Italy. A
subsequent series of decrees culminated in the so-called
February Constitution of 1861 in which the emperor conceded some power to the bicameral Empire's Council (parliament). Its Lower House was to be elected by the diets
of individual lands on the basis of a curial system (great
landowners, burghers, rural communes), and on property or
tax return census. The rationale, widely shared in those
days, was that votes had to be not only counted but also
weighted. The Upper House was to be nominated by the
emperor.

Although the February Constitution recognized the identity of individual lands, it did not recognize the Bohemian
state right; there was also no allowance for the national
aspirations of the non-German nations. The Hungarian diet
did not accept the February Constitution right from the
beginning. After a failed attempt to gain some concessions,

the Czech deputies left the Lower House in protest in March 1863. (Their boycott was to last until 1879). Czech politics turned to the local diets and to the fostering of cultural and educational activities. One of the many ventures in this field deserves special mention: the national gymnastic organization, Sokol (Falcon), founded in 1862. As a counterpart to the German gymnastic organization (the Turnverein), it developed into an important bulwark of Czech patriotic education and self-confidence.

In 1865 Palacký came forward with a piece of political philosophy that outlined conditions under which Czech national aspirations (and indeed the aspirations of all other non-German nationalities in the Empire) could be reconciled with the existence of the Austrian state. The treatise was published under the title *The Idea of the Austrian State*.

In this programmatic work, Palacký first reviewed the rationale of the composite Austrian state as it emerged from the union of the Austrian Alpine lands with the Bohemian and the Hungarian kingdoms. First it was the defence against the Ottoman menace which made this union imperative. Then it was the defence against the Reformation which, however, grew into a repressive regime that then became a part of Austrian tradition. In the nineteenth century both these rationales lost their substance. The contemporary era brought to the forefront the quest for national self-determination and equality of nations. However, in the nineteenth century, where large states were being built up, the small nations living in small states could not maintain their sovereignty. For the small nations it was better to close ranks and find their self-determination within the larger states. Austria was an ideal geopolitical framework for such a coexistence, provided she guaranteed equality for all member nations. In Palacký's view, neither the contemporary centralistic nor the envisaged dualistic Austro-Hungarian solution (the latter alternative was already under serious discussion at that time) would bring internal peace to the Austrian state. The subject Slavic nations would be forced to seek emancipation possibly in the least desirable form of Panslavism. The states are only temporary phenomena, only the nations last for ever.[16] Only a federal state based on the ethnic principle could assure Austria her continued existence. Palacký, however, was aware that the borderlines between individual nations (especially those between the Czechs and the Germans) were not clear-cut and that amongst the former there was a strong feeling for the historical state right; therefore he modified his basically ethnic principle and suggested a federation based on a combination of national, historical and economic conditions. In this combination, as we shall see later, was to be found the main pitfall of all future federalist programmes.

In 1866 friction between Austria and Prussia within the Confederation of German States resulted in a war which brought Austria further humiliation. She had to cede the Venetian province to Italy and leave the Confederation, thus allowing Prussia a further expansion of her influence there. Although this step might have helped Austria to embark on the course suggested by Palacký, the Austrian court opted for a dualistic solution. There were several reasons why Hungarians were always treated with more regard than other non-Germans in Austria. The Habsburgs had to pay a much higher price (in effort, blood and money) to acquire a firm hold on the Hungarian kingdom than for any other of their domains. The Hungarians showed their strength and courage in the uprising of 1848–9; their prestige also was enhanced by the fact that their aristocracy maintained intimate contacts with the court in Vienna. Last but not least, the German minority in Hungary was scattered in enclaves all over the country.[17] This prevented them from making claims to territorial autonomy. The other ethnic minorities in Hungary (the most numerous being Slovaks and Romanians) were not in a position to prevent any deal which would leave them completely at the mercy of the Budapest regime.[18] In May 1867 the Austrian parliament approved the transformation of the Austrian Empire into the Austro-Hungarian monarchy. It was to be in fact a rather loose union; only foreign policy, the armed forces and military finances were to be in common. The common institutions were styled 'Imperial and Royal'.

Although the dualization of the Habsburg Empire was followed by a significant liberalization of its Austrian part, the Czechs felt frustrated with having been relegated to the position of a second-class nation. At the time when dualization was declared, Czech leaders demonstrated their bitterness and defiance with a pilgrimage to Russia, formally for a visit to the ethnographic exhibition in Moscow, in reality to establish contacts in St Petersburg. Although the audience with the tsar observed the usual niceties, nothing came of it; the Russian government assured its imperial counterpart in Vienna that there was no political dimension to that venture.

However, the rights granted to the Czechs by the new constitution and promulgated in the series of laws at the turn of 1867–8 marked a significant step forward: the absolute monarchy was transformed into a constitutional monarchy. The emperor had to swear an oath that he would abide by these laws. All citizens were granted equality before the law, and a wide range of civil liberties, such as freedom of the press, freedom of association, etc.; the judiciary became independent of the administration; the equality of all languages customary in the country was recognized. Those clauses of the Concordat of 1855 which guaranteed the Catholic Church pre-eminence over other Churches and entrusted it with general surveillance in matters of education and marriage were abolished; legal constraints were lifted from the non-Catholic Churches. Thus, in the year 1868, Austria entered her constitutional era. Although for the Czechs this great event was soured by the contrast between the Hungarians' success and their failure, it was nevertheless a kind of spring for their national life. In the sphere of politics, it at least provided a point of departure for more ambitious ventures.

In this more open atmosphere Czech nationalists cooperated with the conservative aristocracy in working out proposals for a more elevated status for the Bohemian kingdom. The emperor seemed to be favourably disposed. His government of the day led promising negotiations with Czech leaders. In October 1871 the Bohemian diet, against the vote of German liberals, approved a project known as the Fundamental Articles (eighteen in number). According to this programme, the lands of the Bohemian Crown were to be granted a status similar to that of Hungary, however with some qualifications in favour of closer cooperation with the other Austrian (Alpine, etc.) provinces. But even this attempt failed. There was concerted opposition to it from strong personalities in the government, Hungarian representatives and, above all, German nationalists who were afraid of losing their privileges; in their protest they hinted at the displeasure of the brand new emperor in Europe, the Prussian king elevated to German emperor, with any weakening of German supremacy in Austria. From 1871 onwards, it was the Bismarckian German Reich which, after the suppression of the republican and federalist tendencies in Germany and after the resounding victory over France, began to play the role of Austria's Big Brother.

6

From ethnic to political nation

School for parliamentarianism. National or class consciousness?

The transformation of Austria into a dual, constitutional monarchy coincided with remarkable progress in industrialization and the growth of the cities. Revolutionary changes in the structure of society and in political arrangements occurred without a revolution. It was a piecemeal process; on the political plane, changes took place against tenacious opposition from the *ancien régime* which, however, was not so inflexible as not to be able to read the writing on the wall, at least at the very last hour. Then it moved ahead, but only as far as seemed absolutely necessary.

What were the reasons for the Habsburg regime's resilience and capacity for adaptation? In principle, a tissue of vested interests, including the landed aristocracy, the army and the Church, united in unbending respect for tradition and loyalty to the sovereign. When great economic changes took place, when the industrial revolution brought the entrepreneur and financier to prominence, the wealthy part of the third estate was taken into partnership in the established alliance of power and prestige. With this opening came a certain degree of flexibility and dynamism. Under the new circumstances, the Austrian government could claim to be ruling above parties, nationalities and classes;

although the treatment of these groups was not even-handed, it could be said that at least between those groups which enjoyed citizens' rights, the government more often than not tried to steer a middle course.

In contrast to the basic and wide-ranging consensus amongst the ruling strata of society (internal squabbles did not dislodge the framework), the subject strata were in many respects divided. Some of their aspirations were so contradictory that the respective issues could not be amicably resolved; thus the emperor and his government could base their policy on balancing counterpoised forces of opposition. Any concession to individual demands had to be carefully thought out in order not to open the lid of this Pandora's box too wide. The danger was not a revolution against the regime, but civil war between opposing forces. In such a social climate the authorities could afford to proceed slower than if they were exposed to a more concentrated opposition. Under the new constitution, the manoeuvring and balancing became more difficult; it also required more skill from those in charge. On the other hand, the extended scope of civil liberties provided the opposition with the opportunity for more unhindered expression of dissent than ever before, which in its turn furthered the government's claim to rule above the parties.

Yet it was only in the Austrian part of the dual monarchy that the situation developed into a complex pattern. In the Hungarian part there was much less scope for political participation beyond the rather narrow élite of members of the ruling nation at the top, let alone for infighting among the subject peoples.[1] In contrast to the Czechs who were able to score some important points in their struggle for national self-assertion, the Slovaks, exposed to systematic Magyarization, had an extremely limited scope for voicing their opinions.

Another reason for this greater complexity in the Austrian than in the Hungarian part of the dual monarchy

was the much higher level of industrialization. It was especially in the Bohemian lands that most of industry was to be
found. Industrialization meant the emergence of the working class and this, in its turn, gave rise to the 'social question'. With it a new dimension entered Austrian politics – a
dimension which in several respects cut across the established ethnic and political fronts within the Empire.

The 'social question' in Austria developed along lines
similar to those in other European countries. The workers'
movement started with spontaneous outbreaks of protest.
The most significant, in 1870, was the ten-weeks-long strike
in Svárov in North Bohemia which ended only after a
bloody intervention by the armed forces. But this kind of
solution seemed unpalatable even to the authorities. A new
law on association allowed peaceful gatherings and associations of workers and, within certain limits, the withdrawal
of labour, i.e., strikes. Thus the workers' unions, at that time
mainly local clubs, were able to operate legally. The found-
ing of political organizations was a more difficult matter.
Following the German model (the Social Democratic Workers' Party of Germany founded in 1869 in Eisenach), representatives of several workers' clubs met illegally in 1874 in
Neudörfel (on the Hungarian side of the border) and
founded the Pan-Austrian Workers' Party, later renamed
the Social Democratic Workers' Party. Of the seventy-four
delegates, ten were ethnic Czechs. As the meeting was not
approved by the authorities, the founders were sentenced
to several months in gaol.[2]

Like similar parties elsewhere in Europe, the Pan-
Austrian Workers' Party stood not only for a change in the
socio-economic system but also for international cooperation and workers' solidarity. Under Austrian conditions this
stance might have been helpful in calming down some of the
nationalistic fervour. The Austrian authorities, however,
needed some more time to test and weigh up, on the one
hand, the possible advantages and, on the other hand, the

risks of admitting a new element into the political arena.

In the first instance, repressive measures were taken against the Social Democratic Party; its second congress was dispersed by the police. In the face of such hostility, some workers advocated direct revolutionary action instead or ogranized struggle with the law. Thus, in many places, anarchist groupings emerged and began to compete with the Social Democrats for membership. But even within that party a controversy over immediate goals and tactics took place. The issue was whether more stress should be laid on economic weapons such as the trade unions and cooperatives, or on the struggle for political power. In terms of ideologies it was the conflict between the formulas of Ferdinand Lasalle and of Karl Marx.

There was yet another dividing factor within the Pan-Austrian Social Democratic Party, namely the ethnic question. Belonging to a particular nation was a strong emotional link, even in the case of people who, in Marx's view, had no fatherland. National consciousness was especially alive where the demarcation between the workers and their employers coincided with the difference between the subject and the ruling nation, where the class contrast and class grievances were accentuated by use of a different language and a sense that the other was an alien. The struggle for the souls of the children (to win them over to the schools of the other nation) was a complicating and disrupting factor in that situation. In order to ease the situation, the Czech Social Democrats decided, with the agreement of their German comrades, to organize their own ethnic party. In 1878, at a clandestine meeting in Břevnov (a Prague suburb), the Czechoslav Social Democratic Workers' Party was founded.[3] Although all participants had to pay for the illegal gathering with several months in gaol, the ethnic articulation of social-democratic movements in Austria became a fact of life.

In the 1880s both national and class issues became more

acute. Fortunately for Austria, in 1879 the emperor entrusted a particularly able politician, Count Taaffe, with the premiership. With patience and assiduity, Taaffe managed to combine respect for tradition with necessary innovations. If, after almost fourteen years of successfully balancing the two, he eventually failed, it was because he attempted to move faster than circumstances allowed.

The first issue which Taaffe and his government had to tackle was the request of the Czech deputies for equal rights for the Czech language with German in schools, administration and the judiciary. Despite opposition from German deputies from Bohemia, some of the Czech demands were met; in administrative matters the Czechs in Bohemia and Moravia were entitled to deal with the authorities in their own language. (In Silesia this principle was subject to certain qualifications.) German, however, was to remain the internal official language. The request of the German deputies to divide Bohemia into, on the one hand, purely German and, on the other hand, bilingual districts, was not granted. The question of which was to be the official internal language and the division of Bohemia on ethnic lines remained the main bones of contention between the two ethnic camps until the very end of the Habsburg Empire.

During Taaffe's premiership, both national camps began more energetically to build up their strength in the fields of culture and education. In 1880, first the Germans and then the Czechs founded private associations which aimed at providing for the expansion of their respective educational facilities. In 1882, the Charles-Ferdinand University in Prague was divided into the Czech and the German University. In 1883 the representative building of the Czech National Theatre (in the style of the great operas in European capitals) was completed. As the construction was wholly financed by private donations, the Czech National Theatre became a symbol of patriotic achievement and pride. In the 1880s, the Czech scholars in the humanities felt confident enough to abandon narrow nationalistic concerns and, like their colleagues in science, began to work more on specialized issues. Their critical attitude did not waver in the face of the cherished fakes of old Czech epics which some patriotic authors produced and presented as ancient texts in order to demonstrate the high level of Czech culture in the past.[4]

In politics the main issue was how to exploit the parliamentary game to which the Czech deputies returned by their re-entry into the Reichsrat (Lower House of the State Parliament) in 1879. In a situation where no nationality and no political party could ever gain an absolute majority, the Czech representatives, dominated by a rather conservative type of liberal (the so-called Old Czechs), found their natural allies in the Polish and conservative Austro-German deputies. It was these three groups together (the conservative 'iron ring') which provided the main parliamentary support for Taaffe's government; the fiercly nationalistic German liberals were more often than not in opposition.

In contrast to the earlier period, in the 1880s the central government began to feel more pressure from the social question. First, it was the fear of anarchists (whose Russian comrades in 1881 had, after all, assassinated Tsar Alexander II) which prompted the government to take repressive measures against all labour associations, a policy which was carried out until the early 1890s. Meanwhile, however, some positive measures were also taken. In 1882, the census for male voting rights to the Reichsrat was lowered from ten to five guldens paid yearly in direct taxes. Thus at least a step was made towards universal suffrage, which was demanded mainly by the Social Democrats. In fact, the enfranchised population increased in the towns by 34 per cent and in the villages by 26 per cent.[5] In 1883 industrial inspection of working conditions was introduced. In 1885, the working day in mines was shortened to ten hours and in all other enterprises with more than twenty employees to eleven hours; children under fourteen were not allowed to work in factories. In 1889, mandatory insurance against sickness and injury was introduced for industrial workers; the existence of the Social Democratic Workers' Party was accepted by the authorities; and, at the congress in Hainfeld, the Social Democrats resolutely parted company with anarchist tendencies. Their programme became a series of campaigns for the education of workers for a class-conscious participation in public life, for universal suffrage, democratic rights and the collectivization of the means of production.

None of the central government's positive measures, however, could bring peace on the labour front, let alone resolve the social question. Taaffe's government believed that it might be more successful in tackling the national, i.e., linguistic, question. In 1890, the Czech and German nationalist deputies from Bohemia were invited to a round-table discussion in order to negotiate a *modus vivendi* between them. To foster a conciliatory mood on the Czech side the emperor approved the foundation of the Czech Academy of Sciences in Prague, a decision which fulfilled a long-standing demand. On the Czech side, however, only the majority political party, the less radical Old Czechs, were invited. After mutual concessions they consented to an agreement in which the German side won one particular advantage, namely the acknowledgement of purely German districts in Bohemia. As the German press hailed this agreement as a victory, the Czech signatories were branded as traitors by the Young Czechs. In the 1891 elections, the Old Czechs paid the price. With only one remaining deputy instead of the customary fifty or so, they were practically eliminated from the parliament. It took time before they regained some of the lost ground.

As it later turned out, the shift from the Old to the Young Czechs was not so much a matter of practical policy as of emphasis on individual points, and of cultural orientation.

Czech history provided ample opportunity to give the Young Czechs a more clear-cut ideological profile. An appreciation of the Hussite period in general, and of John Hus in particular, became emotional elements in Young Czech propaganda. John Hus was presented, anachronistically, as a martyr for freedom of opinion *per se*, not as he really was, a martyr to a quest for a true interpretation of the Bible. The revived cult of John Hus became at the same time a nationalistic and anticlerical symbol.

In the 1880s the political spectrum of Czech society became increasingly variegated. Ethnic, class and party political differences took on more sharply accentuated ideological hues which in their turn brought additional fissions into the groupings which had been united by common interests. The ethno-linguistic issue continued to be only one, if the most hotly debated, concern of Czech politics. Class interests led to the formation of political associations, not only by industrial workers but also by the farmers who organized their own political clubs and, in 1899, their own political party. The Catholics also started to build up their own political parties, in 1894 in Bohemia and in 1896 in Moravia.

On the whole, the Catholic Church exerted a moderating influence on national passions and earned criticism from the radicals in both ethnic camps: amongst the Czechs the criticism came mainly from those who fostered the political cult of Hussitism; the German radicals, organized in the Pan-German Party, launched a propaganda campaign against the Catholic Church under the slogan 'Away from Rome'.[6] The growth of active anti-Semitism was fostered, in particular, by the student club Germania (founded in 1893).

Among the Czechs there was a growing resentment of idle radicalism, which often led to rows and obstructions in the Reichsrat and in the Bohemian diet. The alternative was sought in more positive political work and, above all, in promoting higher levels of education and national consciousness. The most energetic promoter of such a policy of 'realism' was the philosopher and sociologist, Thomas Masaryk, Professor of the University of Prague. In two books: *The Czech Question* and *Our Contemporary Crisis*, published in 1895, Masaryk came forward with a philosophy of Czech history which was to give the Czech struggle for national emancipation a momentous ideological stimulus.[7]

Masaryk realized the need for raising inspiration within political struggle. Looking to the past for suitable paradigms which combined achievement with moral involvement, he found in Czech history two great events: first, the reformist (rather than the revolutionary) aspects of the Hussite period with John Hus and the Unity of Brethren as highlights; second, the national revival which, on the whole, had been successfully completed before Masaryk entered public life. Masaryk saw in these two great epochs of Czech history the embodiment of the national spirit, a spirit which in both these instances showed a particularly humanitarian bent. The humanitarian idea exemplified in the Czech Reformation and national revival was to provide guidance and encouragement in all future Czech undertakings.

Although to a politician or scholar such a normative interpretation of history appeared rather odd, Masaryk's philosophy of history became for many Czechs an effective weapon in their struggle for political emancipation. However airy this philosophy may have been Masaryk himself knew all too well how to combine an imaginative vision with practical, everyday policies in which, as the next twenty-five years were to show, he became the unsurpassed master.

Masaryk's political philosophy, however, was not limited to the national question. With a similar determination he tackled the social question. A book of that title appeared in 1898. Here Masaryk crossed swords with the philosophy of history which fifty years later was to become the creed of his most determined enemies. Masaryk's *Social Question* was, as its German translation indicated, focused on the philosophical and sociological foundations of Marxism. With respect to the practical implications of Marxist teaching, Masaryk took a view similar to that of his contemporary Eduard Bernstein, known amongst orthodox Marxists as the father of revisionism. (Bernstein's book *Die Voraussetzungen des Sozialismus und die Aufgaben der Sozialdemokratie* appeared in 1898).[8] In short, both Masaryk and Bernstein were realistic enough to see that any great vision needs, for its implementation, a lot of deeds great and small, and that it is according to these deeds that the final judgement on the vision would be passed. It was a whole century before Masaryk's and Bernstein's views were fully vindicated.

Of course, Social Democrats throughout the whole of Europe were aware of the gap between vision and practical achievement, and it was the continuous struggle between the two approaches which eventually split the Social Democratic parties in all European countries. The Pan-Austrian Party at the congress in Hainfeld (1888–9) agreed a compromise between the two wings; due to the influence of Karl Kautsky, however, the whole concept was more orthodox than revisionist.

As time went on, however, realism had to be fully taken into account. First, the national question was to be tackled; at the Pan-Austrian Congress in Prague in 1896, the Social Democratic Party was federalized on ethnic lines.[9] But this did not mean the acceptance of the Czech programme of Bohemian state right. On the contrary, the Czech Social Democratic members of parliament, elected on the basis of a law which further extended the suffrage in 1897, explicitly rejected this programme. In response the more nationalistic supporters founded the National Social Party in 1898.

At the Pan-Austrian Congress in Brno (Brünn) in 1899 the Social Democrats proposed the reconstruction of the Austrian monarchy into a 'democratic federal state of nationalities'. Together with universal, equal and direct suffrage, an equal right for all nationalities to their own 'national and cultural' autonomies was considered an essential prerequisite for the emancipation of the proletariat. The idea of a federal Austria was further elaborated by the leading personalities in the Austrian Social Democratic Party, Karl Renner and Otto Bauer (see. p. 136).

The issue of orthodoxy versus 'practicism' came to the forefront later. In 1901, at a congress in Vienna, despite some very radical formulations concerning direct democracy in all walks of public life, substantial concessions were made to the more pragmatic stance. Reform and representative government was the focus of the new programme which was accepted by the Social Democratic parties of the individual nationalities.

The whole situation was favourable to a more pragmatic policy. After the failure of several attempts at conciliation between the Czechs and Germans, the Viennese government was more willing to listen to political movements which were more concerned with other issues than those of national language. Apart from the Catholic political parties it was the Social Democrats who seemed to be more sensible in this respect. However, only in Moravia did the government initiative succeed in bringing both national camps to a compromise over the official use of the respective languages and representation in the land diet. Although the compromise, the so-called Moravian Pact, granted the Germans a disproportionately high representation, the Czech language gained some ground in official use. This compromise, however, could not prevent bloody riots in the streets of the Moravian capital, Brno.[10]

The government gradually took the view that a broader electorate could bring more deputies of ethnically less committed parties to the parliament. But the path towards extension of suffrage was not a straightforward one. The first step was the lowering of the electoral census to four guldens of direct tax and the introduction of a fifth, universal, electoral curia in 1896. Only ten years later, after broadly based campaigns of strikes and mass demonstrations organized mainly by the Social Democratic Party, the new electoral laws introducing universal suffrage to the Reichsrat were passed by both Houses and, in January 1907, were approved by the emperor.

Although the suffrage was universal for males over twenty-four, and was direct and equal as far as their economic situation was concerned (the electoral curias were abolished), it was not equal with respect to the constituencies. Their size varied from about 12,000 to 80,000 inhabitants. These discrepancies resulted in disproportionately small representation of Slavic nationalities and also of the supporters of Social Democracy.[11] Nevertheless it was a substantial improvement in comparison with the previous situation.

Although the expectations of the government were partly fulfilled (in the Czech camp the class- or religion-based parties won almost two-thirds of the vote and the German nationalists in the whole state had a lower share of representation than before), the ethnic strife continued unabated. The Bohemian diet was, because of German obstructionism, unable to operate. In December 1908 Prague again experienced a state of emergency. The German pressure became especially intense against the Slovenes.

There was a conspicuous revival of wider Slavic solidarity in that period. In 1908 in Prague a Slavic Congress was held as a commemoration of the congress organized sixty years earlier. On the Czech side the Panslavic tendencies were particularly represented by the leading young Czech politician Karel Kramář. Also in 1908 Austria unilaterally annexed Bosnia and Herzegovina which she had administered as an occupied territory with the consent of the great powers at the Berlin Congress thirty years earlier. As Bosnia-Herzegovina was a totally Slavic, Serbo-Croat speaking territory, its incorporation into the dual monarchy substantially increased the weight of the Slavic population there. In 1909 the MPs of the Czech, Yugoslav and conservative Ukrainian parties created a common club, open to other Slavic participants. In 1909 Masaryk, as MP of his own Realistic Party (he was elected with the help of Social Democrats who, in his constituency, withdrew their candidate), exposed, in the parliament, irregularities in a political trial directed against the Croat nationalists.

In the increasingly heated atmosphere of nationalistic passions, Czechoslav Social Democracy could not be spared serious repercussions. Although the party's new programme of federalization, democratization and socialization was geared towards ethnic cooperation and not strife, practical issues often led to confrontation. In 1910 the Czechoslav Party recognized a separate Czech Trade Union Central in Prague. The Pan-Austrian Party disagreed and put the matter to the Congress of the Socialist International in Copenhagen. The latter, with 222 votes against 5 Czech votes, carried the motion that in each state the unity of trade unions should be preserved; the Czech stance was branded as separatist and nationalistic.[12] Consequently, before the parliament elections in 1911 some Czech Social Democrats, in a congress in Brno, founded a separate 'centralist' Czech Social Democratic Workers' Party. The 'centralists', however, won only one seat (in Silesia) against twenty-five which went to the 'autonomists'. In terms of votes, the ratio was about 96 to 4.[13]

Thus, within the Czech camp, only the Catholic People's parties with 12 per cent of the vote in Bohemia and 37 per cent in Moravia (they did not compete in Silesia) stood outside the mainstream of Czech autonomists or federalists. In July 1912 a renewed attempt to resolve the stalemate in the Bohemian diet caused by the obstructiveness of the German parties failed. A year later special decrees passed by the central government dissolved the diet and Bohemia was administered by an appointed committee.

In Autumn 1912 war broke out in the Balkans, in that part of Europe which continued to be the only remaining arena for Austro-Hungarian power aspirations. The stuggle for national independence and unification of Balkanic nations took a decisive step forward; for some the goal was almost achieved. Unfortunately for the Habsburg Empire it was the Russian influence which then became stronger in that area, and Austria, had nothing to offer to redress the balance. Plans for 'trialization' of the Empire, creation of a third Illyric (i.e., Yugoslav) state within the monarchy, were too vague; since they were connected with the name of the staunchly conservative and authoritarian Crown Prince Franz Ferdinand d'Este, there was little in them to capture the imagination of the political representatives of the peoples concerned. In particular, the strong Hungarian grip on Croatia was hard to break. Thus, gradually, it was Serbia which became the rallying point for the emancipation of the south Slavic nations in the dual monarchy. And it was a Serb from Bosnia who, on 28 June 1914, in the Bosnian capital Sarajevo, fired the shots which killed the Crown Prince and his spouse. The Austro-Hungarian government was presented with a long-awaited opportunity to settle its account with the hated troublemaker, but the punitive expedition to Serbia turned into a war lasting more than four years, and which soon assumed global dimensions.

The outbreak of war in July 1914 caught the Czech politicians unprepared. At first it was widely believed that the war would be of brief duration. Soon, however, since the great European powers were becoming involved, it became clear that the war would last longer. Although there was still some genuine loyalty to the dynasty, the alliance of the dual monarchy with Germany did not augur well for the Czechs in the event of these two powers' victory. The plans of the Pan-Germans to turn the Bohemian lands into German provinces were well known; therefore a victory for the other side in the conflict appeared desirable. The Czechs living in

Russia and France expressed their anti-Austrian feelings by creating their own combat units within the Russian and French armies respectively.

In Austria itself, the parliament was discontinued and the military authorities began to intervene in the affairs of the civil administration. The Czechs became increasingly irritated by economic hardships which increased their antipathy to the Austrian regime. In the spring of 1915 virtually two whole Czech regiments deserted the Austrian army and went over to the Russians. At that time also, the Young Czech leader Kramář came forward with the idea of an independent Czechoslovak state. In the prevailing circumstances, however, the restructuring of the dual monarchy still seemed to be a more realistic alternative. In May 1915 Kramář and other prominent Czech politicians, including the chairman of the allegedly paramilitary gymnastic organization Sokol, were arrested. In the trial which ran throughout 1916, Kramář and others were sentenced to death. Because of later developments, however, the sentences were not carried out.

The main weight of the political fight shifted abroad where, in November 1915, in the Czech Committee Abroad under Masaryk's leadership, an independent Czechoslovak state was proclaimed as the final aim. From 1916 the Czechoslovak National Council, with Masaryk as Chairman and Eduard Beneš as General Secretary, became the leading organ of resistance abroad. The Slovaks were represented by M.R. Štefánik, a general in the French army. At home a declaration of political aims was out of the question. By the end of 1916 the military situation was so favourable for the central powers (Germany, Austria-Hungary, Bulgaria and Turkey) that they offered the other side peace negotiations. This initiative induced the American President, Woodrow Wilson, to ask the belligerents to account for their respective war aims. In contrast to the rather vague answer from Germany, the Entente (Great Britain, France and Russia) conceived of its aims in concrete form; one of these was the liberation of Italians, Slavs, Romanians and Czechoslovaks from foreign domination. The answer from Austria was the staging of a declaration of loyalty by the political representatives of nations which were to be liberated.

Yet this was the time the dual monarchy began to slacken in its military effort. The new Emperor, Charles I, allowed some power to shift back from the military to the civil authorities. A general amnesty not only commuted death sentences of political prisoners but even released them from prison. In contrast to Austrian relaxation, Germany hardened her stance by escalating the submarine war even against ships under neutral flags. In reply, the United States, itself hit by this uncivilized campaign, entered the war on the side of the Entente. Thus, whilst Germany provoked a new and powerful enemy to make war on the Central Powers, exhausted Austria began to look for peace. However, the German grip over Austria was too strong and the Pan-German nationalists in Austria pressed for closer attachment of the Alpine and Bohemian lands to the German Empire; changes in the constitution were to be enforced. The Emperor Charles and his government, however, all too aware of the abrupt collapse of the Russian monarchy in March 1917, played safe and decided to reactivate the existing constitution and convoke the parliament in the composition it had had after the 1911 elections.

Meanwhile, Czechoslovak resistance gathered momentum. Abroad, it was the Czechoslovak armed forces operating in Russia, France and later in Italy, which gave the Czechoslovak National Council an impressive attribute of statehood. It was, above all, the achievement of Czechoslovak legions in Russia that contributed substantially to the status of Czechoslovakia as a belligerent power.[14] At home writers took the initiative in political matters. Their manifesto of May 1917 was an appeal to the Czech MPs either to stand up firmly for the defence of national interests or to resign.

The MPs obliged and at the opening of parliament put forward a declaration demanding the transformation of the dual monarchy into a federation on the basis of natural rights of national self-determination (Czechs and Slovaks together), national rights strengthened in the Czech case by inalienable historical rights. Czechoslovak Social Democrats fully supported this declaration, reaffirming this stance at the so-called Peace Congress of the Socialist International in Stockholm; their leader, Bohumír Šmeral, who was a staunch supporter of an internationalist orientation of the party, resigned from the leadership.[15]

The Austrian authorities were not able to respond in time to the offer which might have saved at least a vestige of dynastic unity, a kind of dynastic presidency over a confederation of virtually independent states. The Bolshevik Revolution in November 1917 eased the position of the Central Powers. The Peace of Brest-Litowsk of March 1918 allowed them to shift a part of their armies (especially the still-formidable German battalions) to the Western Front. The relief, though substantial, came too late. Austria was already exhausted and the Emperor Charles attempted to achieve a separate peace by secret negotiations. The Germans, however, intercepted these efforts and Charles did not feel strong enough to withstand German pressure.

In October 1918 the situation developed with immense speed. At the outset the Czech MPs in the Austrian parliament declared that the Austrian authorities were no longer to negotiate with them but with Czechoslovak representatives abroad. On 14 October, the Czechoslovak National Council declared itself the provisory Czechoslovak government and on 17 October Masaryk drew up the declaration of independence which envisaged Czechoslovakia as a republic. At home, the question arose of the extent to which the new state should be socialist. By declaring a general strike for 14 October, the Social Democrats and the National Social Party attempted to acquire a stronger position on that issue. Their separate action, however, was opposed by the other parties and was only partially successful. Eventually they decided to toe the line and wait for common national action which came a fortnight later. Meanwhile (on 16 October) the Emperor Charles announced in a manifesto the transformation of the Habsburg Empire into a federation. On 21 October the Austro-German National Council declared itself the parliament of the supposed Austro-German state in that federation. On 25 October the leaders of the main Czech parties at home were allowed to leave for Geneva where they met the leaders of the resistance abroad. On 28 October the Austro-Hungarian government signed the unconditional capitulation. With scenes of great jubilation, national independence was declared in Prague. Three days later the Czech leaders in Geneva agreed that the independent state should be a republic with Masaryk as the president designate; the composition of the government was also agreed. On 30 October the Slovak leaders founded the Slovak National Council which adopted a resolution demanding the right of self-determination and endorsed the principle of Czechoslovak unity. On 11 November the Emperor Charles abdicated.

A great epoch in Central Europe came to an end. A dynastic empire which had shown an extraordinary vitality for almost four centuries outlived its *raison d'être*. Paradoxically, it was the Czechs, with the historian Palacký as their most articulate representative, who first suggested a new rationale for the Habsburg Empire, a rationale which should have enabled it to survive into the age where national consciousness became the main bond of loyalty.

In his call for federalization, Palacký was by no means a lone voice. In the late 1860s Count Belcredi had also envisaged a new, but more rudimentary, re-articulation of the Empire: the 'Big Five' components of it (Germans, Magyars, Czechs, Poles and Croats) should be based on historical political units. (It may be worth mentioning that, in 1918, when it was already too late, a Hungarian, Oskar Jaszi, came forward with a similar idea.)

More eleborate concepts cropped up by the turn of the century. There were, on the one hand, the so-called Austro-Marxists, such as Karl Renner and Otto Bauer, and, on the other hand, conservatives such as the Catholic ideologist Ignaz Seipel, or the pro-Austrian Romanian from Transylvania, Aurel Popovici. All wrestled with the problem of how to reconcile the existence of a multiethnic state with the claims of individual nationalities for self-determination and at the same time how to preserve those historical lands which appeared as geographically and economically well-demarcated units.

One strategem to resolve this complex question required a combination of regional autonomy for ethnically homogeneous areas and corporate cultural autonomy based on personal membership in the ethnically mixed areas. It was Renner in particular who devised a complex scheme for such arrangements. On the other hand Popovici conceived of fifteen ethnic regions supervised by a strong central power. The most radical view, however, was taken by Otto Bauer. Whilst Renner upheld the idea of the Austrian Empire as a geographic and economic necessity, Bauer was ready to meet the most extensive claims of the Slav nationalities. In his own words: 'The organization of mankind into autonomous national communities enjoying, organizing, and developing their national cultural goods is the final national aim of international Social Democracy.'[16]

However, nothing came of these well-intended suggestions. The German nation which had been the main beneficiary of the Austrian Empire throughout its whole life span was indeed its chief grave-digger. It was above all the Germans of the Bohemian lands who, with their fervent linguistic nationalism, prevented the more conciliatory and conservative Austro-Germans from making sensible concessions to the other nationalities. On the other hand, the Czechs, especially those of Bohemia, vehemently opposed any attempts to divide their historical lands according to the ethnic principle. The only partners treated by the Austro-Germans as equals, the Magyars, were even less disposed to find a sensible *modus vivendi* with the other nationalities. The dual monarchy created half a century earlier gave the Habsburg Empire only a temporary respite. Eventually, both Cisleithania and Transleithania had to give way to the successor states which were all, rightly or wrongly, conceived of as nation states.

Trying out democracy. A nation state or state of nationalities?

As a new state, the Czechoslovak Republic faced new problems; the old ones, however, were only partly resolved, and some acquired a new shape.

The existence of the Czechoslovak state was internationally acknowledged and its boundaries were fixed by the Peace Treaties of St Germain with Austria (10 September 1919) and of Trianon with Hungary (4 June 1920). These treaties brought a resounding victory for Czech political aims. The new state comprised the three Bohemian lands in their historical borders with a few small additions[17] plus the northern part of the Hungarian kingdom out of which two new lands were created: Slovakia and Subcarpathian Russia (often simply described as Ruthenia). The reason for the inclusion of the latter was that of all the neighbouring states Czechoslovakia appeared to be the least awkward choice.[18]

The only historical precedent for the geographical extent of the Czechoslovak Republic was the Great Moravian realm a thousand years earlier. Although during that time the linguistic affinity between the Slovaks and the Czechs remained close and, from the time of the Reformation, cultural contacts were frequent, nevertheless their much closer contact with the Magyars in the common

Hungarian state gave Slovak society a shape which was different in several respects from that of Czech society. The lower economic and educational level in the Hungarian kingdom as a whole, combined with the denial of cultural self-determination to the Slovaks by the ruling Magyar nation, left the Slovaks less prepared for the role of a political nation than the Czechs.

As a result, Slovak statehood had to start from scratch. Czech help proved essential, but was not without its problems. With the consent of a particular sector of the Slovak population in which the Protestant intelligentsia played the dominant role, the Czechoslovak Republic was constituted as a unitary state, under the assumption that there was one Czechoslovak nation with two languages. (As we saw in Chapter 5 (see p. 103), Slovak as a literary language was standardized about eighty years earlier). Not all Slovaks, however, accepted this position. Some maintained that Slovaks had their own national identity and, although they did not deny the need for a common state, they required an autonomous status for Slovakia. Czechoslovakia should in their view be written with a hyphen: Czecho-Slovakia. The Slovak claim for autonomy referred to the agreement made between the Czech and Slovak émigrés in the USA during the war (the so-called Pittsburgh Agreement of 30 May 1918).

The main supporters of Czechoslovak unity among the Slovaks were the Protestant intelligentsia from whose ranks the most articulate Slovak politicians in various parties were recruited. On the other hand, the Catholic Slovak People's Party led by Andrej Hlinka, a clergyman, became the autonomist party *par excellence*. This was the main reason why it could not cooperate with its predominantly Czech counterpart, the Czechoslovak People's Party. The struggle between the centralists and autonomists, however, was most bitter among the Slovaks themselves. If the Czechs added fuel to the fire, it was more by neglect or high-handedness than by intent. Although Czech help, especially in education and administration, was appreciated by all Slovaks, the liberal secular culture of the Czechs was viewed with mixed feelings. The Slovak People's Party wanted religious, Catholic schools, whilst the government insisted on state schools. The Czech laxity in religious matters was often irritating to Slovaks. Equally resented was Czech economic policy, or rather the lack of it, with respect to Slovakia. The Slovak enterprises were treated as equal to the Czech ones; it was up to market forces which of them were to prosper and which were to perish. The latter was more likely to happen to Slovak than to Czech firms. In the credit shortage caused by the deflationary policy the Slovak enterprises were particularly vulnerable. Nevertheless, in spite of all these irritants, most Slovaks tended to vote for the political parties which were constituted as common Czechoslovak parties; they were considered to be in a better position to redress the Slovak grievances.

The problem, which was not so much a new one as the obverse of an old one, was that of the two nationalities in the Bohemian lands. Now the Czechs became the masters and their language the official language of the state. The Germans were not allowed to constitute their own ethnic territories which would be linked with the new, small, exclusively German-speaking Austria. The victorious powers of the Entente, especially France, wished to satisfy the ambitions of their Czechoslovak ally, which was supposed to become an important link in the chain of states (a *cordon sanitaire*), checking the possible future expansion of the two giants, the Germans and the Russians; the scattered nature of the German-inhabited territories in the Bohemian lands and the geographic separation of most of them from the Austro-German lands provided obvious reasons for rejecting the German request.

The Germans in Czechoslovakia started their post-war political existence with passive resistance. Their leaders rejected the offer to join the Prague National Committee which soon adopted a provisional constitution and created a provisional (Revolutionary) National Assembly. The first public act in which the Germans in Czechoslovakia took part was the municipal elections in June 1919, held in the 'historial' lands (Bohemia, Moravia and Silesia) according to the principle of proportional representation. There were also good economic reasons for a gradual softening of the negative attitude on the part of the German-speakers, who entered the new state much better equipped, culturally and economically, than the Czechs. It was still the Czechs who, especially with respect to the establishment of higher education, had to catch up with the Germans. As far as the language question was concerned, Czechoslovakia accepted and conscientiously abided by the provision of the peace treaties guaranteeing all national minorities use of their own language in all contact with the respective authorities wherever their numbers exceeded 20 per cent of the population. As far as the Germans were concerned, this was the case for the state as a whole.

The social question appeared as an old problem in a new setting. The issue dividing the centralists and autonomists in the Social Democratic Party was resolved in favour of the latter. In fact, they received more than autonomy and became centralists of a new kind in the new state. The ethnic roles were reversed. It was now the German Social Democrats who joined the other Germans in claiming the right to national self-determination. Yet the inter-party division on ethnic lines was soon overshadowed by division over the question of how the working class was to fight for its emancipation. The aftermath of the war in which production substantially declined, inflation was rampant and many rich became richer and many poor poorer was radicalism in all its forms. As in other industrialized countries, the social democratic (or socialist) parties were split between those who wanted to achieve their aims in cooperation with the nonsocialist parties and those who wanted to force through their programmes single-handedly. The ballot was unlikely to give a clear answer.

In what was now the Czechoslovak (no longer the Czechoslav) Social Democratic Party, the struggle gathered momentum in 1919. At a congress in December 1918 the reformists still won the day; the motion was carried that the party should participate in a national coalition government and press for socialization of large landed estates, mines and some big industrial enterprises. The climate for social reforms appeared favourable. Even the 'bourgeois' parties accepted that some reforms must be passed. The eight-hour working day and unemployment insurance were the first measures introduced. At the same time, and throughout 1919, workers' councils spontaneously sprang up in the mining industry. In February 1920, the Social Democrats and National Socialists (the former National Social Party) succeeded in legalizing this situation. In addition, the law in question made a provision for district councils granting workers' councils access to the accounts of their enterprises and a 10 per cent share in the net profits for social purposes. Further legislative measures concerning workers' co-determination in the industrial sector were prevented by fierce infighting within the Social Democratic Party. Reform activity shifted to the extension of social insurance. By 1929, all employees were covered by some kind of sickness and old-age benefit schemes. Czechoslovakia became one of the most advanced countries in this field.

With respect to changes of ownership, the reform programme in agriculture was the most extensive. Here the Social Democratic programme of land reform to transform the large estates into cooperatives had little chance of materializing. It was the Agrarian Party which pushed through its concept of land reform, and in 1919 this became law. Although implementation was very slow and the result was far from revolutionary, Czechoslovak land reform was none the less a significant levelling measure. The expropriation for compensation at a very low (pre-war) price affected estates exceeding 150 hectares (370 acres) of arable land and 250 hectares (618 acres) of land in general. Cheap credit was to be granted to small buyers. By 1930, 14 per cent of all landed property in the state was distributed amongst 583,000 small holders; this number was more than a third of all farms at that time. A further 5 per cent of landed property was distributed amongst larger estates, mainly in the form of so-called residual estates sold as a political reward to people of merit.[19] This programme was managed by the Landed Estate Board, a powerful economic arm of the Agrarian Party, renamed the Republican Party of Farmers and Peasants in 1921 when its Czech and Slovak constituent parts were merged. Led by an extraordinarily talented farmer-politician, Antonín Švehla, this party became the backbone of all coalition governments of independent Czechoslovakia until World War II.

Owing to the German refusal to join the Prague National Committee, the provisional National Assembly (parliament) was an exclusively Czech and Slovak matter. In addition, the remaining sizeable ethnic minorities such as the Magyars in Slovakia and the Ruthenians were absent. The Czech part of the parliament was composed on the basis of the results of the 1911 elections, whilst the Slovak part was constituted by the cooption of a number of Slovak political leaders.

The provisional (Revolutionary) National Assembly unanimously adopted the constitution which proclaimed Czechoslovakia a democratic parliamentary republic with universal, equal direct and secret suffrage and proportional representation at all levels of government, national and local. The president of the republic was to be elected every seven years by the two chambers of parliament, the National Assembly and the Senate. Although in the wording of the constitution the power of the president was kept within narrow limits, the fact that Masaryk was elected President gave the presidency significant weight.

In the first parliamentary elections according to the new constitution in 1920, all nationalities in Czechoslovakia represented by their own political parties took part. The socialist parties of all shades and ethnic groups won 47.6 per cent of the vote. Their divisions along ethnic and ideological lines, however, did not permit concentrated action on their part. The Marxist left in the social democratic parties of all ethnic groups attempted to win the upper hand by a mounting wave of strikes. The trade unions, dominated by the left, tried to force the national socialist and Christian trade unions either to join their ranks or abandon their work. Occasionally, during the strikes and also as a result of ethnic tensions, bloody confrontations occurred. Under these circumstances the National Assembly passed a law enabling the administration to take more vigorous measures to protect personal freedom against terror and intimidation at public meetings and similar occasions. At the same time, to relieve the tension, a law granted employees in enterprises with more than thirty workers the right to elect workers' councils. They were to be concerned with social issues within the individual firms.

In Czechoslovakia, as in all other countries, the Marxist left followed the example of the Bolsheviks in Russia. It was the Leninists idea of world-wide revolution which inspired their activists. After a bitter struggle in which the courts, the police and eventually, when a violent strike broke out, even the army, had to intervene, the social democratic, Marxist, left constituted themselves (in May 1921) as an independent party which adopted the name Communist Party of Czechoslovakia. Unlike the Social Democratic Party, the Communist Party became a party of all nationalities in Czechoslovakia, stressing the multiethnic nature of the state to the point of the right to secession.[20] It was a class-based party *par excellence*.

At the outset, it seemed that the Communist Party might take the majority of Social Democrats with it; but as the general situation in Czechoslovakia improved (her success in this respect was in marked contrast to all neighbouring countries) and the economy experienced a boom period, the Social Democrats began to regain ground. In 1925 the Czechoslovak and German Social Democratic parties together won 14.7 per cent of the vote in the elections for the National Assembly (the Lower House of the Czechoslovak parliament), with the Communists achieving 13.2 per cent. The Social Democrats emerged still stronger in the 1929 election, with 19.9 per cent of the vote against the Communist 10.2 per cent.

Meanwhile two important shifts occurred. On the class front the dedicated Stalinists within the Communist Party managed to outmanoeuvre their opponents and gained a firm hold on the party. The anti-Stalinists did not want to yield to the pressure of the Communist International and among other things wanted to keep the 'Red Trade Unions' independent of the Communist Party. But after an internal struggle which coincided with Stalin's coming to absolute power in the USSR after Lenin's death, the Communist Party of Czechoslovakia became, in 1929, under the leadership of Klement Gottwald, an unreservedly obedient tool of Stalin's policy.[21]

On the ethnic front, the German minority began to take a more positive attitude towards the Czechoslovak state. In 1922, the club of German MPs split into two clubs with symptomatic labels: Combat Community (with seventeen members) versus Working Community (with about forty members).[22] In 1926 the German Agrarian and Social Christian parties, representing almost half of the German vote in 1925, entered the government. As the German Social Democrats followed suit in 1929, the share of the so-called activists in the German electorate increased to three-quarters. (The share of the German vote which went to the ethnically undifferentiated Communist Party is not taken into account.) Meanwhile at the re-election of Masaryk as President of the Republic, a strange combination of opponents emerged. Only the Communists put up a counter-candidate. The Czech National Democrats, German nationalist parties and the Slovak People's Party (the autonomists) cast a blank vote. The German activists voted for Masaryk.

Social, or rather class-related, and ethnic issues, however, were not the only divisive issues among the problems which confronted the Czechoslovak Republic in the first decade of its existence. For a while, religion also became a source of conflict. Although the national revival of the early nineteenth century laid more stress on national than on religious loyalties, the Hussite/Protestant tradition in Czech history provided a welcome source of inspiration for patriotic endeavour on account of its political and cultural achievements. It was, in particular, Masaryk who stressed this point. During World War I, the memory of the Hussite warriors was successfully fostered in the Czechoslovak legions fighting against the German and Austro-Hungarian armies. On the other hand, a close link between the Habsburg dynasty and the Catholic Church and what many saw as the lukewarm participation of the Czech (Catholic) People's Party in the drive for national independence were damaging to the cause of Catholicism. Owing to these circumstances, following yet another campaign called 'Away from Rome', about 20 per cent of the Czech population left the Catholic Church in the early 1920s. Apart from those who joined the Protestant Churches (the main body was now the Evangelical, i.e., Protestant, Church of the Czech Brethren) and those who remained without any religious affiliation whatsoever, a new element appeared in the religious differentiation of the Czechs: the dissident Catholic clergy founded the national Czechoslovak Church aiming at a resumption of the Hussite tradition. The ensuing struggle for ecclesiastical buildings and other property, often conducted in a very ungentlemanly way, added to the turbulences of the post-war years. Thus when, in 1921, the Czechoslovak parliament passed a law to protect personal freedom against terror during public meetings, this law explicitly mentioned religious terror, in addition to social (class-based) and ethnic (nationalistic) terror, as one of the main threats to peace in the country.

Religious strife soon calmed down without any loss of life – something which unfortunately cannot be said of the class and ethnic struggle in their most hectic periods. Its last appearance was the departure of the papal nuncio from Prague in 1925 in protest at President Masaryk and the majority of the cabinet (the People's Party members disapproved) officially participating in the solemn ceremony in remembrance of John Hus who had been burnt at the stake in 1415. In response, diplomatic relations with the Vatican were broken off. But three years later a *modus vivendi* was negotiated with the Vatican; the Holy See agreed to redraw the boundaries of dioceses in order to coincide with the state's borders, a point of particular importance for Slovakia which until then had been under the ecclesiastical jurisdiction of the archbishop in Hungary. Otherwise only occasional polemics and a slow trickle of defection from the Catholic Church in the Bohemian lands continued as a reminder of an old ideological strife that was fading away.

However, the Czechoslovak (in fact almost wholly Czech) People's Party, created by the merger of two separate Catholic parties a week before the proclamation of the Czechoslovak Republic, developed, under the skilful leadership of Monsignor Šrámek and with its main strength in Moravia, into a respected partner in all government coalitions. Although several attempts were made to bring about closer cooperation of the Czechoslovak People's Party with the Slovak People's Party, they all eventually failed. As within the Social Democratic fold before the war, the centralists and autonomists were only occasionally able to make common cause.

In this context it should be pointed out that the Czechoslovak centralists of all shades worked out a routine for settling their differences by negotiation and compromise. As
Šrámek once put it, 'We have agreed that we shall always
come to an agreement'. The participants in this consensus
were the five Czechoslovak parties: the Republicans (Agrarians), Social Democrats, National Socialists, People's
Party, and National Democrats (ranged according to the
size of their electoral support). The framework, however,
was not rigid: occasionally one or two parties stayed away if
outsiders from the German and/or Slovak camp could be
brought into the government. Except where there was an
interim 'officials' (bureaucrats) cabinet, the prime minister
was always an Agrarian. At the request of President
Masaryk, Eduard Beneš, as a specialist who, if needed,
counted as a National Socialist, was continuously in charge
of the Foreign Office until his election as President in 1935.
The cooperation of the Agrarians with the two Socialist
parties (interrupted between 1925-9) was known as the red-
green coalition. In the 1930s it also included the respective
German parties.

In 1929 the Czech Catholics and Christians at large had
an opportunity to manifest the longevity of their tradition.
According to the prevalent opinion of the scholars of those
days it was on the 28 September 929 (and not six years
later as is now assumed) that the most cherished Czech
saint, Duke Wenceslas, met a martyr's death. The great festive millenial commemoration arranged for that day and
year was also an opportunity for reflection. Was the Christian tradition still a unifying factor in the Czech nation? As
the Czechs seceded from the supranational Habsburg
Empire, were they not following the path of the fratricide
Boleslav rather than that of his saint victim? In 1929 all
reflections of this kind appeared more or less academic.
Ten years later, and then again after a further ten years,
reflections on these topics became more intriguing.

With the advantage of hindsight 1929 was the brightest year in Czechoslovak history. For more than a decade the Czechs, united with the Slovaks, enjoyed the independence of their state. The state rights of the Bohemian Crown were vindicated; so also was the quest for national self-determination of both branches of the Czechoslovak nation. Although not everything was right with Slovak participation (a week after the millenial celebration a prominent radical Slovak autonomist, Tuka, was sentenced to fifteen years' imprisonment for plotting with Hungary, and the Slovak People's Party left the government in protest), the parliamentary elections three weeks later brought the centralist parties in Slovakia a resounding victory. Furthermore, the communist vote in the whole state was reduced and the continuous participation of the German representatives in the government pointed towards an ethnic reconciliation which would be more far-reaching than any other since the inception of parliamentarism under the Habsburgs' reign. Nationalists in all ethnic camps lost their influence. A year after St Wenceslas' millenial day, the Czechoslovak Social Democrats included the demand for cultural autonomy for national minorities in their party programme. Last but not least, in 1929 the Czechoslovak economy experienced the top of a boom. Industrial production and exports peaked and the social dimension of prosperity was manifest in the completion of a comprehensive scheme of social insurance. As a mark of confidence and a sign of pride, Czechoslovakia adopted the gold standard for her currency.

Czechoslovakia could indeed be proud of many of her achievements. However, her fate was not in her own hands. A fortnight before her currency became convertible to gold, 'Black Friday' on the New York stock exchange gave the signal for a world-wide economic crisis of extraordinary severity. Czechoslovakia with her high dependence on foreign trade (a quarter of her GNP went to exports) was particularly vulnerable. But the economic crisis was only the background on which other and greater disasters were to feed. The world around Czechoslovakia, almost all her neighbours, turned their back on democracy or rather on that façade of parliamentarianism which still allowed them some claim to be considered pluralistic. German nationalism in the new populist and racist form became more virulent than ever; Germany's noisy and unscrupulous bid for more 'living space' set in. The great powers of the West, whose goodwill had been essential for the creation of Czechoslovakia with borders suggested by her leaders, began to lose their grip on the international situation; their vigour was on the wane. On 30 January 1933, Hitler became Chancellor of the German Republic. A year later, a fascist-type regime was established in Austria. Soon Czechoslovakia became a refuge for those persecuted by the new regimes in the two neighbouring states. In the early years of her existence it was the anti-Bolshevik Russians and Ukrainians, in the 1930s it was the anti-fascist Germans, Austrians, and Jews in particular, who found asylum in Czechoslovakia which was then an island of pluralist democracy in Central Europe.

In such a situation the German minority in Czechoslovakia began to be more than ever torn apart between those who preferred democracy and those who preferred national unification in an authoritarian state. The tide was running against the former. In October/November 1933 the Czechoslovak government disbanded the German National Socialist Workers' Party (its much more important counterpart in Gemany was styled the 'National Socialist German Workers' Party) and the German National Party (which, too, had its mightier counterpart in Germany). But before that happened, a leading representative of the Union of the German gymnastic societies (Turnvereine) in Czechoslovakia founded a new German nationalist organization called Sudetendeutsche Heimatsfront (Sudeten German Fatherland Front). Althought its original support basis and political orientation were traditionalist rather than a Nazi type of nationalist, the Heimatsfront gradually developed into an instrument of Hitler's expansive policy. In 1935, in order to conform with electoral laws, the Heimatsfront was renamed the Sudeten German Party (in Slovakia and Ruthenia 'Carpathian German Party') and in the subsequent parliamentary elections of that year won two-thirds of the German vote in Czechoslovakia. The 'activists' parties, which in the 1929 elections were supported by three-quarters of the German electorate, became minorities in that ethnic camp.

Meanwhile the Czechoslovak centralist camp was, on the one hand, shattered by internal dissent, on the other hand, strengthened from an unexpected quarter, the communists. On the whole, in the mid-1930s, a substantial restructuring of political forces in Czechoslovakia came about. The main events illustrating the various turning points can be outlined as follows.

At the presidential elections in May 1934, in which Masaryk was re-elected as usual with a large majority, his only opponent was the communist candidate Klement Gottwald. 'Not Masaryk but Lenin' was the communist slogan. Before the parliamentary elections in May 1935, the Czech National Democrats led by Karel Kramář, a hero of the Czech resistance during World War I, merged with two smaller right-wing parties in the Party of National Unity which was to become a fierce nationalistic antidote to advancing German nationalism. The electorate, however, was unimpressed with the *tour de force* manifested in fascist-type symbols (blue shirts uniform, fascist salute, etc.) and a noisy election campaign. The National Fascist Community (they stood for election for the first time) also failed to make any impact (gaining only 2 per cent of the total vote, more in Slovakia than in the Czech lands).

A more serious rift in the Czechoslovak camp occurred when in November 1935 Masaryk, because of illness, offered his resignation and recommended Beneš as his successor. The latter, however, was not favoured by the Czech wing of the Agrarian Party (the Slovak representative, Milan Hodža, supported Beneš) and confrontation between the right and left seemed inevitable. As neither side could count on a majority, the casting vote could have remained, undesirably, with the Sudeten German Party. Combat voting was averted by the timely intervention of the Vatican which recommended the Slovak People's Party to vote for Beneš. Scenting defeat, the right withdrew its candidate. In December 1935 Eduard Beneš was elected President by an even higher majority than Masaryk. The communists also cast their vote for him.

The reason for the change of communist policy towards what, in their view, was a bourgeois candidate, has to be sought in international developments. On 2 May 1935 France and the USSR signed a treaty of mutual assistance. On 16 May Czechoslovakia concluded a similar treaty with the USSR. Soviet help to Czechoslovakia, however, was conditional on French assistance. Stalin did not want to become involved without another, stronger, capitalist ally. In those days the Czechoslovak government did not know that Stalin would have preferred an agreement with Hitler; only when Hitler ignored Stalin's overtures did Stalin decide, reluctantly, to play the French and Czech card instead. For the Czech right-wing parties as well, a tripartite alliance was more acceptable. The Communist International, at its congress in August 1935, followed the shift in Soviet policy. The struggle against fascism was declared its primary aim, with the united front of all antifascist forces as the main weapon.

The three subsequent years were taken up with an uphill struggle against the rise of Nazi Germany. The story of the latter is too well known to need repeating here. Only two points have to be stressed in this context. Firstly, the demands of the Sudeten German Party, fully supported by Hitler, were based on the principle of self-determination for the German minority, an argument which even people well-disposed towards Czechoslovakia found difficult to refute; among some French and British politicians there was even an uneasy feeling that the inclusion of a sizeable German minority in the Czechoslovak state according to the terms of the peace treaty (which their governments had imposed upon Germany) had not been justified.[23] Secondly, the demand for Sudeten German self-determination was aimed, in fact, at full subordination of that ethnic group to Hitler's personal dictatorship. This was only the first step towards Germany's domination of the whole of Czechoslovakia; and this, in its turn, was to be only a stage in Hitler's bid for hegemony in Europe as a whole.

Czechoslovakia grew increasingly isolated. Her allies in the Little Entente, Romania and Yugoslavia, had no interest beyond the rationale of that Entente, which had been created as a counterweight to possible Hungarian irredentism and/or a restoration of the Habsburgs in 1920. Hodža's plan for a Danubian confederation, envisaged at that time, was stillborn. The corporatist regime in Austria relied more on Italian help, and Hungary could be won over to cooperation only in return for substantial territorial concessions. In a series of negotiations, Beneš and his government tried hard to satisfy the Sudeten German Party with far-reaching concessions, but whenever something was conceded the demands were increased. 'We must always demand so much that we can never be satisfied', said the Sudeten German leader Henlein to Hitler on 29 March 1938.[24] Meanwhile, the Sudeten German Party unleashed a campaign of terror against democratic Germans and against the Czech officials in the borderland. Frightened Agrarian and Christian Social parties disbanded (as did one smaller party also) and joined the Sudeten German Party. Only the German Social Democrats withstood the pressure but even they had at least to leave the government in order to facilitate negotiations between the Czechoslovak authorities and the Sudeten German representatives.

The declared aim of the Sudeten German Party was the enrolment of all members of the German minority in Czechoslovakia into a corporate body which was to direct all aspects of its members' lives and which should be authorized to found compulsory social, economic and cultural groups.[25] Later, reparations were required to be paid for damages caused by alleged injustices perpetrated against the Sudeten Germans since 1918 and Czechoslovakia was asked to grant the Sudeten Germans complete freedom of choice in matters of allegiance to the German nation and to its *Weltanschauung*.[26]

Although the acceptance of these demands meant a complete renunciation of Czechoslovak sovereignty over a particular part of her population and the creation of an organization both territorially and personally totalitarian within her territory, in fact of a state within the State, the Czechoslovak government eventually, under pressure from the Western powers, was ready to make this almost suicidal sacrifice.

Yet Hitler did not actually want to bring the negotiations to a sucessful end. He would have preferred to resolve the situation by a war in which he could destroy Czechoslovakia at one stroke and show the world the efficiency of his military might. Only fears of war on the part of the British and French governments and also of Hitler's ally, Mussolini (who was apparently not yet prepared for his fateful venture), persuaded Hitler to pursue and achieve his aims piecemeal and without war. The role of the British and French governments in forcing Czechoslovakia to surrender to Hitler's demands is too well known to be discussed here, as is the price which the two countries had to pay for their ill-conceived appeasement of an adversary whom no concessions could appease.

On 29 September 1938 in Munich, the dictators of Germany and Italy and the Prime Ministers of the United Kingdom and France signed the agreement according to which Czecho-

slovakia was to cede to Germany its German-inhabited bor-
derlands. The Czechs were neither invited nor consulted.
The verdict was presented to them as an ultimatum. The
new frontiers of smaller Czechoslovakia were supposed to
be guaranteed by the four powers, but an agreement on this
matter did not materialize.

For Czechoslovakia the only alternative was to fight single-handedly. As the quick mobilization on 23 September
1938 and then the great mass demonstrations in Prague
against the capitulation showed, there was widespread
readiness to fight – and Czechoslovakia was well armed.
Was there any chance to win or at least sustain a prolonged
war until the international constellation would change?
After the annexation of Austria in March 1938, Germany
engulfed the western (Czech) part of Czechoslovakia not
only from the north and west but also from the south; there
the Czechoslovak border was not yet fortified. Furthermore,
Poland and Hungary which bordered Slovakia and Ruthenia
on the north and south respectively, also had their territorial claims on Czechoslovakia;[27] it was most unlikely that
they would stay neutral. In terms of population the combined strength of the hostile neighbours was more than 100
million against the 15 million in Czechoslovakia; of the latter, moreover, more than 3 million were Germans and
700,000 Magyars. Only 5 per cent of the 3,000-kilometre-
long Czechoslovak border ran alongside a friendly power
(Romania). Under these circumstances, the war might perhaps have preserved Czechoslovakia's morale and prestige
but not her existence. It was only rational to pose the question whether the losses of population and the wholesale
destruction would be worth such a heroic gesture.

Beneš himself anticipated that Hitler's further expansion
would eventually force Britain and France to fight, making
the chances of Germany's defeat greater and, consequently,
Czechoslovakia might have a better chance to recover than
if she were destroyed in war. Thus, after having taken mili-

tary advice and with the consent of the government, President Beneš signed the capitulation and soon after resigned. In the first days of October 1938, Czechoslovakia surrendered her border territories. Less than six months later she was dismembered and disappeared for six years from the map of Europe.

After twenty years of endeavour, the Czechoslovak experiment with fully-fledged pluralistic democracy, which looked so promising in 1929, came to an abrupt halt. The fight, however, did not end there. Against heavier odds than ever, it was to take on different forms and different strategies.

7

In the frontline again

Between Swastika and Red Star. Disturbing the balance

As a result of the Munich ultimatum, Germany annexed 38 per cent of the Bohemian lands with about 34 per cent of their population; almost one-fifth were ethnic Czechs. The Hungarian territorial claims were resolved by German-Italian arbitration in Vienna; Hungary obtained a southern strip of Slovakia and Ruthenia with over a quarter of their total population, only slightly more than a half of them declared themselves to be Hungarians in 1930. At the same time Czechoslovakia was forced to cede to Poland the eastern, and economically most valuable, part of what still remained of Silesia which belonged to the Bohemian lands.

The rest of Czechoslovakia was transformed into Czecho-Slovakia in which Slovaks were recognized as a separate, self-governing nation; a similar autonomous status was granted to Ruthenia. Everywhere political pluralism was substantially reduced. However, Hitler allowed no time for the viability of this tripartite arrangement to be tested. In the night of 14/15 March 1939, under the menace of a devastating assault on a defenceless country (guarantees of its territorial integrity envisaged by the four powers in Munich had been rejected by Germany), the Czecho-Slovak government surrendered, and accepted for the remaining parts of Bohemia and Moravia the status of a Protectorate of the

German Reich. A day earlier, Slovak leaders made a deal with Hitler, and Slovakia was constituted as an independent state under German protection. The Ruthenians wanted to save themselves by a similar arrangement, but Hitler was no longer interested in that area and agreed the incorporation of Ruthenia into Hungary.

When, at the beginning of September 1939, Germany attacked Poland, and France together with the United Kingdom declared war on Germany, the Czechs found themselves in a situation similar to that of 1914. Their country was under a foreign power; their free political representatives were abroad and their only effective military participation in the conflict was in organizing army and air-force units for the states which were at war with those of their homeland. Yet there were also some significant differences. The Czechs had at least a vestige of a separate polity; the Protectorate of Bohemia and Moravia. Its head was officially styled 'Staatspräsident'. But the Bohemian lands were, in fact, divided, according to the earlier wishes of radical German nationalists, into two parts. One of these, the so-called Sudetenland, and some other minor territories were directly incorporated into the Reich, and despite a sizeable Czech minority, German was the exclusive language there; the other part was the Protectorate, with only about 3½ per cent of ethnic Germans, and was supposed to be bilingual – German and Czech (in that order) were its official languages.

Furthermore, political pluralism was abolished in the Protectorate. All adult males were called upon to join the collective organization Národní Souručenství (National Partnership); with the exception of communists, representatives of all Czech political parties, with the Agrarians foremost amongst them, were involved. The main task of this movement was to support the State President and his government to steer a middle course in the policy for survival: on the one hand, to keep at bay what in their view would be premature acts of defiance and, on the other hand, to prevent any take-over of leading positions by the small, vociferous fascist groupings, a kind of lunatic fringe. The general belief in the country was that the Protectorate was a temporary arrangement which had to be survived at minimum cost and loss of face. The justification for this attitude can be summarized as follows: The Czechs were betrayed by their allies and forced to extradite their armaments and fortifications and disband their armed forces. Thus they were pushed against their own will into a situation in which only a few of them could escape and join the Allied armies. At home the resistance forces had to wait until a propitious moment to strike presented itself. A German observer gave the following poignant summary of the situation:

> As long as the war lasted, neither side had reason to want an open conflict; relative quiet served the interests of both. While the German administration was interested in exploiting the working capacity of the Czech population to the utmost, and for this reason in keeping it relatively content materially, it wanted to lull or kill off its political and intellectual life as completely as possible. The Czech leaders, for their part, saw that their interest lay in keeping the political awareness of their people as alert as possible, holding collaboration to a minimum, 'throwing sand into the cogwheels' and resisting all efforts and inducements at Germanization . . .
>
> This also explains the motives of most members of the Protectorate government and of numerous Czech civil servants, who remained at their posts not out of opportunism or selfishness but to serve the national cause and then, perforce, slipped into collaboration. The great majority of them believed that they could serve the future of the Czech nation best by remaining in their places. However, they often found themselves facing the painful dilemma of deciding at what point collaboration with the Germans ceased to serve the national cause and became treasonable. Like other peoples under German occupation, they never found a satisfactory solution to the dilemma.[1]

How difficult the middle course could be was, however, revealed very soon when mass demonstrations broke out on the occasion of the 21st anniversary of the Czechoslovak Republic (28 October 1939) and then during the burial of a student shot at that demonstration by German police. Hitler's revenge was swift. Nine student leaders were summarily executed (all of them belonged to the political right) and 1,200 students were sent to concentration camps. All Czech establishments of higher education were closed down allegedly for three years, but they were not opened when the time elapsed. This was the first step in Hitler's plan to Germanize the Czech nation. As Hitler put it, 'by firmly leading the Protectorate, it ought to be possible to push the Czech language in about twenty years back to the level of a dialect'.[2] There could be little doubt about it that German domination over the Czechs was aimed at the latter's disappearance not only from the political but also from the ethnic map of Europe.

Everybody knew that the fate of Czechoslovakia depended on the outcome of the war. In principle, there were no fundamental differences of opinion between the leaders at home and abroad. The State President, Emil Hácha, and the Protectorate government under Prime Minister Alois Eliáš saw themselves as caretakers; most were in secret contact with the government in exile. However, as the war proliferated and became more merciless, the pressure on the domestic authorities increased, both from the German side and from the government in exile. Under the new acting Reichsprotector Reinhard Heydrich, tough measures were taken against the Czechs. On 27 September 1941 Prime Minister Eliáš (the German secret police had collected evidence of his contacts with Czechoslovak exiles) was arrested and, three days later, sentenced to death; martial law was declared. Far-reaching arrests of political and cultural representatives of the Czech nation followed. More systematic measures were also taken to exterminate the

Jews in the Protectorate.

Heydrich decided to tighten German domination of the Czechs with a calculated shock wave of terror. Its impact was focused on the educated strata, intellectuals, teachers, army officers and representatives of cultural and gymnastic organizations (Sokol in particular). On the other hand, manual workers and peasants were to be won over to collaboration by preferential treatment, especially with respect to the rationing of consumer goods, extended social and recreational facilities, etc. The Protectorate government was restructured and its position weakened. A German took over the combined Ministry of Economy and Labour and a dedicated pro-Nazi (a former colonel in the Czechoslovak army) became Minister of Education. President Hácha was persuaded to make an emotional appeal warning the Czech population against anti-German actions. The link between the government in exile and the Protectorate government was broken. Beneš asked for the resignation of Hácha and his government and denied them further legal authority. They, however, considered such a step a further stimulus to escalated repression and terror and felt bound to stay in charge.[3]

Meanwhile, Beneš succeeded in arranging recognition of the Czechoslovak government in London on an equal footing with other governments in exile. He had to overcome quite a few judicial obstacles, i.e., not only the signature of the French and British representatives on the Munich Agreement, but also his own abdication as president, and the international recognition of Hácha's presidency and of the independent Slovak state. The participation of the Czech army and air-force units on the British side played a substantial role in his success; on 18 July 1941, recognition was granted by the UK and also by the USSR. Twelve days later the USA followed suit.

The relative calm which characterized, at a superficial level, the Czech social climate at home after Heydrich took over was not a good advertisement for the Czech cause among the Allies. The contrast with the situation in other occupied countries was obvious. Something spectacular had to be undertaken. Against objections from the resistance leaders at home, President Beneš, as the supreme commander of armed forces, authorized a group of Czech paratroopers to assassinate Heydrich. On 27 May 1942, the order was successfully carried out but at a cost which far exceeded the gain. A campaign of drastic reprisals and serious menaces of still worse to come was mounted with the aim of capturing the paratroopers and those who had helped them. Although many knew the secret, only one – a paratrooper not directly involved in the assassination – succumbed to his fears for his family and to the temptation of a reward, and offered the German police a clue on how to trace the hidden paratroopers. The Orthodox church in Prague where they were hidden in the basement was besieged and, after a gun battle in which they used all their cartridges, they committed suicide. Everybody who had been in touch with the paratroopers was executed. Many hostages from amongst the Czech political and cultural élite, taken when the war broke out, suffered the same fate. Everybody who was deemed to have approved the assassination was also put to death. At that time also the death sentence passed on Eliáš was carried out. Altogether, 1,331 persons were killed by order of the summary courts. Furthermore, two villages Lidice and Ležáky, were razed to the ground, their adult male population killed, their women sent to concentration camps (in the smaller village, Ležáky, women too were shot dead) and children were submitted to racial examination to determine whether they were to be re-educated or killed. Another 252 persons were massacred in Mauthausen concentration camp. The transport of Jews to the extermination camps was stepped up. The arrests and executions were a serious blow to the resistance movement.[4]

More important for the future of the Czechs were developments in the international field. Here it was the USSR which entered into the forefront of post-war consideration. As we have seen, the USSR would have preferred to survive the war in a neutral position in the hope of then exploiting the mutual exhaustion of the capitalist belligerents. This had been the main reason for the Stalin-Hitler Non-Agression Pact of 23 August and 28 September 1939 with its secret clause on the division of power spheres in Eastern-Central Europe. This was also the reason why, at the time, communist refugees from Czechoslovakia refused to join the Czechoslovak army and air-force units in France and Great Britain. Hitler, however, decided otherwise; yet it was mainly his own folly that he waged war on two fronts simultaneously (a repetition of similar blunders made by Wilhelmine Germany in 1914), eventually bringing unprecedented disaster upon Germany.

Before that happened, about 360,000 Czechoslovak citizens perished in prisons, concentration camps and on different war fronts. Of this number about half were of Jewish origin.[5] As elsewhere under Nazi occupation, the Jews were first to be destined for the final solution.

In this context a few words have to be said about the predicament of the Jewish community in Czechoslovakia. During the hundred years or so that had elapsed since Joseph II had begun to allow them to leave the ghettos, the Jews succeeded more or less in integrating themselves into their respective ethnic environment. This at least was the case with Bohemia and Moravia (and also with the Alpine Austrian lands), where the Jews found their environment more congenial for socio-cultural assimilation than in other parts of the Habsburg Empire. This difference was later demonstrated by the population censuses. Whereas in Bohemia and Moravia most Jews declared their nationality as either Czech or German, in Slovakia, where the Jews constituted a higher percentage of the population (4.1 per cent

in Slovakia against 1.1 per cent in the Czech lands) they preferred to declare themselves as Jews not only by religion
but also by nationality.

Assimilation enabled the Jews to take an active part in
the public life of the country in which they lived. From the
mid-nineteenth century until World War II the Jews not
only played an important role in the economic development
of Bohemia and Moravia but also significantly contributed
to the cultural performance of that nationality with which
they assimilated. Exceptionally, such as with the Prague
Jewish writer Franz Kafka (1883–1924), their work has been
considered a contribution to both national cultures.

The assimilation did not mean, however, that the Jews
were everywhere accepted as genuine Czechs or Germans.
Medieval prejudices only slowly gave way to more enlightened views and attitudes. To a large extent it was jealousy
of the successes achieved by a number of Jews in economic
and professional walks of life that made old habits die hard.
The atmosphere of inter-ethnic rivalry was a further impediment. The inclination of the Jews to be rather cosmopolitan
in ethnic outlook and also their greater upward social mobility made them more likely to adopt the language and culture
of the upper, ruling strata in society. This was, more often
than not, German, but in Slovakia it could also be Magyar.
Under the circumstances anti-Semitism tended to taint the
patriotic fervour of those ethnic Czechs who were economically less favourably placed. Significantly, it was Thomas
Masaryk who did not hesitate to intercede on behalf of the
Jews when they became victims of outbursts of hatred. In
1899/1900, there occurred the famous lawsuit against a
young Jew by the name of Hilsner. He was charged and sentenced to death for an alleged murder, to which the popular
press, in a vilification campaign, ascribed ritual motives.
Masaryk, seconded by the Czech poet J.S. Machar, vigorously denounced the campaign as absurd.[6]

In spite of such events, on the whole a more sensible

approach and tolerance prevailed in both national ethnic camps. Jewish participation in the social democratic movement and in various ethnic cultural activities was not a negligible factor in this development. Only the emergence of German Nazism in the 1930s brought a disastrous reversal of this trend.

The story of the Nazis' anti-Jewish barbarism is too well known to be retold in this context. All that need be remembered here is the impact of Hitler's extermination policy on Czechoslovak Jewry. Despite the unrestrained anti-Semitic propaganda of a small Czech fascist group, the Czech authorities in the Protectorate implemented only with the utmost reluctance the anti-Semitic measures imposed upon them by their German masters. This, however, could not prevent the Germans from pursuing their anti-Jewish policy in the Protectorate. In Slovakia, which was in a better position to withstand German pressure, there were (as will be shown later) enough willing collaborators in the establishment ready to perpetrate anti-Semitic atrocities.

As a result, the Jewish religious community which, according to the Census of 1930 comprised on the territory of post-war Czechoslovakia (i.e., not including Ruthenia with her 102,000 Jews) 254,000 people, was, between 1940–5 virtually wiped out. The Nazi extermination, however, was directed not only against those who were Jewish by religion but also against those who were Jewish by descent, irrespective of whether they had converted to another religion or remained without any religious affiliation. This would increase the number of victims of the holocaust by a few further thousands.

The 44,000 or so Jews who reappeared in Czechoslovakia, between 1945 and 1947 were mainly those who survived either by hiding or by emigration, or even in some concentration camps. Most of these remaining Jews joined the two waves of general exodus from Czechoslovakia (each comprising about 140,000), which took place as a result of events in 1948 and 1968 (which we shall turn to later). In 1980 only 9,000 Jews were believed to be living in Czecho-slovakia.[7]

In order to understand post-war developments in Czecho-slovakia, we must look briefly at the shifts in public opinion amongst Czechs as a result of Munich and the Nazi occupa-tion. President Beneš partly reflected these shifts, partly helped them to become more widespread. It was also Beneš who articulated these shifts in a programmatic way and who, by his widely recognized authority, set aside the still significant but less articulated and less energetic opposition to his policy. We shall refer in this context to Beneš's American lectures of 1939 and to articles written in England between 1940 and 1942 which were later published together in Czech under the title *Democracy Today and Tomorrow*.

In this book Beneš expressed his concern with the depressing weakness of the Western democracies (his per-sonal experience of this was overwhelming) and identified its main origin in the lack of any social dimension to a capi-talist economy. He saw the remedy in some degree of social-ization and economic planning. He believed that in this respect the West could learn from the USSR, whereas the USSR could learn from the West in the political sphere. He assumed that the dictatorship of the proletariat was meant as a temporary measure which, in due course, would be 'auto-matically' replaced by some kind of democracy.[8] In his opinion, an East-West *rapprochement* would be the general trend on an international scale, and any future Czecho-solvakia should take an active part in it. Another cause of the weakness of democracies was, in Beneš's opinion, too great a number of political parties and the low moral stand-ards of their representatives. In post-war Czechoslovakia their number should be limited to at most three: the conser-vatives, the socialists and the centre.[9]

With specific reference to Czechoslovakia, President Beneš was concerned mainly with international and internal security. International security required a better guarantee than the tripartite treaty with France and the USSR. The main precondition for internal security was, in his view, a greater ethnic homogeneity. As recent history has shown, the existence of a sizeable German minority proved to be the main stumbling block for Czechoslovakia's stability.

Like Masaryk earlier, Beneš also envisaged ceding to Germany some German-inhabited territories which were not necessarily needed for strategic reasons, in order to reduce the number of ethnic Germans in Czechoslovakia. Unlike Masaryk, however, he conceived of the idea of transferring the rest to Germany. After almost a hundred years of strife in which, despite many attempts, no compromise could be achieved, the combination of the two methods seemed to him, and also to many of his compatriots, the only way out of the impasse. In World War II, as in World War I, cession of territory by a state which won the war to a state which lost it was out of the question; thus the expulsion of the German minority from Czechoslovakia appeared as the only alternative. The communists who, in the 1920s, had defended the rights of ethnic minorities until the right to territorial secession had been won, now became the most ardent supporters of such a transfer. Did not Generalissimus Stalin set an example by deporting about ten nationalities from their homeland in southern Russia and the Caucasus to Central Asia?

With respect to international security, President Beneš realized that the future Czechoslovakia would need more friendly neighbours than was the case in 1938. The change in the Polish leadership (the result of the crushing defeat by Germany in September 1939) provided an opportunity to resolve the issue of the border by agreement and to initiate close cooperation between the Polish and Czechoslovak governments in exile. The respective negotiations between Beneš and the Polish Premier Sikorski started as early as 1940 and went as far as to envisage a kind of confederation.

But Beneš was well aware that in the European constellation even the combined forces of Poland and Czechoslovakia would not be a sufficient deterrent against a more powerful aggressor and therefore wanted to bolster this pact by the participation of a greater power, the USSR. Polish-Soviet relations, however, were rather tense; the Polish government wanted assurances concerning the inviolability of Poland's eastern borders, but this, insofar as it affected a great number of Ukrainians and Belorussians in these areas, was unacceptable to the Soviet Union. The Polish leaders were also more suspicious and, as it turned out, more realistic about the Soviets' ulterior motives.

President Beneš, although he did not completely trust Stalin, nevertheless believed that, on the strength of his outgoing policy towards the USSR and towards Stalin personally, the latter would be induced to reciprocate; Stalin on the other hand knew well how to pretend goodwill where there was none. Beneš also showed more understanding for Soviet ethnic claims and therefore, without much hesitation, yielded to Stalin's pressure and agreed to cede Ruthenia to the USSR. Benes tried to reconcile the Polish government in exile and Soviet representatives, but eventually he had to give up and decide whether he wanted closer cooperation with Poland or with the USSR. Given his own political philosophy, and in view of the comparative strength of the two countries in question, it was clear that his decision was to opt for the Soviets. They also made the abandonment of the Czecho-Polish treaty a condition of their later deal with Czechoslovakia. Furthermore, the Soviet decision to build up their own resistance organization in Poland, hostile to those domestic resistance forces that cooperated with the Polish government in exile, was for Beneš a serious memento.

However, there was yet another impediment in the way of a Czechoslovak treaty with the USSR. There was an Anglo-Soviet agreement that neither side would conclude any treaties with other states before the end of the war. It took some time before this problem was cleared up. In December 1943 President Beneš finally went to Moscow and there signed a treaty of friendship, mutual assistance and post-war cooperation between Czechoslovakia and the USSR. This act was followed by an exchange of views between President Beneš and Czechoslovak communist leaders in exile in Moscow (the main one being Klement Gottwald), in which Beneš offered them two government posts. The communists, however, first wanted to resolve the organization of political parties and of local government in post-war Czechoslovakia. Both sides envisaged a reduced number of political parties, but each in a different way. President Beneš suggested a merger of the three parties of the left: Communists, Social Democrats and National Socialists. The communist leaders, however, wanted to eliminate parties of the right. Although the issue was not resolved at that meeting, the communists finally won the argument. In post-war Czechoslovakia only four political parties were allowed: the Communists, the Social Democrats, the National Socialists and the People's Party. This meant that the 'right-wing' political parties (Agrarians, National Democrats, Tradesmen's Party, etc.), who before the war represented almost 40 per cent of the Czech electorate, were banned from political life. Similarly the other idea put forward by the communists, namely the new local administration by National Committees elected in public meetings, was eventually pushed through. Concerning the Czech-Slovak relationship, the agreement between Beneš and Gottwald seemed to have been most difficult,[10] but the status of Slovakia was eventually resolved with respect to what was going on in the country itself.

In constituting itself as a separate state, Slovakia saved itself from the humiliation and oppression to which the Czechs were exposed, but lost credit because of collaboration with Hitler. In contrast to the Czechs whose army was disbanded, the Slovak army joined the German campaign against the USSR; furthermore, despite protests on the part of the Catholic Church (the Vatican and some bishops) and on the part of the Slovak Lutheran Church,[11] Slovak authorities took an active part in expropriating and mal-treating the Jewish population and transporting them to German and Slovak extermination camps. The most zealous and merciless persecutors were the so-called 'Hlinka's guards', the paramilitary organization of the Slovak People's Party; they were the epitome of what has been dubbed the 'clero-fascist' regime. The treatment of the Czechs and their expulsion from Slovakia was also a blot on the record of the Slovak state, whose President, Dr Josef Tiso, was a Catho-lic clergyman.

Pro-Czech sympathies, however, did not entirely disap-pear in Slovakia; with the continuing war and growing hard-ships, and also with declining prospects for German victory, the idea of a reconstitution of the Czechoslovak state became increasingly popular. With the change in the course of the war after the battle of Stalingrad (13 September 1942–2 February 1943), Czechoslovak partisan units began to operate in Slovakia. In December 1943 representatives of the Czechoslovak resistance in Slovakia together with the Slovak communists created the clandestine Slovak National Council which, in agreement with the Czechoslovak govern-ment in exile, was to prepare an uprising against the clero-fascist regime and the Germans. Owing to the advancing Soviet armies and the intensified activity of the partisans, the German army began to occupy Slovakia. This fact pre-cipitated the uprising that started on 29 August 1944. A sub-stantial part of the Slovak army took part in it. Yet, after two months of heroic fighting, the Czechoslovak forces were defeated. Their captured military leaders were executed and the population in the area affected by the uprising was exposed to brutal repressions. Many villages were utterly destroyed.[12]

The Czechs, having no army of their own (7,000 government troops had no military significance), had to wait much
longer for a more resolute act of defiance than the scattered
though increasing partisan activities could provide.[13] Thus
it was only on 5 May 1945 that an uprising broke out in
Prague. The Czech National Council which led it proceeded
with reasonable caution dictated by the circumstances; it
did not refuse the help of General Vlasov's 'Russian army of
liberation' created from the Russian prisoners of war fighting on the side of the Germans (this help was essential in
saving Prague from a devastating assault by a nearby German SS army corps) and accepted the capitulation of the
remnants of the German army in Prague. For these two acts,
however, the Council was reprimanded by the Czechoslovak
government which, on the communists' instigation, favoured
a more resolute revolutionary show in Prague. Eventually
the Soviet armies, which had travelled from Saxony more
than 100 kilometres distant, entered Prague as liberators,
whilst the American army which, at the time of the Prague
uprising was only 30 kilometres from Prague, was obliged
not to cross the line fixed by the agreement of the Soviet
and American military commands. The timely intervention
of Vlasov's army became a non-event in official Czechoslovak historiography.

The March before this happened, President Beneš and
his government in London moved to Moscow where final
agreement about the arrangements in post-war Czechoslovakia were concluded. The Czechoslovak government
was to be made up of representatives of all permitted
parties under the chairmanship of a crypto-communist (formerly Social Democrat) whose pro-Soviet stance was obvious.
Another crypto-communist, commander of the Czechoslovak
army units in the USSR, was made Minister of National
Defence and an overt communist was put in charge of the
Home Office.

All recognized political parties (in the Czech part of the

state the Communists, Social Democrats, National Socialists and the People's Party; in Slovakia the Communists
and the Democrats), had to form a permanent coalition
called the National Front. Apart from that, the Social Democrats and National Socialists were induced to form a socialist
bloc with the Communists. Furthermore, secret communists
in each of the two parties were to watch and possibly influence their policies. The provisional parliament was constituted of equal numbers of MPs from each political party,
members of the National Front.

The Czechoslovak government, as agreed in Moscow,
moved to Czechoslovak territory on 3 April 1945. There, in
Košice (East Slovakia) it announced its first programme
which was, in general, similar to President Beneš's ideas as
expounded in his book *Democracy Today and Tomorrow*.
Yet, the communists succeeded in giving this theoretical
framework their own content: it represented the first stage
in their bid for total power. On 10 May 1945, the government moved to Prague and the Czech National Council
resigned.

Thus, in May 1945, Czechoslovakia made another entrance
onto the stage of history. With the exception of Ruthenia,
which had been ceded to the USSR, Czechoslovakia was
reconstituted in her pre-war borders. What was not
reconstituted, however, was any wide-ranging political and
cultural pluralism. The new and, so to speak, Third Czechoslovak Republic, appeared as a kind of compromise
between East and West, a compromise which, not only
according to Beneš's dreams but also according to those of
many of his co-citizens, was to become a bridge between the
two very different parts of modern Europe. However, Stalin
had no interest in making bridges. His aim was further
expansion of his empire. As with the swastika, so with the
red star, no compromise was possible.

East or West? The new rebirth

The idea that the communists could be accommodated within a pluralistic framework implied significant concessions to the spirit of tolerance. The demand for revenge was given an ideological backing; class and nationalistic hatreds were elevated into virtues. Masaryk's bequest of humanitarian democracy was put in jeopardy.

The six years of German occupation and repression, with their calculated waves of terror, left their mark on the Czechs. The threat of total eradication as a nation from the map of Europe was alarming. There was no secret about Hitler's plans for the Czechs, whereby some would be Germanized and others transferred elsewhere. There was widespread longing to avoid any recurrence of such a threat. Bitter memories of the betrayal by the West in 1938 and of the great economic depression of the 1930s pushed many to the left of the political spectrum. German war propaganda against the Soviet Union and Bolshevism was counter-productive. In such circumstances Stalin's pact with Hitler in 1939 was often dismissed as a mere tactical manoeuvre.

As the communists espoused the cause of Czech nationalism and expressed the will to cooperate with the 'progressive' democratic parties, many people wanted to believe that this apparent change in the communist attitude in favour of a limited pluralism was genuine. Furthermore, many trusted the wisdom of President Beneš; was he not the closest collaborator of the cherished Masaryk, the most meritworthy founder of the Czechoslovak Republic? And did not Beneš make good the Munich disaster, having returned victoriously to Prague? Was he not the architect of a new, more secure Czechoslovakia? Like Masaryk, Beneš became a kind of father-figure, although one with much less emotional appeal. He was the only internationally well-known and recognized Czechoslovak politician, a man of extraordinary diligence and energy in pursuit of his aims. No other politician was in a position to grow to comparable standing and authority. Although he did not shun consultation, Beneš relied predominantly on his own judgement. It was not difficult to put aside those who disagreed.

But trust in communist intentions and in President Beneš's wisdom were not the only deciding factors. For many, and to be fair not only in Czechoslovakia, there was much confusion concerning the concept of socialism. It was often not realized that there was a yawning gap between socialist aims, such as more equitable distribution of work, of income and of power, and the means by which those aims were to be achieved, e.g., centralized ownership, planning and management of economy and dictatorship of a one-party *apparat*. Only later did it emerge that these measures lead not to the achievement of socialist objectives, but to the opposite. Many people also imagined that by joining the Communist Party they would be in a position to influence it from within. In a significant section of the Czech population there flourished the grand illusion that a democratic road to socialism in Czechoslovakia had been found.

The communists' plan involved two consecutive revolutions: first a national one, then a socialist one. In the first revolution, however, the bourgeoisie was already to be deprived of all effective power. The regime of a 'people's democracy', agreed upon in Moscow and formulated in the Košice programme, provided a wide range of opportunities for such a venture. In the first year of the reconstituted Republic there was no elected parliament and lawmaking was a matter for the leaders of the National Front parties; the prime movers amongst them were the two communist sections (Czech and Slovak) supported by crypto-communists, mainly from the Social Democratic Party. All basic legislation then took the form of presidential decrees and the details were regulated by decrees of individual ministers. The most important of them fell into the domain of the Home Office which was firmly held by a communist. The democratic parties found themselves limited to a kind of rearguard action. The President of the Republic tended to take a nonpartisan stance, as if it were a genuine parliamentary democracy.

Futhermore, the principle of direct democracy (election by acclamation or ballot of those present at the meeting) pushed through by the communists for the election of local councils (in official parlance National Councils) gave the activists, who were mainly the communists, the advantage of organized presence and psychological pressure. Under these circumstances shifts in public opinion were reinforced by demagogy, intimidation and personal terror on the part of the communists against their opponents.

The official view was that something had to be done in order to prevent any repetition of the German assault. Anyone who had collaborated with the Germans had to be punished and the German minority should not have any further opportunity to destroy the state. These motives of precaution and revenge suited the communist strategy extremely well. Retribution for collaboration was seen by the communists as a weapon against all kinds of enemies. As their leader, Gottwald, put it, 'This is an immensely sharp weapon with the help of which we can reach to the very roots of the bourgeoisie . . . to chop off so many scions that only the stump remains.'[14] The expulsion of Germans and the resulting fear of possible retaliation was bound to make Czechoslovakia more dependent on the USSR.

Collaborators were dealt with in special courts, in the Czech lands based on a presidential decree, in Slovakia on a decree of the Slovak National Council which acted as a supreme organ of Slovak self-government. The extraordinary retribution courts were active for two years. Altogether over 130,000 complaints were lodged; 713 persons were sentenced to death, 741 to life imprisonment and 19,888 to prison sentences of varying duration.[15] The official figures do not, however, include victims of summary 'revolutionary' retribution performed without serious scrutiny of the case by the communist-sponsored 'Revolutionary Guards' and similar groupings.[16]

The issue of the German minority in Czechoslovakia was to be resolved on an international level. At the conference of Potsdam in the late summer of 1945, the USSR, US and UK allowed Czechoslovakia to expel her German minority. Of over 3 million people (according to the census in 1930, 3,207 thousand) more than half a million left, or were expelled from, the country before the organized transfer. The latter was implemented during 1946 and according to the official figures comprised 2,165 thousand people.[17] Also many German 'anti fascists' (only the communists and social democrats were recognized as such) who, as a matter of principle, were not scheduled for the transfer, were induced to emigrate. Thus the census of 1950 reported only 165,000 Germans left in Czechoslovakia. A special office headed by a communist was entrusted with the resettlement of the depopulated areas and with the allocation of the confiscated property. This gave the communists an effective propaganda tool.[18]

The problem of the Hungarian minority, Slovakia's pre-war border with Hungary having been restored, was to be resolved partly by the exchange of population (there was a Slovak minority in southern Hungary), partly by re-Slovakization. However, only a little over 70,000 people were exchanged, and re-Slovakization was stopped in 1948. More significant was the repatriation of Czechs and Slovaks from various countries, amounting altogether to 121,000 of whom 40,000 were from the USSR .[19]

Thus, as to its ethnic composition, Czechoslovakia, especially its Czech part, achieved near-homogeneity. Furthermore, the pre-war relationship between Czechs and Slovaks was modified by an explicit recognition of Slovaks as a separate nation and by granting Slovakia wide-ranging autonomy.

Socialist measures began to be introduced in autumn

1945. On 28 October (the anniversary of the birth of the Czechoslovak Republic in 1918) all banks and more than a half of all industrial assets were nationalized.[20] The subsequent monetary reform, needed to check inflationary pressures resulting from demand stored up during wartime and to alleviate the burden of debt, was combined with a general restructuring of prices and wages; the result was a substantial levelling of real wage differentials.[21] At the same time the apparatus for the planning of the national economy was created. Post-war economic reconstruction was to be achieved over the two years 1947 and 1948, for which the first Czechoslovak plan was launched.

Meanwhile, the time came for the provisional parliament to be replaced by an elected one. In the general election of May 1946 the permitted political parties organized in the National Front contested altogether 300 seats, of which, corresponding to its share of the population, Slovakia had 69. As a percentage of the votes cast the results were as follows. In the Czech lands: Communists 40 per cent, National Socialists 24 per cent, People's Party 20 per cent and Social Democrats 16 per cent. In Slovakia: Democratic Party 62 per cent, Communists 30 per cent, and the remainder went to the two minor parties, hastily organized before the elections; one of them being the Labour Party, i.e., social democrats who refused to merge with the communists at the time of the Slovak uprising.[22] The contrast between the polls for the communists in the two parts of the state was significant. As, however, in the state as a whole the Communists were the strongest party, an overt communist, Klement Gottwald, instead of a crypto-communist, Fierlinger, became prime minister. Furthermore, the number of communists in the government was increased.

The government programme of the middle of 1946 proclaimed nationalization to be completed. However, it was agreed that the agrarian reform introduced before the war was to be revised and the commercial network simplified. This seemed to be a sensible completion of the type of socialism agreed by the Košice programme. In reality, it was merely a prelude to something quite different.

All the political parties were interested in soliciting the favour of the electorate. Foreign aid (mainly UNRRA),[23] a good start to the production drive in 1946, and a reasonably good harvest in that year provided the opportunity for a fair increase in real income. A fierce discussion as to whether to encourage such an increase by raising wages or by lowering prices ended in favour of the latter alternative. The 1947 harvest, however, not only fell short of expectations but dropped considerably below the 1946 level. Czechoslovakia had to restructure her imports. The Ministry of Finance estimate of the total damage caused by the drought in 1947 equalled approximately 7–8 per cent of the national income. The need for a remedy gave individual parties the opportunity to promote their political aims. After hard bargaining the communists succeeded in introducing an emergency levy on property and on the increase in the value of property (the so-called 'millionaires' ' levy). A special 'Drought Fund' was set up. Yet the yield of the levy amounted to only one-eighth of the expenditure of the fund.[24]

Meanwhile, another subject of disagreement arose with the US invitation to the Czechoslovak government to participate in the benefits of the Marshall Plan. The noncommunist parties saw in this offer an excellent opportunity to receive economic aid and to strengthen Czechoslovakia's international position. Neither were the communists, at the beginning, averse to this approach. They agreed at the meeting of the Council of Ministers on 4 July 1947 to accept the invitation to the preliminary talks in Paris. Stalin's summoning of Czechoslovak representatives to Moscow, however, changed their mood. It was impressed upon them that joining the Marshall Plan would be considered a hostile act towards the Soviet Union. As a result of this the Czechoslovak government withdrew from the preparatory conference in Paris and refrained from joining the scheme.[25]

In autumn 1947 yet another economic issue, the reorganization of the wholesale trade, was raised. The communists argued that the wholesale network was too dense and increased the cost of distribution unnecessarily, and that many firms attempted tax evasion, especially in view of the 'millionaires' levy, and were also operating extensively on the black market. Again, after hard political fighting, the communists succeeded in substituting a government agency for private wholesale enterprises, at least in the textile sector. Another cause of dissent was the continuation of agrarian reform. Yet the most serious matters were yet to come.

In September 1947 the communist police, following the pattern in other 'people's democracies' (the strings being pulled by Moscow) began to 'uncover' reactionary plots. Slovakia was the most suitable terrain and her majority Democratic Party was the ultimate target. This party was to be purged and the system of self-government was to be reorganized so that the other two small parties and mass organizations such as the trade unions could take part in it. The communists, however, scored only a partial success: their nominees in the guise of mass organizations did not get in. In the new system of self-government, however, no single party had a majority.

Since there was no scope in the Czech lands of 'uncovering' plots, the communists prepared one of their own. Also in September 1947, an attempt was discovered to assassinate three democratic ministers with bombs disguised as perfume. As it turned out the plot was organized by a Communist MP with the knowledge of the Communist Party Politburo in Prague. The communist-dominated Ministry of the Interior did its best to hamper the investigation undertaken by the Ministry of Justice headed by a national socialist. Eventually, the main culprits were to be brought before a trial scheduled for March 1948. Meanwhile, however, as will be shown later, the communists were to be successful in a nation-wide coup and gain absolute power in the state as a whole. As a result it was the investigators of the assassination plot who were sent to gaol.[26] It is difficult to fathom the rationale of this extraordinary venture. Did the communists really want to assassinate the three ministers, or did they intend to fabricate a case in which they could foist responsibility on to another target? The latter would more probably be their style of doing things.

Not everything went well for the communists up to the end of 1947. In the Czech lands the social democrats replaced their crypto-communist chairman by a seemingly more democratically minded person. Tensions between communists and noncommunists grew. The opinion polls revealed a substantial decline in pro-communist sympathies, but as the institution responsible for the opinion polls was under the jurisdiction of a communist-led ministry, the results of its enquiry were not publicized.

Last but not least, at that time there was yet another issue which revealed the differences between individual political ideologies within the Czechoslovak community. At stake were the basic ideas of the Five Year Plan for which the Social Democratic and the Communist parties prepared their respective drafts.[27] The main bone of contention was the communist wish to make Czechoslovakia a heavy industry workshop for the whole Soviet bloc, irrespective of cost. The National Socialists supported the Social Democrats' alternative. The People's Party, being in favour of a free market economy, did not take part in the discussion.

With the beginning of 1948 the political strains became even more marked. They focused upon two particular questions: control of the security apparatus and the structure of any future legislative assembly.[28] The communists offset their decline in popularity by increasing the number of posts they held in the security apparatus at the expense of the other parties; their Home Office minister refrained from reinstating demoted democratic officials in spite of repeated government rulings to this effect.

As a protest against this policy, ministers of three democratic parties (the National Socialists, the People's Party and the Slovak Democrats) decided to end cooperation with the Communists and resigned. Two Social Democrats followed later, but the others adhered to the Communist side. However, as the parliamentary elections due to be held that year were likely to increase the non-Communist vote, the resignations gave the Communists a welcome opportunity to forestall the polls and to stage their *coup d'état*. They unleashed a vigorous campaign for further extension of nationalization and agrarian reform in favour of small peasants, a campaign in which the communist-dominated trade unions, workers' militia and peasants' committees became the main agents of intimidation. Before that happened, however, the Communist Party *apparat*, in cooperation with the police, secret police, trade unions and other communist-dominated organizations, reduced to powerlessness all possible centres of opposition against the communist *coup d'état*. The border was closed, factories and offices were occupied by the communist-led 'action committees'; searching and arrests began. The ailing president failed to give the democrats the expected support. They, in turn, had become so accustomed to the president's decisive lead, that they did not know how to act effectively without his authoritative direction.[29] In the climate of rising terror, even the convention of parliament to resolve the crisis failed to take place, and the president was not allowed to broadcast his message to the nation.

Beneš shrank from the prospect of calling in the army. As at the time of the Munich crisis in 1938 he wanted to avoid bloodshed. At any rate, the communists in the armed forces, with their men in key positions, had taken all precautionary measures against this contingency. Some twenty-five generals were relieved of their duties. As in 1938, so in 1948, the challenger had formidable foreign support. The Red Army could enter Czechoslovakia from almost all sides of her border and no help could have been expected from abroad.

After some bargaining the president eventually accepted the resignation of the democratic ministers. He also accepted the new government composed totally of communists and their collaborators from the other political parties. From mid-1947 they had managed to organize in all of them a pro-communist left. Thus by a well prepared and broadly staged *coup d'état* (in their language the 'Victorious February'), the Communist Party established its absolute rule in Czechoslovakia.[30]

The National Socialist and the People's parties were thoroughly purged and their numbers reduced to a few thousand each (the Communists styled it a 'gentleman's agreement'). Futhermore the National Socialists dropped the epithet 'National' from their name. In the Social Democratic Party the pro-communist leadership was reinstalled and merged with the Communist Party. However, despite great pressure, almost two-thirds of the membership refused to take part in the merger.[31] In Slovakia the Democratic Party was disbanded and the pro-communist Slovak Renewal Party founded instead. The already insignificant Freedom Party was reduced almost to nonexistence.

Thus the elections of spring 1948, which had earlier been expected to result in losses to the communists, were contested by only one common list of the communist-dominated National Front. For the voters the only alternative was the blank vote; but there was no guarantee that their number would be fairly counted. Only 13 per cent of the vote in the Czech lands and 15 per cent in Slovakia were reported as not the cast for the National Front.[32] In 1948 universal equal suffrage, a great achievement of the Social Democrats forty years earlier, turned under communist domination into a cynical parody.

From 1945 to 1948 the undisguised class struggle had been directed mainly against big business. Only large industrial enterprises and finance institutions were nationalized in the first instance; all other property was confiscated not overtly as a measure against the class enemy, but only when there could be brought against the respective owners charges of collaboration with the occupying forces, i.e., of betrayal of their ethnic loyalty.

The bulk of the owning class, the few remaining capitalists and the small craftsmen, shopkeepers and farmers were expropriated only after the communist takeover in 1948. About 300,000 formerly self-employed, approximately 5 per cent of the labour force, became workers. Approximately another 100,000 workers were recruited from formerly nonmanual employees and professionals, victims of purges. However, in order to staff the civil service, the armed forces and managerial posts with class-conscious men and women, there was a flow of approximately the same magnitude from the blue- to the white-collar workers' categories.[33] The rhetoric hailed it as the culmination of the class struggle. In fact it was the annihilation of a prostrate, defenceless loser. With respect to agriculture it took about ten years for the entire operation to be completed and for the former owners to be thoroughly proletarized.

Meanwhile, various groups became particular targets for repression: officers who during the war fought on the Western Front and also those who had come in contact with the Soviet intelligence service; partisans who fought in the Spanish Civil War; prominent or potentially dangerous members of the noncommunist parties; the Catholic clergy; alleged Trotskyites; other enemies within the Communist Party. To demonstrate the continuation of the class war, all kinds of actual or potential opponents of further nationalization and, eventually, also collectivization of farms, likewise became targets. Under instructions from Soviet experts the Czechoslovak state security apparatus fabricated several centres of conspiracy; their alleged members were induced by physical torture and psychological pressure to plead guilty. The supposed ringleaders and persons deemed most dangerous were executed.

The number of death sentences passed and carried out at that time was kept secret but there are good reasons to believe that they run to several hundreds. Suffice it to give here only two names: a woman, the National Socialist MP, Dr Milada Horáková, and one of the most distinguished Czech soldiers in World War II, General Heliodor Pika. The hanging of eleven leading communists because of their alleged conspiracy for the Western imperialists only underlines the monstrous absurdity of the whole action.

The total number of victims sentenced by various types of courts or sent to labour camps by administrative decisions of local authorities has been estimated to be well over 100,000,[34] much more than under 'retribution' in 1945, if the expulsion of Germans is considered separately. A similar number of persons escaped into exile. In contrast to the situation after the defeat of the Bohemian uprising in 1620, no one was officially allowed to leave.

A policy of repression was also used against the Churches. The prime target was the Roman Catholic Church, to which in 1947 three-quarters of the Czechoslovak population were affiliated. The communists knew that they could not destroy it at one stroke and they attempted to undermine it by driving a wedge between the episcopate and the rank-and-file clergy.

Hoping to gain the allegiance of the clergy, the communist government was not interested in the virtual separation of the Church from the State. In continuing to pay the salaries of the clergy the state reserved to itself a powerful weapon in influencing their behaviour. After a round of negotiations between government officials and the Catholic episcopate in 1949, there was complete deadlock. The representatives of the Church hesitated to declare full loyalty to the State, because in their minds it implied a schismatic separation from the rest of the Catholic Church and the pope in Rome. On the other hand the communists complained of intervention by the Vatican. They later even accused it of fostering espionage in the 'people's democracies'. The communists accordingly initiated and sponsored an association of loyal priests, the so-called Peace Committee of Catholic Clergy. (After its disintegration in 1968, it was reconstituted in the early 1970s and renamed according to the Papal Encyclical of 1963 'Pacem in Terris'!)

As the Communist Minister of Information announced, religious freedom would be fully respected, but the task of educating children was the task of the state, which it would carry out 'in the spirit of our scientific truth of Marxism/Leninism'; he further rejected the right of the Vatican to interfere in affairs of education, in Church property, in the punishment of priests according to Canon Law, etc., and defined the relationship of Czechoslovakia to the supreme authority of the Roman Catholic Church as a purely international matter. Consequently, obedience to the orders of the pope, if in contradiction with communist policy, became obedience to a foreign power and therefore high treason.

As most priests refrained from joining the Peace Committee, punitive measures were taken. During the period 1949–51 religious orders were dissolved, Church administration and the pastoral activity of clergy were put under state control, and priests who had not taken the oath of allegiance to the government were dismissed. In the event that they opposed government policy, they were imprisoned. These measures most affected the bishops whose offices, as a result, were left vacant.

Under such conditions this new *Kulturkampf* was a one-sided battle, the Church being without any effective defence. In comparison with neighbouring Poland, for instance, the Catholic Church was immensely weaker in her command over her membership, and she could reach through her pulpits only a small proportion of the population. This was apparently the main reason why the communists could afford a greater resoluteness in the Czech lands than in Poland. The struggle, however, was hardest in

Slovakia where the population was more religious and, in several instances, did not hesitate to defend their priests physically from arrest or deportation.

The pressure on the other Churches was less severe. What mattered was that their leadership was not foreign. Moreover, there was enough goodwill in the ranks of the Czechoslovak Church to make cooperation with the communists possible. The main Protestant Church, the Czech Brethren, in its turn, was too small and yet too entrenched in its Presbyterian constitution and its members' loyalty to merit disruption. There was also a degree of sophisticated collaboration with the communist authorities exercised by its leading theologian, Hromádka, widely known abroad, which eased the position of this Church. In spite of all this, however, even the non-Catholic Churches were subject to watchful state control. Religious education was squeezed out of schools; the exercise of pastoral work was made dependent on the consent of the state supervisory office as was also any activity extending beyond the compass of individual parishes.[35] Too often government consent was withdrawn from individual ministers.

There was another reason why the Catholic Church was singled out for harsher treatment than the others. In their wish to present their policy as the culmination of the progressive trend in Czech and Slovak history, the communists tried to interpret the Hussite reformation as a kind of social revolutionary movement which was articulated in religious terms and symbols only because of the spirit of the time. Consequently, the whole Protestant Reformation too was viewed more favourably than the Catholic periods in Czech and Slovak history. Yet following this strategem the communists performed a disservice to the Protestant cause. Contrary to their intention, having turned the Catholic Church into a suffering Church, the communists purged it of opportunistic elements and re-established its moral standing and prestige. More than anything else they contributed to its full rehabilitation amongst those Czechs who had until then harboured reservations concerning its past record.

It was the Catholic Church itself which made the most welcome and rewarding step towards interdenominational reconciliation, towards healing the traumatic wounds of the past. At the Second Vatican Council in 1962–4 Cardinal Karel Beran explicitly criticized and apologized for the repressive measures of the Counter-Reformation. In the growing mood of Christian ecumenism the communist attempt to single out the Catholic Church for particular repression backfired. For, as we will see later, Catholicism in Czechoslovakia, after thirty years of repression, experienced an extraordinary rivival.

What eventually proved most disastrous for the communist cause was the fact that the great constructive economic effort was not accompanied by any commensurate improvement in living standards or, most important, in the quality of life. The manual workers were the first to show their disappointment. When the monetary reform of June 1953 confiscated a substantial part of their savings, the workers demonstrated in several industrial cities.[36] Their public protest signalled a watershed in the drive for ideological conversions.

A few years were to pass before the communist intellectuals began to show their dissatisfaction with the system. Although Czechoslovakia was now what the new constitution of 1960 called a 'socialist republic', for the great mass of people there was no improvement in living standards. On the contrary, the subsequent years showed an interruption of economic growth. Economic reform became an urgent issue, and unorthodox ideas began to crop up in the planning and later also the party apparatus. A palace revolution was in the making.[37]

Why and how this was possible is explained by the institutional structure of the power élite. The communist élite has its hard core: the Party, the police and the army; it controls the traditional hierarchy of civil servants and local government; finally it has its outer fringes consisting of mass organizations such as trade unions, unions of youth, of women and of professionals such as writers, artists, journalists, etc.

The relative importance of individual core organizations is not invariable. Fluctuations in their respective powers, albeit of small intensity, occurred between 1948 and 1968. In the first two years party officials with their secretary at their head, were at the top. Beginning in 1950 however, the State Security body (i.e., the political police), controlled by Soviet agents, bypassed the party apparatus under the auspices of the 'workers' president' of the state, and thus grew more powerful than any other component of the power élite.

However, as the police authority derived its strength from the USSR, its ascendency depended on the relative position of the police there. As this was considerably weakened after Stalin's and especially Beria's death in 1953, the position of the police in Prague in turn suffered a setback too. Only gradually, however, did the party apparatus regain its ascendency in Czechoslovakia. It was probably not fully restored until Novotný became First Secretary of the Party and President of Czechoslovakia in 1957. Holding the main threads of contact with the Kremlin, Novotný could not be easily circumvented by other contacts with Moscow, as had so often happened in the previous president's terms of office. This, in my opinion, was the first precondition for autonomous development in Czechoslovakia.

Meanwhile, internal factors started to operate as well, first in the outer fringe of the power élites. Although institutions of this type enjoy only a limited range of power, their main task being to keep their members in line politically, their members often enjoy wider influence by virtue of their professional activities. Thus the first articulate act of criticism which took place at the Congress of Writers in 1956 and later at the students' First of May celebrations, won unprecedented publicity.

Officially acknowledged writers were in many respects a privileged group. Why then did they initiate criticism and eventually become the most vociferous group in the movement? Similarly, students who became representatives of their organizations had the best prospects of getting good jobs in the power élite. Why did they start to speak on behalf of other people?

Firstly, the reason was, in many instances, the awakening of conscience which came after the period of Stalinist terror had ended. Secondly, there was the yawning gap between theory and practice, between official claims and doctrinal statements on the one hand and practical achievements on the other. Many writers, and some student leaders, discovered that they could no longer pretend that they did not see these discrepancies.

Evidently there were other people who had similar or even stronger views and who, in addition had direct economic and political grievances. Although they were still silent, they gradually became receptive to the criticisms within the fringe of the power élite; eventually their sympathy revealed itself in the hour of crisis.[38]

There was yet another, perhaps more politically significant, difference of opinion within the communist power élite, concerning the Czech-Slovak relationship – the ethnic backbone of the state. Since in 1946 the Slovaks had been less inclined than the Czechs to vote communist, the communists had supported the centralization of all decision-making in Prague. In the early 1950s the Slovak communist leaders who did not toe the line were sentenced, as bourgeois nationalists, to long-term imprisonment or even death. The post-Stalin thaw came to Czechoslovakia belatedly but when it did come the Slovak communist nationalists who survived the purge were released from prison and rehabilitated. However, Slovak autonomy was not renewed. This aroused misgivings in the Slovak communist leadership as a whole. The conservative communist leadership in Prague had thus to face two enemies at the same time: the reformists in their own ranks and most of the Slovak party into the bargain. In due course the combined pressure of Slovaks and reformers led, at the beginning of January 1968, to Dubček, a Slovak, becoming First Secretary of the Communist Party of Czechoslovakia.

The marriage between the reform wing of the Czech communists and the Slovak Communist Party did not last for long, however. When Soviet military intervention put an end to the whole Czechoslovak experiment, the Slovaks adapted more quickly. Their earlier cooperation with the Czech reformists had been rewarded by a change in the constitution. The unitary Czechoslovak Socialist Republic was transformed into a federation of Czech Socialist and Slovak Socialist republics.[39] The Soviets were quick to realize that this was what mattered most to the Slovaks. They also quickly grasped that they could exploit the lack of unity and thus rule more effectively. They consented to the constitutional change and, with Dubček out of the saddle, the Slovak communists abandoned the cause of reform. Thus, whereas in 1948 it was the Czechs who were favoured by the Soviets, in 1968 Soviet preference went to the Slovaks. No wonder that the latter could then be more relaxed about what the communists called the 'normalization'.

Although the communist leadership under Dubček tried to avoid any confrontation with the USSR (they remembered the unfortunate Hungarian uprising in 1956) they nevertheless failed to achieve Soviet acquiescence. Furthermore, the East German communist leaders were alarmed at the extent of the liberalization in Czechoslovakia, especially that in the political sphere. After seven months of a cautious broadening of civil liberties the armed forces of five member states of the Warsaw Pact (the USSR, Poland, East Germany, Hungary and Bulgaria) invaded Czechoslovakia

in the night of 20/21 August 1968, in order, as the official
version reads, 'to secure the socialist system in Czechoslovakia and to ensure the security of the whole socialist
community'. At that time the military preparedness of
Czechoslovakia was even more hopeless than in 1938 and
1948. The Czechoslovak armed forces had been integrated
into the military machinery of the Warsaw Pact; the Soviets
knew all their secrets, and also, numerically, the Czechoslovak army was no match for the invading forces.

However, seven months of liberalization and the Soviet
invasion were enough to electrify the nation into a mighty
response to the assault. Everywhere the invading armies
met with defiance. The press, radio and television were all
still in the hands of the reformers and continued to report
events, so encouraging the people not to yield; instructions
aimed at confusing the invaders were immediately carried
out. Attempts to stop the tanks and to hold discussions with
the Soviet soldiers about their hostile action had some
effect: the Soviets had to replace some units which had
become infected with 'heretical' ideas. But there were also
mortal casualties among the Czech enthusiasts. Solidarity
and the morale of the Czechoslovak people were at their
height.

The Soviet plan to impose a new 'workers' and peasants'
government' which would then put the deviant leadership
on trial, misfired. In view of the spirited response of the
population, and on the insistence of the new President of
the Czechoslovak Republic, Ludvik Svoboda, who during
World War II was the supreme commander of the Czechoslovak army in the USSR, the Soviets settled for a negotiated
capitulation by Dubček's team, which meanwhile was
imprisoned in Moscow.[40]

The year following the invasion was a depressing anti-
climax. Gradually all the liberties which had been achieved
were stifled. Nothing could better illustrate the depths of
national desperation than the public self-immolation of two

students, Jan Palach and Jan Zajíc. Although their protest found a resounding echo amongst the people, the regime made every effort to suppress the memory of these events.

The Soviet armed intervention against the 'Prague Spring' completed the process of alienation of the Czechs and Slovaks from Soviet Russia. Whilst between 1945 and 1948 the advance of the pro-Soviet communists was predominantly brought about by the Czechs and Slovaks themselves, in 1968 their comeback was to be reimposed upon Czechoslovakia by force from abroad. Those who were supposed to have requested Soviet 'help' have not dared, up to the time of writing, to declare all their names in public. Another 120,000 to 140,000 people went into exile.[41]

A sense of powerlessness and dashed hopes together produced a widespread malaise amongst the Czechs and to some extent also amongst the Slovaks. Most turned their backs on any kind of politics whatever. Some focused all their effort on improving their personal lot, on relentless acquisition of means to, and symbols of, a comfortable life. This was a means of escape which the authorities found quite acceptable. For the communist regime gave up its indoctrinating zeal; it no longer insisted on manifestations of loyalty, but contented itself with political disinvolvement on the part of the citizen, whose acquisitive drive it was ready to accept as legitimate behaviour. In order to facilitate this shift from political involvement towards personal acquisitiveness, the regime began to be lenient about various kinds of minor economic offences.

Those who did not want to play this game tried to build up a framework of their own culture. Some Czech dissidents dubbed it a 'parallel polis', but in fact it was neither parallel nor a polis. It was an alternative culture. In contrast to the official culture, it was pluralistic both in form and in ideological orientation. Every kind of art and every shade of opinion found a place within it. Not only criticism of current events and practices but also a critical reappraisal of the past played an important role in its themes. The three successive surrenders, in 1938, in 1948, and in 1968, and the expulsion of 3 million Germans constituted the main sore points in the collective consciousness. The sense of shame or even guilt combined with the quest for scapegoats who were sought not so much abroad as at home. No one, however exemplary his historical record might be, has been immune to criticism. Great breaks with the past within the life span of one generation, coupled with a sense of helplessness, had traumatic effects which those who were effected tried to sublimate in this way.

By the end of the 1980s the extent of the alternative culture in Czechoslovakia was impressive. It was kept alive by the enormous effort and enthusiasm of those who were spending their time and energy in writing, retyping and distributing what has become known as *samizdat* literature. It comprised not only novels, poetry, drama, etc., but also historical, sociological, philosophical and other writings. Several literary and scholarly periodicals provided a forum for discussion. Although the circulation of *samizdat* literature at home was limited, about a dozen Czech and Slovak publishing houses abroad gave it the widest possible publicity.

At the beginning of 1989 eighteen independent movements in Czechoslovakia were reported in the West. The best known has been the oldest of them, Charter 77. It was founded as a loose pressure group in January 1977 and the membership in mid-1989 was about 1,500 signatories. Charter 77 functioned as a spontaneous voice of conscience. Its main aim was to remind the Czechoslovak authorities of the necessity to observe the laws and international agreements, particularly those concerning human rights, to which Czechoslovakia has been a signatory. This applied especially to the so-called Helsinki Agreement of 1975. A special branch of Charter 77, largely independent, however, of the main organization, was the Committee for the Defence of the Unjustly Prosecuted, founded in 1978.

Of the more recent groupings the most remarkable was the Movement for Civil Liberties, founded in October 1988 as a loose association of independent political groups and clubs. Its Manifesto stood for political pluralism, a new democratic constitution, overhaul of the legal system, protection of the environment, freedom of intellectual activity and belief, independent trade unions, de-militarization, and national sovereignty within an integrated democratic Europe.

One particular feature of this alternative culture was the revival of religious consciousness. This was most clearly manifested in an increasing number of churchgoers and mass participation in religious pilgrimages but this trend could also be seen in the themes of *samizdat* literature. Significantly, it was Roman Catholicism which became most attractive. Just as Hitler's propaganda backfired when it picked upon Bolshevism as the main enemy, likewise the communist campaign against Catholicism.

Although from time to time sporadic voices were to be heard, both at home and in exile, criticizing the Protestant tradition and extolling the Catholic Counter-Reformation, majority feeling and, indeed, the official position of the Catholic Church is for tolerance and mutual understanding. In his ecumenical message for Easter 1988 the Primate of Bohemia, Cardinal František Tomášek, announced a Ten-Year Programme of Spiritual Renewal. In it he made the following statement:

> When looking to the past we all have reason to call for mercy and forgiveness. The Catholic Church does not disguise its share of guilt for the regrettable chapters of our history (put forward, for instance by Cardinal Beran at the Second Vatican Council, regarding the burning at the stake of John Hus and the violence accompanying the recatholization of Bohemia after 1620). We hope that our ten-year programme will help us to avoid protracting discords of the past into the new millenium.[42]

On the opposing side of the Christian tradition, thirteen prominent Czech Protestants wrote an open letter in June 1988 to the Central Committee of the Communist Party of Czechoslovakia. In it they stressed their solidarity with Catholic demands for the restitution of their educational and publishing facilities and for the reopening of monasteries; they also acknowledged that the Catholics had been exposed to harsher repression than they themselves had suffered. Last but not least the Protestant speakers expressed their shame for the fact that they had not stood up earlier for their Catholic fellow Christians.[43]

Thus a start has been made on the healing of a wound which had remained open for more than three hundred years. Tolerance ceased to be a matter of indifference, of declining religious beliefs, but, on the contrary, reappeared as the result of a deeper, more understanding and empathic religious sense, the fruit of adversity and suffering.

The communist regime in Czechoslovakia seemed not to be so much concerned with suppressing the alternative culture as with isolating it from the bulk of the population. This, however, was more easily done with *samizdat* literature than with popular music and – this was particularly irritating for the regime – with the religious revival. Particpation in religious rites and the wearing of religious symbols became an expression of protest in which anyone not interested in promotion dependent on political screening was able to indulge in without risk. The brunt of repression was borne by those who organized religious meetings, seminars, etc., whether they were clergymen or laymen.

As far as literature was concerned, contacts with those in exile, though resolutely discouraged, were seen as a lesser danger than the domestic dissemination of what were deemed to be harmful ideas. Pressure was most severe on those participants in the alternative culture (it would not be appropriate to call all of them 'dissidents') who were not known abroad. The harsh treatment of such people spread fear which was an effective deterrent to the silent majority who, having seen the danger, were all the more motivated to seek comfort in consumerism.

In the conditions of a command economy, however, even this orientation constituted some risk for the regime. The example of a more affluent West with easier access to the cherished symbols of wealth discredited any claims for the superiority of the socialist economy and helped to spread disbelief in official views and statements even amongst those who were genuinely uninterested in politics. Fortunately for the regime, the difficulties which citizens had to over-come, whether they wanted to find self-expression in the acquisition of consumer goods and symbols of affluence or in participation in the alternative culture, required so much energy that little was left over for other concerns. This made surveillance easier, but it provided yet another reason for frustration. Coupled with the traumatic effects of past breaks in continuity, accumulated frustration threatened to burst through the apparently calm surface. Conditions were ripe for a new dramatic event.

Miracle of the 'velvet revolution'

As is well known, Czechoslovakia was not the only country of the European West that was brought under the domin-ation of the USSR. Apart from Austria, all the eastern part of Central Europe was in a similar position. In all these countries there was much dissatisfaction and a great longing for change. The dissenters, however, were not able to syn-chronize their actions. Upheavals and revolts in individual countries occurred at different times. The East Germans, driven to action by a high degree of exploitation, were the first to rise against Soviet domination. Their uprising of June 1953 was, however, quashed by the Soviet tanks. A more formidable uprising, amounting indeed to a revolution, three years later in Hungary suffered a still more revengeful defeat. At the same time the Poles managed to win a short-lived and limited respite from the brutal dictatorship. Then, there was a twelve-year lull until, in 1968, the Czechoslovak communists attempted a peaceful, and as they hoped, negotiated emancipation. But greater freedom was not negotiable with the Soviets. Only with the coming of the 1980s did the Poles, due to specific circumstances, manage to establish an institutionalized form of dissent. Alliance of the working class with the Catholic Church in effective opposition to the communist regime turned the Marxist-Leninist dialectics upside down. But even this unprecedented venture did not suffice to bring about a substantial breakthrough.

The impulse towards a real and essential change was to come from the Soviet Union itself. Already before this happened most people in the satellite countries had taken the view that without some internal change in the Soviet Union there was little hope of any substantial improvement in their own countries. However, any change in a country whose social fabric was frozen by firmly established despotism, imbued with a paranoic fear of any innovation, was considered by many to be an unrealizable dream. Nevertheless, in the late 1980s the unbelievable became reality. The Soviet Union itself awoke from its torpor and began to look for inspiration in the West, to assimilate Western ideas and ways of life. Gorbachev's attempt at thorough reform at home was followed by abandonment of the Brezhnev doctrine claiming the right to interfere in other countries of the Soviet power bloc; these were the starting points which put in motion the process of change which was to embrace the whole Soviet empire.

But how could this happen? Why should the despot, of his own volition, cease to be a despot? Furthermore, regardless of what he might have undertaken at home, was it not in the interest of the USSR to keep all its satellites on a short lead? Did they not have a vital function to perform in providing economic and military support, a kind of glacis, for the Soviet Union?

The reason for change in Soviet foreign and domestic policy has to be looked for in the coincidence of progressive internal decay with shifts in the international constellation of forces. In the mid-1970s Stalin's transformation and subsequent mismanagement of Russia revealed its devastating consequences on a large scale. Side by side with the persistence for the bulk of the population of a miserable quality of life, demographic decline and ecological disasters assumed proportions that could no longer be disguised. Although the relevant data were kept secret, there were enough people, both in the 'nomenclatura' and elsewhere, who grasped the extent of the nationwide calamity. The yawning gap between the achievements of the West and those of the East became alarming.

It was not the first time that the Russian power élite was confronted with such a perception, with a situation in which the remedy had to be sought abroad, significantly from the West, as always. So it was at the time of Peter the Great; so it was with the Tsars after losing the Crimean War; so it was at the time of the February Revolution of 1917. But Western wisdom used to be only half-learned and was easily forgotten. When Lenin, and later Stalin, assumed command of Holy Russia, it was only the technology of the West that they envisaged for adoption; the traditional despotism of Russia was to be toughened rather than relaxed. Marxism, that Danaëan intellectual gift of the West, provided a delusive ideological weapon for such a purpose. Thus when Gorbachev launched his reform campaign, it seemed possible that he would just follow the old pattern: the path already trodden by earlier Russian Westernizers, only either to stop half-way or to lose sight of their original destination entirely. However, it gradually became clear that his reforms were meant seriously and promised to be comprehensive; they should touch the very nerve of Russian tradition, the heart of the Russian psyche.

External circumstances have provided Gorbachev with adequate space for manoeuvre. It has become clear to him that the 'capitalist' West is no real threat to his country. The leaderships of both superpowers, the USSR and the USA, have realized that if there is any external danger to either of them, it lies outside of the two respective power blocs. From 1950 to 1985 the share of the so-called North in world population declined from 30 to 20 per cent; this tendency continued throughout the whole of the eighties and is not likely to stop in the near future. The revival and militancy of Islam has made demographic pressure from the South still more alarming. Meanwhile about a dozen sovereign states of the so-called Third World have been acquiring a dangerous amount of striking power, whether in atomic, chemical or other sophisticated weaponry; a new, terrorist type of warfare has become endemic in many parts of that part of the world and threatens to upset civilized relationships both between nations and between individuals. Furthermore, mass immigration to the northern countries by peoples with substantially different values and understanding of human cohabitation, makes their satisfactory cultural integration into those countries increasingly difficult. No wonder that the leading politicians, both in the West and in the East, are beginning to grasp that *vis-à-vis* the South they all are in the same boat. The consequences are clear: Why should the USSR keep the iron curtain? Why should it not use the opportunity to shift resources from military to civil purposes? And why should the West not help Russia in this laudable endeavour?

As the Soviet leaders wanted to tackle their problems of stagnation and decay seriously they could not keep them secret any longer but had to bring them out into the open. Thus, in spite of many risks, they became more trustworthy not only to their own peoples but also to the West whose benevolent attitude they needed. There is a certain logic in Gorbachev's *glasnost* and *perestroika*. Yet the liberalization of a multiethnic, despotic empire whose constituent parts are at very different levels of civilization reveals another kind of logic. Whatever may happen with Gorbachev's grand design, the changed power structure in the world with the growing pressure from the 'Third World' will persist; consequently more elbow-room will be available for spontaneous action in the communist-dominated countries outside the USSR.

In the context of this book it would be out of place to discuss in more detail the fascinating turning point that Europe experienced toward the end of the 1980s. This topic certainly will attract much attention and will be amply analyzed at various levels of sophistication. Here we have merely to mention briefly that the opportunity to free themselves was first grasped by the Poles and Hungarians and that soon afterwards the spirit of defiance broke out in East Germany, Czechoslovakia and, to a lesser extent, in Bulgaria. Everywhere the transformation developed more like a game of chess than like a revolution, although the temptation to use arms against the demonstrating people was not absent. Only Romania was to tread the bitter path of a real, bloody revolution. But the magnitude of change in all these countries rightly deserves the epithet 'revolutionary'.

The label fits not only what happened in individual countries of the Soviet sphere but also with respect to Europe at large. The traditional division of Europe between the pluralistic West and the monocratic East, a division that was accentuated when Russia became communist-dominated, has been called into question. Although at the time of writing the whole process is not yet over and the abolition of the socio-cultural and economico-political division between Eastern and Western Europe may turn out to be incomplete (Russia may preserve quite a lot of her particularities; Gorbachev failing, she may even again become more autocratic), one thing appears certain: the end of the Marxist-Leninist-Stalinist totalitarian structure of power in Europe.

Nations which had been incorporated into the Soviet sphere of domination by force are now in a position to shape their lives without foreign interference. Although no nation in the world can escape foreign influences (it has been shown in this book how strong these influences were in the course of the whole of Czech and Slovak history), the fact that there is no Big Brother in ultimate command and no iron curtain that runs across Central Europe is an enormous step forward for national self-assertion.

In Czechoslovakia, the decisive change occurred in the last week of November 1989 and took the form which has been described as a 'velvet revolution'. Although dissent had been grumbling underground for many years, the breakthrough closely followed the events in East Germany which in their turn had been triggered by the opening of the Hungarian border with the West and the resulting exodus of East Germans by that route. From outside it was a typical domino theory effect. From inside it was the culmination of the process of revulsion against an oppressive and fatuous regime.

As has been said earlier, the main expression of dissent in Czechoslovakia was the alternative culture; its spectrum ranged from the revitalization of religion through various kinds of art, and even pop music. The vanguard was Charter 77, to which a broader Movement of Civil Liberties acceded in 1988. In both emerged, as the leading personality, the playwright Václav Havel. (This was not the first instance in Czech history in which writers had to take over from politicians who had failed; the Writers' Manifesto of 1917 and the writers' congress in 1956 were the most conspicuous earlier examples.) Uncommitted to any political party but showing great moral courage and endurance (apart from continuous harassment he spent altogether five years in prison), Havel captured the imagination of all who were longing for genuine change and liberation, in particular that of the younger generation.

It was in the first instance the students and apprentices, the future white- and blue-collar workers, who challenged the police state in the streets of Prague. On the 17 November 1989, their officially authorized gathering to commemorate the fiftieth anniversary of the Nazi atrocities and the closure of the Czech establishments of higher education turned into a protest march in the course of which they were savagely beaten up. The police brutality triggered off many more protests in which more and more people took part. People quickly began to shake of their fear. Theatres replaced their usual programmes by political debates with their audiences. Meanwhile, some of the communist leaders, reading the writing on the wall and realizing that this time Soviet help would not be forthcoming, began to negotiate with the leaders of the opposition. For a while Alexander Dubček, the figurehead of the 1968 emancipation attempt, reappeared on the stage, but soon the hero of the people, Havel, moved into the limelight. As leader of the newly created, broadly based, democratic movement 'Civic Forum' which organized a short strike and brought up to half of the population of all the larger cities on to the streets, Havel and his colleagues were able to negotiate with the Communist Party a retreat from its leading position, the dismantling of its army, the 'workers' militia', the installation of a coalition government and the promise of free elections for mid-1990. The Civic Forum in the Czech part of the state was echoed by a parallel movement, The Public Against Violence in Slovakia.

It all happened so quickly and without violence that to many it looked like a miracle. On the 29 December Václav Havel was unanimously elected by the communist-dominated Parliament President of the Republic with mandate until the new, democratically elected Parliament would make its decision. After having ousted some of the most conservative and compromised leaders from the party, the communists embarked on a tactic aimed at the preservation of their own existence for a less rainy day. They made concessions in the

hope that the reconversion to normalcy of the economy
from its present highly distorted condition would cost their
opponents a good deal of popularity. This would give the
communists a chance to recover some ground and even
allow them some kind of a comeback. In this they would
hope to have the cooperation of camouflaged fellow-travellers,
and of former supporters still managing to remain in the
power apparatus. This time, however, they have no Stalin or
Brezhnev who might throw his sword into the balance. Most
people and above all the younger generation are hostile to
communism and it is their hostility that will decide the issue
in the long run.

As a friend of mine who experienced the exhilarating
week of November in Prague put it, 'It was our children who
brought us freedom'. Indeed the courageous and admirably
disciplined intervention of our young people, especially students, in the 'velvet revolution' was crucial. All of us, including they themselves when grown up, must not betray their
youthful dedication to the principle which, before the communist takeover, had been the promising device of our
national emblem and since then, for most of us, mere wishful
thinking: 'The Truth prevails'. Václav Havel turned this
Masarykian motto into a stimulus for everyday behaviour:
'Living within the Truth'.[44] And this is what the 'velvet revolution' was all about.

It remains to be seen how quickly the Czechs and Slovaks
will be able to overcome the demoralizing effects of having
been crushed between the Swastika and Red Star, and to
what extent their institutions will be reframed in such a
manner as to promote the principle proclaimed at the finest
hour of their second national rebirth.

Summary

As we have seen, all the main conflicts in Czech and Slovak history have had strong ideological connotations. Even in the perennial struggle for power and wealth, carried on mainly between the king and the estates, both sides looked for ideological support in a tradition: the king in the tradition of the Roman Empire, the estates in that of customs established when the king had been weak. Yet three times in the history of the two nations the internal strife assumed ideological proportions on a large scale.

The first conflict of this kind occurred in the ninth century when, in the territory of Great Moravia, the Greek-Orthodox practice of Christianity clashed with that of the Roman Catholic Church; in terms of ecclesiastical language it was a clash between the Slavic and Latin liturgies. The conflict of liturgies left some traces for two more centuries; then, as the focus of Czech political life was transferred to Bohemia, it was superseded by issues resulting from the polarity of the Church and State, of Pope and Emperor. Meanwhile, the contest between Christianity and paganism, which had lasted for two or three centuries, was brought to an end with the complete victory of the cross.

The polarity between spiritual and temporal powers that reached its climax in the struggle for the investiture offered Bohemian rulers the opportunity to strengthen their prestige and power within the loose-knit structure of the Holy Roman Empire and the German kingdom. On the other hand, the Slovaks whose territory had been incorporated into the Hungarian kingdom were severed, for the whole millenium to come, from the political framework of the Czech nation, and from involvement in all matters of the Empire that this framework implied.

In the fourteenth century, the Czechs transcended the political and cultural confines of the Holy Empire and established direct contacts with the main cultural foci of Western Europe, France and later also England. Under King Charles (as Emperor Charles IV) of the Luxembourg dynasty, the Bohemian state reached its largest extent in history. The Czechs were able to enjoy the Gothic sunshine as one of the prominent nations in Europe.

With the sunshine, however, also came the shadows. The new cultural vogue spreading from the south, the Renaissance, tended, with its worldly interests, to undermine Gothic values with their particular stress on devotion and piety. The clash of values caused intellectual and spiritual upheaval in many countries, but nowhere was the reaction as strong as amongst the Czechs. Here the call for reform of the Church which had deviated from the path of Christ by letting itself be seduced by the lust for power and wealth, was taken up by the people as a whole. Only in Bohemia and Moravia were the intellectuals, gentry and common folk in a position to make common cause and to challenge, with formidable might, the Papacy and Empire alike. The forces of the Hussites, however, became overstrained; the resulting meagre compromise provided too narrow a basis for sustaining the impetus.

Nor could the Reformation in other parts of Europe, though sympathetic to the Hussite tradition, help the Czechs to regain their former strength. In the final confrontation of the Protestant north with the Catholic south, the Czechs, together with their German cohabitants in Bohemia and Moravia, fell victim to their fading endurance and resolve.

The penalty was two hundred years of life in limbo. Embracing baroque culture, with its new religious devotion and artistic exuberance, the Czechs were able to find some consolation but little, if any, ground for self-assertion as a nation. The Czech language and national consciousness retreated to the lower echelons of the social fabric, to the peasantry and common urban folk; because of general conditions at that time, they were not in a position to make a wider impact.

It was only the new breezes from the West, the Enlightenment and Romanticism, that provided new stimuli for the Czechs. Enlightened absolutism opened the door for upward social mobility and also created conditions for fast technological progress; Romanticism pointed to yet another object of devotion apart from religion – devotion to a national culture identified by language and tradition.

Thus the way was made for a new venture. The revival of national language and tradition took on a higher, spiritual, justification. Enhanced mobility gave this national revival active support from the hitherto neglected social classes. What eventually, in the 1840s, emerged as a new political factor was not a new nation, as has sometimes been suggested, but a thoroughly restructured nation. It was no longer the aristocracy but the middle class that took the lead. Later, more than in other nations of East-Central Europe, farmers and industrial workers also took an active part in the political and cultural life of society.

Fortunately for the Czechs, in 1860 the Habsburg monarchy abolished absolutism and in its Austrian (Cisleithanian) domains started experimenting with parliamentary rule. Within fifty years the Czechs were able not only to emancipate their culture from German tutelage and to build up their own economic strength but also to acquire expertise in political life in the modern state. Thus, when the last hour struck for the Austro-Hungarian Empire, and the multiethnic state that was dominated by two nations (Germans and Magyars) comprising only over a third of its population, collapsed in World War I, the Czechs, supported by the Western Allies, were able to re-establish their independent state.

Yet, on this occasion, the Czechs seem to have over-reached themselves. Although they struck a deal with the Slovaks and built the new state in cooperation with them, the cohabitation of the two closely related peoples was not without problems. A thousand years of living apart left deep differences in the cultural outlook of the two nations. But a more serious problem for the Czechoslovak Republic was the presence in the state of a sizeable German minority (over 20 per cent of the population). As long as the regimes of neighbouring Germany and Austria were democratic, the policy of cooperation with the Czechs won widening support amongst the Germans in Czechoslovakia. When, however, most Germans were converted to the aggressive and racist nationalism preached by Adolf Hitler, more and more Germans in Czechoslovakia, too, became infected with the virus. Even the godfathers of free Czechoslovakia, France and Great Britain, felt constrained to give way to Hitler's fury and blackmail. The recalcitrant Czechoslovakia was looked upon as a troublemaker. For the sake of peace she was sacrificed to the power that was not seeking peace at all. Fortunatley for Czechoslovakia, Hitler overreached himself much more than the Czechs had done earlier; after immense suffering inflicted upon many nations, he was utterly defeated and his work destroyed.

The Czechs were liberated again; but the shock of betrayal on the part of the West, and the experience of German occupation exacerbated by terror, pushed the bulk of public opinion away from the traditional understanding of democracy and pluralism. Racial hatred and genocide gave way to class hatred and retribution for collective guilt. From the concentration camps of the swastika the road led eventually to the labour camps of the red star. The Slovaks were even more perplexed. Having saved themselves from direct submission to the Nazi empire by proclamation of their own state, they were to follow Hitler's path anyhow. It was of no help to them that they were more suspicious than the Czechs of the honest intentions of their Slavic Big Brother.

The decade 1938 to 1948, with World War II and its aftermath, brought the Czechs and Slovaks much more comprehensive changes than had been the case with the decade covering World War I and the subsequent turmoil and reconstruction. In 1918 Czechoslovakia emerged as a new state within one and the same civilization – liberal, pluralistic and capitalist, articulated into sovereign nation states with a more or less loose link to the Christian tradition. In 1945 Czechoslovakia was reconstituted as a state under the shadow of a new division of Europe. All attempts to strike out on her own were in vain. In 1948 Czechoslovakia was incorporated into a totally alien civilization which for thirty years had already been tightening its totalitarian grip over the lands of the former Russian Empire.

In the aftermath of World War II the new social and political formation on Russian soil was presented with the opportunity to expand towards the West. Under the colours of Marxism-Leninism, all the Slavic nations, including the Finno-Ugric and Romance enclaves, were attached, each as a kind of satellite, to the 'indissoluble union of free republics forged together for ever by the Great Russia' (as the new Soviet anthem put it). The scope of ideological differences attained unprecedented dimensions. Never before had Europe been so abysmally divided.

Like other East-Central European countries, Czechoslovakia was to experience ideological confrontation with shattering effects on her way of life and self-confidence. For the third time in their history the Czechs were plunged into a crisis of the utmost gravity. At the outset, many of them were prepared to change tracks and allow themselves to be led by the star of the East. But as early as ten years after the communist takeover of all power in state and society, the transfer from the civilization of the West to that of the

East appeared unpalatable to the vast majority of the Czechs. This was even more the case with the Slovaks who, right from the beginning, were much less prone to succumb to the lure of Soviet civilization.

After a further ten years, the Communist Party of Czechoslovakia itself began to resent its satellite status. Defection from the Soviet camp, however, was not envisaged, only a kind of internal reform, and even this was to happen in agreement with Big Brother. Yet the latter was not prepared to allow any deviation from his own norms.

Twenty years later, the new Soviet leader, Mikhail Gorbachev has himself picked up the idea of reform and started to implement it at home. The communist leadership in Czechoslovakia, however, the appointees of the late Brezhnev, stuck to the model of bygone Soviet orthodoxy; they believed and hoped that the new breeze from the East was merely a temporary aberration.

In comparison with 1968, the situation twenty years later seemed to be reversed. Then people supported reform and hated foreign influence. Now, they had nothing official to support at home and rather hoped for a foreign challenge – naturally in the opposite direction from that of 1968. Meanwhile, people looked for compensations: economic shortcomings had to be overcome by stepping up the hunt for ostentatious consumption; lack of freedom had to be offset by a new kind of venture which was ingenious but extremely demanding – the development of an unofficial, alternative culture. Thus the conflict of ideologies went on. The crossroads seemed to become a roundabout.

But the stalemate at the surface was misleading. By the end of 1989 the series of challenges, the chain reaction of the Gorbachevian revolution in the USSR reached Czechoslovakia. The 'Velvet Revolution' of late November 1989 opened for Czechoslovakia the only sensible exit: rejoining Europe. As Thomas Masaryk once put it: Lux ex Occidente – the Light comes from the West.

Chronology

AD	
c. 830	First Christian churches in present-day Moravia and Slovakia
845	Fourteen Slavic noblemen from Bohemia baptized in Regensburg
863	Constantine (Cyrillus) and Methodius arrive in Moravia
880	Methodius Archbishop of Moravia
c. 907	End of Great Moravia
935	St Wenceslas' death
950	Boleslav I accepts Emperor Otto's suzerainty
973	Bishopric in Prague founded
1085	Bishopric in Nitra reconstituted
1212	Bohemian rulers become hereditary kings (Golden Bull of Sicily)
1306	End of the Přemyslid dynasty
1310–1437	Luxembourg dynasty
1344	Bishopric in Prague elevated to archbishopric
1346–78	Charles (as Emperor Charles IV) King of Bohemia
1348	University founded in Prague
1356	Golden Bull of Charles IV
1409	University reform; John Hus elected rector
1415	John Hus burnt at stake in Constance
1419	First defenestration in Prague
1420	Four Articles of Prague
1420–31	Five Crusades against the Hussites defeated
1434	Compacts of Basle
1457	Unity of Brethren founded

1458–71	George of Poděbrady King of Bohemia
1471–1526	Jagiellon dynasty
1485	Treaty of Kutná Hora (religious peace)
1517	St Wenceslas' Treaty (peace between estates)
1519	Lutheranism penetrates to Bohemia
1526	Ferdinand Habsburg elected King of Bohemia
1526–1918	Habsburg dynasty
1547	Power and wealth of royal boroughs broken
1575	Bohemian Confession (Lutherans and Brethren)
1609	Emperor Rudolph's Charter (freedom for all Protestants)
1618	Second defenestration of Prague. Uprising of Protestant nobility
1620	Uprising defeated
1621–7	Protestantism banned from Bohemia and Moravia; trials and confiscations of property
1648	Peace of Westphalia. Counter-Reformation intensified
1740–80	MariaTheresa Queen of Bohemia
1749	Beginning of centralization and Germanization
1780–90	Enlightened absolutism of Joseph II
1781	Toleration Edict. Abolition of bondage
1786–91	Beginning of the Czech national revival
1804	Austria becomes Empire in her own right
1844	Bohemian Repeal
1848	Campaign for Bohemian autonomy. June uprising. Slavic congress in Prague. Constituent Assembly in Vienna. Abolition of corvée
1848–1916	Francis Joseph I Emperor
1860	End of absolutism
1867	Austro-Hungarian Settlement (dual monarchy)
1867	Austria becomes constitutional monarchy
1907	Universal equal suffrage introduced
1914–18	World War I
1918	Czechoslovak Republic constituted
1929	Peak of prosperity
1938	Munich Agreement, dismemberment of Czechoslovakia
1939–45	Protectorate of Bohemia and Moravia. Slovak

state. World War II

1945–8	Czechoslovakia reconstituted. Reduced pluralism. Partial socialization
1946	Retribution. Expulsion of Germans
1948	Communist *coup d'état*
1950–4	'Class war' intensified; fabricated trials. Further socialization
1960	Czechoslovakia proclaimed socialist republic
1968	Attempt at emancipation (Prague Spring). Invasion by the Warsaw Pact armies. Czechoslovakia becomes a dual federation
1969–70	Political purges
1977	Charter 77 founded
1980s	Development of the alternative culture
1989	The 'Velvet Revolution'

.... Lands of the Bohemian Crown in the XIV - XVII Centuries: Bohemia, Moravia, Silesia and Lusatia.

———— Present Day Czechoslovakia.

- - - - Ruthenia (Part of Czechoslovakia, 1919-1939)

Notes

Chapter One

1. However, the Frankish annalist Fredegar reports that there existed (on the territory of present-day Czechoslovakia) an earlier political entity which lasted for 35 years (*c*. 624–59). It was ruled by a Frank who had come to that country as a merchant and who, as its ruler, waged successful wars against the Frankish Empire. According to the Polish historian G. Labuda (*Pierwsze państwo slowiańskie. Państwo Samona* (The First Slavic State. Samo's Realm), Poznań, 1949) the centre of Samo's realm was in Moravia, which thus became the basis for further development of a Slavic state in the area.
2. For some more on the sources to the topic see F. Graus, *Die Nationenbildung der Westslawen im Mittelalter* (Sigmaringen: Jan Thorbecke Verlag, 1980) pp. 41–51.
3. The annals mention the following events: about 820 the Moravian ruler Mojmír was baptized by the Bishop of Passau Reginhar who in 831 undertook a visitation of Mojmír's domains. Between 830 and 850 more than thirty churches were built under the auspices of the Archbishop of Salzburg in what is now western Slovakia and western Hungary (the latter then know as Pannonia) by the local ruler (Pribina) whose seat was in Nitra. In 845, Regensburg saw fourteen Bohemian chieftains baptized. Ruins of churches of that epoch were uncovered in various places in Moravia proper.
4. For a discussion of the respective roles of Hiberno-Scottish and Frankish missions in Moravia see Z.R. Dittrich, *Christianity in Great Moravia* (Groningen: J.B. Wolters, 1962) pp. 47–

52. In the following narrative I follow mainly Dittrich's account of the Great Moravian epoch in Czech history.

5. The term appeared in Constantin Porphyrogenitus, *De Administrando Imperio, 13*; for detail see R. Dostálová, *Megale Moravia*, in *Byzantinoslavica*, 27, 1966, pp. 344–9.

6. Z.R. Dittrich, *Christianity*, p.208 ff.

7. L.E. Havlík, *Velká Morava a středoevropští Slované* (Great Moravia and Central European Slavs: Prague: ČSAV, 1964).

8. For the sake of completeness it has to be added that for almost 300 years (1346–1635) yet another ethnically mixed region, by constitution a twin region, Upper and Lower Lusatia, was a lateral land of the Bohemian Crown. At that time, the upper strata of the Lusatian population were already mainly German-speaking, whilst most peasants still spoke a particular Slavic vernacular, known as Sorbian. From this, during the Reformation, two literary tongues crystallized: the Upper and the Lower Lusatian Sorbian languages. Since 1635 both Lusatias have been a part of various German states (Saxony, Prussia, German Empire and currently the German Democratic Republic). Meanwhile the number of Sorbian-speakers has dwindled to less that 50,000.

9. Although the schism between Eastern and Western Christianity had its roots in the Graeco-Latin dualism of the earlier epoch, the divide did not become less acute with the new ethnic structure. The present-day distinction between the Serbs and Croats bears witness to the strength of this particular division.

10. For an interesting discussion of contradictions in annals relating to the earliest period of Czech history see O. Králík, *Labyrint dávných dějin českých* (Labyrinth of Ancient Czech History; Prague: Vyšehrad, 1970).

11. This point is discussed at length by J. Slavík, *Vznik českého národa* (Origin of the Czech Nation), vol. I (Prague: Pokrok, 1946).

12. This point is stressed by Slavík, esp. pp. 46–53.

13. Králík, pp. 94 and ff.

14. According to a chronicle this happened on the anniversary day of St Wenceslas' death, an occasion which the Slavnikids celebrated.

15. At that time, canonization was not yet centrally regulated, but their position as saints, acknowledged by the episcopate of the area, was accepted by the Church as a whole.

Chapter Two

1. Jan Slavík, a sociologically oriented Czech historian, maintained that the original form of the realm was a predatory one; there were no fixed rules, either for taxation or for the administration of justice, etc. The ruler (duke or whoever) governed with assistance from, and representation by, his military retinue, known as the *ministeriales*, who enjoyed a considerable licence in enforcing the will and authority of their master. Only gradually, with the civilizing role of Christian institutions and also with the formation of more or less autonomous estates, did the government become less arbitrary and begin, progressively, to observe some rules. With this suggestion, Slavík clashed with Marxist historiography, which after 1948 dominated the field in Czechoslovakia and which for the most ancient epoch of Slavic society (as indeed for any other ancient society in the world) presupposed the existence of a primitive communal (or communist) social formation where people, in contrast to the subsequent formation, were free. With respect to further development, Slavík, like the Marxists, characterized Czech society as feudal. Although the Marxists laid stress on the socio-economic aspects which they believe to be the basis of all social and cultural development, and Slavík understood feudalism more or less in political terms as a hierarchical pyramid of domination, for both feudalism means a comprehensive category in which almost all types of lordship can justifiably be characterized as feudal.

   Other, non-Marxist historians (especially those who belonged to the so-called positivist school of historiography, sometimes also known under the name of its most prominent representative, Jaroslav Goll), were more cautious with the general term 'feudalism'; if they had to use it, they tended to do so with reference to its etymological meaning. Thus the term 'feudalism' was used primarily with respect to the existence of fiefs, i.e., holdings of land or offices handed over on the condition of reciprocal services or other obligations. In that sense not all medieval social relations were feudal. Thus the positivists came closer to understanding social structure as a configuration of various elements and relationships rather than conceiving of it in terms of a more or less uniform social formation.

2. The precise constitutional position was as follows: the king of the *regnum Teutonicorum* (The King of the Germans) was king of the union of the six German tribal duchies plus Lombardy and, from 1033, also Burgundy. The elected king became Emperor Designate with the title *Romanorum rex*; once crowned by the pope at Rome he became Roman Emperor. The term 'election', however, refers to the theory rather than to the reality. More often than not, it involved a power contest, or, in earlier times, the acknowledgement of a hereditary succession. The number of electors also varied according to circumstances (originally all direct feudatories of the king, lay and ecclesiastical, were entitled to vote) and often various groups of electors opted for different candidates who then tried to decide the issue by force of arms. The journey to a coronation in Rome was very often a demanding military expedition in which various opponents of the respective claimant for the imperial title had to be tamed. This may serve us as a reminder that the efficacy of constitutional arrangements in the Middle Ages was questionable.

3. For craftsmen who had settled in villages bondage seems to have been more a personal dependency than an attachment to the land. Everybody who was not free (i.e., who was not a member of a higher estate) had to belong to somebody who did enjoy the status of freeman or to a royal borough. The term *servi* often used in the sources of the epoch cannot be understood as slaves in the sense of people totally owned as a movable object (*instrumentum vocale*). Even in earlier times when the term 'slave' really meant precisely that, such slaves, who were prisoners of war or were being sold because of poverty, were treated as a commodity for export rather than as a means of domestic production.

4. Slavík, vol. I, esp. pp. 11–16 and 135–47.

5. Charles was definitely not a Renaissance man, nor were his

transalpine subjects. However, in his reply to the first Petrarch's letter inviting him to take over rule in Italy, Charles could not resist the charm of Petrarch's affected style and attempted (with the help of the classicists at his disposal) to adorn his scholastic argumentation with a colour typical of Renaissance 'humanism'. Yet in his realistic appreciation of the Roman heritage, Charles quoted Augustus rather than a philosopher or poet when he wrote: *Nescitis quanta bellua sit imperium?* (Don't you know what a monster is to govern?); quoted from : J. Šusta, *České dějiny II., 4., Karel IV.*, (Prague: Laichter, 1948) pp. 316–19.

6. The confrontation between Wenceslas IV and Archbishop John of Jenstein attained its height when the king attempted to elevate a particular West Bohemian abbey to a bishopric against the will of the archbishop. The archbishop's general vicar, John of Nepomuk, who is understood to have been most instrumental in frustrating Wenceslas' intention, payed dearly for his courage. After having been tortured he was drowned in the river Vltava. The archbishop himself went into hiding for some time. Three hundred years later, the memory of John of Nepomuk's martyrdom was to play an important role in the fight for the formation of the Czech religious tradition. The story is referred to on p. 90.

7. Šusta, *České dějiny II, 4, Karel IV*, pp. 261–3.

8. *ibid*.

Chapter Three

1. In this book it is not possible to go into more detail. The following books in English may be consulted: M. Spinka, *John Hus at the Council of Constance* (New York: Columbia University Press, 1965) *John Hus and the Czech Reform* (Hamden: Archon Books, 1966) and *John Hus: A Biography* (New Jersey: Princeton University Press, 1968); R.R. Betts, *Essays in Czech History* (London: Athlone Press, 1969) a posthumous edition of articles.

2. However, this alignment does not mean that all German masters were against the reform. Indeed, the most original and influential German-speaking master was Nicholas of Dresden,

whose radicalism in several respects surpassed that of the Czech reformers.

3. Quoted from J.M. Klassen, 'The nobility and the making of the Hussite revolution' in *East European Quarterly* (Boulder, New York: 1978) p.67.

4. The Hussite lords actually returned to the ancient practice common before the investitute contest (see p. 17).

5. Quoted from O. Odložilík, *The Hussite King: Bohemia in European Affairs 1440–1471* (New Jersey: Rutgers University Press, 1965) pp. 4–5.

6. Although scholarly opinion is divided on the issue, it seems most probable that Taborite religious radicalism was mainly due to two influences: the teaching of radical masters from Prague University, such as Nicholas of Dresden and the young (in contrast to the mature) Jacobellus de Misa (Jakoubek of Stříbro) on the one hand, and contacts with Waldensian communities in South Bohemia on the other. For detailed evaluation of this issue, see H. Kaminský, *A History of the Hussite Revolution* (Berkeley and Los Angeles University Press, 1967). pp. 141–220.

7. The diet, summoned in 1421 to the royal borough of Čáslav, and attended not only by all the Hussite factions but also by most Romanists, elected a committee of twenty governors. Its composition characterized the shift in the relative power and prestige of individual estates. Eight representatives were from royal boroughs, seven from the gentry, and only five from the baronial ranks. To make the reversal of importance still more explicit, the burgomaster and councillors of the Old and New Town of Prague were placed first on the roll.

Within Prague, the radical faction, led by John Želivský, favoured the so-called Great Community, i.e., the general assembly of burghers (as a rule, but not necessarily at that time, owners of houses in Prague), while the moderates rallied rather to the 'seniores' (Senior Community), a body of burghers enjoying social, economic and political prestige in the city. Both these communities acquired importance at the expense of the traditional administration represented by the city councillors. Naturally the Great Community, as an unwieldy body with irregular attendance, could not exert much direct power, but it had considerable influence, especially in cases of emergency. Otherwise the main initiative seems to have been with the Senior Community, although executive power remained with the councillors. For a systematic attempt to sort out both primary and secondary sources on what may be described as constitutional issues in the capital city, see especially F. Seibt, *Hussitica. Zur Struktur einer Revolution* (Köln-Graz: Böhlau Verlag, 1965) pp. 133–45, and K. Hrubý, 'Senior Communitas – Eine revolutionäre Institution der Prager Hussitischen Bürgerschaft in Bohemia' in *Jarhbuch des Collegium Carolinum*, Band 13 (Munich and Vienna: R. Oldenbourg Verlag, 1972) pp. 9–43.

8. All three secular estates, barons, knights and royal boroughs, had a stake in what was going on in the revolution. To what extent the peasants, who were the most numerous socio-economic group, were affected, is difficult to assess. A few sources, not always clearly worded, indicate that in the high days of revolution, villages became recognized as communities participating in some matters concerning the country's administration, but the practical impact of this position is difficult to evaluate. Those who settled in the towns or who joined the Taborite and Horebite armies found some prospects of individual advancement. It is, however, impossible to draw a reliable picture of the general economic situation of the Czech peasantry. It seems that the disorders in the country resulting from the war were more to their disadvantage than to their advantage: fighting armies and the mutual devastation of property were the biggest nuisance for them while the lightening of the tax burden resulting from the neglect of tax collections for central government may have been outweighed by the exaction of extraordinary contributions by the warring parties. (There are many complaints to this effect in the documents of that epoch, complaints directed against both sides in the conflict). As far as the peasant's attitudes are concerned, it may be reasonably assumed that at the beginning many of them expected from the reform an improvement in their lot. In so far as their religious needs were catered for by the Utraquist clergy, they may have felt satisified by having obtained in the communion from the chalice an equal religious status with the clergy, and lower ecclesiastical dues (the contribution to the Curia was abolished) may also have been

appreciated. Unfortunately, there is not enough evidence on how the peasant majority of the Czech nation coped with what, in contrast to the experience of the three higher secular estates, may have been an ordeal rather than an opportunity for advancement.

9. Quoted from F.G. Heymann, *George of Bohemia, King of Heretics* (New Jersey: Princeton University Press, 1965) pp. 8–9.

10. Such as Nicholas of Dresden.

11. The roundabout way of obtaining consecration for Utraquist clergy was not only an impediment to the smooth running of ecclesiastical administration, but was also harmful for the prestige of the Utraquist establishment.

12. George of Poděbrady used especially the services of Martin Mair who himself devised a scheme of imperial reform, of Fantino de Valle who was destined to protect the king's interests in Rome, and of Antonio Marini of Grenoble, a former French diplomat.

13. As reported by Viktorin Kornel of Všehrd, a lawyer and humanist (c. 1460–1520) in his *O práviech, o súdiech i o dskách země české knihy devatery* (Nine Books on Law, Courts and Land-registers in Bohemia; 1495/9; modern edition Prague: 1874).

14. However, as Z.R. Dittrich drew to my attention, the term 'second bondage' could be misleading because it implies a return to a situation several centuries earlier. In Dittrich's view, the extension of bondage at the turn of the sixteenth century was due to the failure of the emphyteutic law to develop the cash economy fully, to the gradual weakening of cities and to the abundant supply of cultivable but sparsely populated land. Thus it was a structural shift rather than a structural change, and one which was substantially influenced by the increasing political power of the aristocracy.

15. As the colophon-date reveals only the time of completion of the manuscript which the anonymous printer used as his copy-text, the date of the printed edition is not certain. But it is assumed that it was indeed the earliest Czech printed book, produced in the early 1470s. (G. Painter and D. Chrástek, *Printing in Czechoslovakia in the 15th Century* (British Museum, 1969) p. 10.

16. The Czech language was widely used especially in diplomatic and commercial contacts with Poland and Hungary.

Chapter Four

1. The cultural contrast between northern and southern Europe, however, has to be put into a more long-term perspective. There had always been a significant difference between Mediterranean and Nordic peoples. The north-south migrations of various Germanic and Scandinavian tribes seems to have effected only a partial levelling. Another contribution in that direction was the unificatory pastoral work of the Church. The Catholic-Protestant split stopped the levelling process of acculturation and revitalized some of the earlier particularities. The different shape of baroque and, above all, divergent socio-economic developments illustrate the point. It has to be borne in mind, however, that between the two parts of Europe lay a large area in which both type of culture lived in interwoven enclaves and thus, in a geographical sense, side by side.

2. Although both the government of Bohemia and the government in Moravia were in Catholic hands, the scope of tolerance in Moravia was significantly wider. Not only was the Unity of Brethren able to consolidate its position but also foreign Christian denominations such as the Anabaptists found a safe haven there.

3. The most prominent leaders of the radical Protestants in Bohemia were Václav Budovec (a Czech) and Josef Mathias Thurn (a German). After defeat in the uprising in 1619–20, Budovec, owing to his advanced age, did not leave the country and a year later was executed; Thurn left the country and spent most of his life in the military service of the anti-Habsburg armies.

4. Unfortunately, the Moravian estates joined the Bohemian cause too late to provide effective help in the war. The leader of the Moravian Protestants, Karel of Žerotín, did not consider the time right for a military confrontation. Only when a younger member of his family overthrew the Moravian government was hesitation put aside.

5. The enlightened aristocrat was Georg Erasmus Tschernembl. Abolition of bondage was one of his suggestions. But neither the estates nor the imperial side could accept it, although the idea was discussed with the peasants who had taken up arms in order to protect themselves against the ravages caused by mercenary armies on both sides of the conflict.

6. Of the executed leaders of the Bohemian uprising three were barons, seven were knights and seven were burghers (amongst them the rector of the Charles University); it was again the third estate that was hit most severely.

7. Wallenstein's saga is reported tellingly in J. Pekař, *Valdštejn, 1630–1634*, Dějiny Valdštejnského spiknutí, 2 vols., (Prague: Orbis, 1934). German translation, *Wallenstein, 1630–1634, Tragödie einer Verschwörung* (Berlin: A. Metzner Verlag, 1937).

8. The feud between, on the one hand, the Jesuits and, on the other hand, the Franciscans and Dominicans had ideological overtones. The Dominicans and Franciscans argued that alternative philosophical interpretations of Catholic theology, a token of pluralism for those elect for higher knowledge, would enhance the academic prestige of the university. Although the Jesuits took the point, they maintained that, under the given circumstances, such a situation would be interpreted as representing a lack of unity amongst the Catholics and this would be a greater evil than some loss of academic brilliance. S. Sousedík, *Valerián Magni 1586–1661* (Prague: Vyšehrad, 1983). p. 44 ff.

9. The fact that the author might have been a Roman Catholic did not make the book trustworthy; it might have been translated or adapted by a heretic. The Key had two later editions, one in 1749 and the last one under the title *Index Bohemicorum librorum prohibitorum et corrigendorum alphabeti digestus*, in 1760. B. Wiždálková, *Konkordance Koniášových klíčů, indexu, Jungmanna a knihopisu* (Prague: Státní knihovna ČSR, 1987).

10. Josef Pekař, *Bílá Hora* (Surrey: Rozmluvy, 1986) p. 99. (First edition Prague: Vesmír, 1922).

11. Before the Thirty Years War the average corvée required from the holder of one land track was four to twelve days per year. But the faltering of the money economy due to inflation

and extension of the landlords' direct holdings (the dominical) at the expense of the peasants' holdings (the rustical) forced the landlords to require more work from their subjects. In 1680, a royal letters patent, which was intended to limit the arbitrary extension of corvée, put its ceiling at three days per week. Another letters patent of the same year, however, forbade peasants to address their grievances directly to the king; appeals were to be made to the counties which were fully controlled by the landlords. In such a situation any regulation of corvée was illusory. O. Odložilík, *Československá vlastivěda*, vol. IV (Prague: Sfinx, 1932) p. 526.

Bondage, tightened by new decrees, became applicable to children also. Only with their landlord's permission could they enter an apprenticeship in the crafts. Such consent was required for marriages as well. In addition, peasant levies were substituted for the use of mercenaries as soldiers.

12. Pekař, *Bílá Hora*, p. 99, translated from Czech.

Chapter Five

1. In the 1650s the relationship of the old to the new baronial families was in Bohemia 169:128, in Moravia 27:30; with respect to the gentry the ratio was 457:116 and 30:35. J. Purš and M. Kropilák (eds.), *Přehled dějin Československa* (History of Czechoslovakia; Prague: Academia, 1982) pp. 184–5.
2. There was a special rule for children of mixed marriages. If the father was Catholic, all children were to be Catholic. If the father was Protestant, only his sons were allowed to follow his religion.
3. Jews were freed from the obligation of wearing a specific mark on their dress, they were admitted to all crafts and professions, allowed to attend higher-level Christian schools except for theology, and, under certain conditions, were permitted to move out of the ghettos. The number of Jews allowed in the country, however, was only slightly increased.
4. Purš and Kropilák, p. 508.
5. A well-articulated reflection of the reinvigorated national consciousness was presented by the German philosopher Johann Gottfried Herder. His writings became popular amongst

Slavic intellectuals. His hypothesis that the Slavic peoples were of a peaceful nature was especially well received.

In English-language literature, Johann Gottfried Herder is often presented as an oddity who incited the Central European peoples to irrational behaviour. This view, however, merely reflects the lack of Continental experience in the British Isles. Language as the main means of mutual understanding and participation in a common culture proved to be the main symbol and demarcation mark of national identity. The last 150 years of European history have demonstrated a clear-cut trend towards adaptation of state boundaries to ethnic boundaries or, though to a lesser extent, vice versa. The respective dates are contained in J. Krejčí and V. Velímský, *Ethnic and Political Nations in Europe* (London: Croom Helm, 1981) pp. 61–73. After World War II, a similar tendency could be seen also in other parts of the world, especially in South Asia.

6. Although we must not forget that national awakening was a collective work, a result of the enthusiasm of multitudes, Palacký's outstanding scholarship and vision and his political skill provided the Czech struggle for national self-determination with its own ideological backing.

7. For a brief general account see, for instance, P. Brock, *The Slovak National Awakening* (University of Toronto Press, 1976).

8. The Irish motif in the Czech struggle for national emancipation in ethno-linguistic terms was exploited most vociferously by Karel Havlíček whose radicalism and journalistic skill made his views widely read and shared. Havlíček made a paradigm of the Irish struggle against English domination, referring to it in his newspaper, often in a cryptic way. In order to avoid censorship he dressed Czech girevances in Irish garb and published reports as if they were sent from Cork or Tipperary whilst they in fact mirrored events taking place, or demands originating, in Bohemia.

9. The concept of nation in respect to its basic dimensions, ethnic, political and psychological, is discussed at length in J. Krejčí and V. Velímský.

10. S.Z. Pech, *The Czech Revolution of 1848* (Chapel Hill: Univer-

sity of North Carolina Press, 1969) p.111.

11. *ibid.*, p. 87.

12. *ibid.*, p. 102.

13. The election of the Constituent Assembly of 1848 took place after difficult bargaining about the extent of the vote. Eventually the electorate was conceived of quite broadly, although with not enough precision. For example, the vote was extended to 'independent' workers. The vote for a single chamber was to be cast by the diets of individual lands.

14. Prague was one of those places where the widely travelled Russian anarchist-revolutionary M.A. Bakunin tried to ignite the fire of world revolution.

15. O. Urban, *Česká společnost 1848–1918* (Czech Society 1848–1918; Prague: Svoboda, 1982) p. 83.

16. In this treatise Palacký put his idea (which he expounded on various occasions elsewhere) in the following concrete way: 'We were here before Austria, we shall still be alive when she no longer exists.'

17. In 1910 ethnic Germans constituted over 10 per cent of the total population in the Hungarian kingdom.

18. As Croatia was a kingdom in its own right, though closely linked with Hungary, Croatians were in a comparatively better position to preserve their national identity.

Chapter Six

1. The official title of the Austrian part of the dual monarchy was 'The Kingdoms and Lands Represented in the Reichsrat' (i.e., Imperial Council). In popular usage, however, the abbreviated name was used; it referred to the geographical position with respect to the small river Leitha which, close to Vienna, demarcated the border between Austria and Hungary. The Austrian part was known as Cisleithania, the Hungarian as Transleithania.

2. The standard work on the origins and development of the Austrian Social Democratic Party is L. Brügel, *Geschichte der österreichischen Sozialdemokratie*, 5 vols., (Vienna: Wiener Volksbuchhandlung, 1922/5).

3. An outline of the history and of the main problems of the

Czechoslav and Czechoslovak Social Democratic Parties,

Systemwandel, Hundert Jahre tschechoslowakische Erfahrung (Berlin-Bonn: Dietz Verlag, 1978).

4. As in many other nations, inpiration from the glorious past was usually sought in the heroic epic of bygone ages. Where there was none, Romantics produced their own fakes. In 1816–18, three Czech manuscripts were 'discovered', all of outstanding poetic quality, but all of them products of contemporary writers. They pictured ancient Czech society as democratic and strong, able to withstand foreign pressure. The manuscripts obviously reflected the ideal of the epoch in which they were written. They were enthusiastically received by the public and the critical scholars had a hard time convincing their fellow-countrymen that the manuscripts were not written in antiquity but a short while before being 'discovered'.

5. J.K. Hoensch, *Geschichte Böhmens von der slavischen Landnahme bis ins 20. Jahrhundert* (Munich: Beck, 1987) p. 368.

6. *ibid.*, p. 396.

7. There is a vast literature on Masaryk as a thinker and a statesman. Suffice it here to mention the memorial volume, *T.G. Masaryk in Perspective, Comments and Criticism*, written by experts in the various fields of Masaryk's activity, edited by M. Čapek and K. Hrubý (Ann Arbor: SVU Press, 1981).

8. Bernstein's importance for the Social Democrats in Czechoslovakia has been particularly stressed by J. Krejčí's 'Schlussfolgerungen' in *Sozialdemokratie und Systemwandel*, pp. 207 ff.

9. As in many similar instances elsewhere, class loyalties could not be substituted for ethnic loyalties on a mass scale. After 1896 this experience was repeated many times. Towards the end of the twentieth century the preponderance of ethnic loyalties became particularly conspicuous in countries which adopted Marxism-Leninism as the philosophy of the state.

10. The riots in Brno in 1905, in which the army had to intervene, resulted from clashes between the participants in a German rally from all parts of Austria, on the one hand, and, on the other hand, the Czechs demonstrating for the foundation of a Czech university in Brno.

11. On average, one German MP represented 40,000 people, one

Polish 52,000, one Czech 55,000 and one Ukrainian 102,000. In the Bohemian lands, Social Democrats needed, for one MP, over 13,000 votes whereas the other parties only required more than 7,000. (R.A. Kann, *The Multinational Empire*, New York: Columbia University Press, 1950, vol. II, p. 223, and O. Urban, *Česka společnost 1848–1918* (Czech Society 1848–1918), Prague: Svoboda, 1982, p. 530.) In the whole of Cisleithania, the Germans obtained 43 per cent of seats whereas their share in the population was only 35 per cent (Hoensch, p. 399).

12. O. Urban, pp. 560–1.
13. *Dějiny Československa v datech* (History of Czechoslovakia in Dates; Prague: Svoboda, 1968) pp. 464–6.
14. The story of the 40,000-strong Czechoslovak Legion in Russia is one of the most extraordinary of World War II and indeed of the whole of Czechoslovak history. Recruited from Austro-Hungarian prisoners of war of Czech and Slovak ethnic nationality in order to fight on Russia's side for the national independence of their homeland, they had to stop this fight when, in March 1918, the Bolsheviks concluded the peace treaty with Germany and her allies in Brest-Litowsk. The Legion was supposed to be transported over the Pacific Ocean to the battlefields of France. En route, however, misunderstandings with local Bolshevik authorities multiplied and the attempt to disarm the Legion and to redirect its movements provoked a confrontation, as a result of which the Czechoslovak Legion took control of the transport centres in the Middle Volga and the Ural regions, and of the whole Trans-Siberian railway. This move, which the Bolshevik army was not in a position to prevent, allowed Admiral Kolchak to establish his power base in West Siberia, but he could hold it only as long as the Czechoslovak Legion acting on behalf of the Allied command were willing to provide him with their support. As the Czechoslovaks preferred not to be involved in internal Russian matters and as the Kolchak's dictatorial reign and terrorist methods appalled them, the gradual withdrawal of their Legion from Siberia also meant the end of Kolchak. For more detail in English see V.M. Fic, *The Bolsheviks and the Czechoslovak Legion: the Origin of their Armed*

Conflict, March–May 1918 (New Delhi: Abhinav Publ., 1978).

15. After the war Šmeral joined the Communist Party but even there he could only play a leading role for a short while. An intellectual, used to developing his own ideas, he was not fitted for a party which was to become the tool of a strategy decided outside the country.

16. Otto Bauer, *Die Nationalitätenfrage*, p. 531 quoted in R.A. Kann, p. 170.

17. Altogether three small areas inhabited by the Czech-speakers were added to the historical Bohemian lands: two from Lower Austria (North Vitoraz and Valtice) and one from German Upper Silesia (Hlučín). However, the so-called Czech corner in the Kladsko region of German Silesia remained with Germany.

18. The constitutive acts were as follows: on 12 November 1918 the Ruthenian emigrés in the US held a plebiscite in which they expressed the wish that, if there was no prospect of an independent Ukraine with which their homeland could be united, it should join Czechoslovakia as an autonomous territory. A gathering on 8 May 1919 of the councils of the local populations in Ruthenia approved the result of the plebiscite. On 16 November 1919 the General Statute (constitution) for 'Subcarpathian Rus' (sic) was proclaimed by the Czechoslovak government. A new civil administration, however, could be established in Ruthenia only with effect from January 1922. At the Census of 1930, the 709,000 people living in Ruthenia declared their nationality as follows: Russians or Ukrainians 63 per cent, Magyars, 15 per cent, Jews 13 percent, Czechoslovaks 5 per cent, Germans 2 per cent.

19. See V. Beneš, 'Czechoslovak democracy and its problems' in V.S. Mamatey and R. Luža, p. 90, and J. Krejčí, 'Die Wechselwirkung von Wirtschaft und Politik' in J. Krejčí, *Sozialdemokratie und Systemwandel*, p. 69.

20. Resolution of the 5th Congress of the Comintern, June 1924.

21. The whole story of the birth and Bolshevization of the Communist Party in Czechoslovakia is told in detail in Z. Suda, *Zealots and Rebels, A History of the Ruling Communist Party of Czechoslovakia* (Stanford, California: Hoover Institution Press, 1980) pp. 37 ff, and J. Rupnik, *Histoire du Parti communiste tchécoslovaque* (Paris: Presses de la fondation nationale des

sciences politiques, 1981) pp. 47 ff. Both books also contain accounts of the ephemeral impact of the Hungarian Communist revolution on the development in Slovakia and Ruthenia.

22. *Dějiny Československa v datech* (History of Czechoslovakia in Dates), p. 306. On further development of the Czech-German relationship in Czechoslovakia see esp. J.W. Bruegel, *Czechoslovakia Before Munich. The German Minority Problem and British Appeasement Policy* (Cambridge: Cambridge University Press, 1973).

23. Unfortunately, the Czechoslovak government was slow to meet the legitimate demands of the German activists, whose main concerns were: higher public spending in German-inhabited regions which were more affected by unemployment than were the Czech regions: an adequate share for German workers of employment in public works and services; and some minor concessions in linguistic matters. The Agreement of February 1937, concluded between the government and the three German activist parties, was too little too late. However, even if more had been done, it would hardly have had any influence on the course of events which was dictated by outside forces.

24. V.S. Mamatey and R. Luža, p. 158.

25. The draft of a Bill submitted to the parliament on 27 April 1937, quoted in E. Wiskemann, *Czechs & Germans*, 2nd edition, (London: Macmillan; New York: St Martin's Press, 1967), p. 257.

26. Passages of the Henlein's eight-point Programme declared in Karlovy Vary in March 1938. For more detail see V. Olivová, *The Doomed Democracy* (London: Sidgwick & Jackson, 1972) pp. 215–16.

27. Poland laid claim to three territories of which one was of particular strategic and economic importance for Czechoslovakia. It was a strip of land in the eastern part of Silesia that remained Austrian after the bulk of that land had been ceded to Prussia in 1763. People there spoke a dialect which was transitional between Polish and Czech. Only in the course of the nineteenth century did they begin to consider themselves either Poles or Czechs according to what their school attendance made of them. Later the Polish ethnic element was

strengthened by large-scale immigration of workers from Galicia. By the end of World War I, apart from a small minority of German-speakers, both Slavic nationalities were about equally represented in the contested territory. After the war a bitter dispute emerged concerning partition of the territory between the two successor states (Czechoslovakia and Poland). First a plebiscite for the area was envisaged. Eventually, however, it was the Ambassadors' Conference of 18 July 1920 in Paris (an annex to the Peace Conference) that apportioned the contested territory to Czechoslovakia. Apart from some historical considerations, it was taken into account that what was then the only railway line between the Czech lands and northern and eastern Slovakia lead through this area. Also the fact that the mines and plants there formed an integral part of the vital Moravian-Silesian coal-and-steel complex was an argument in favour of Czechoslovakia. At the time when Czechoslovakia was compelled to yield to the Munich dictate, she also had to comply with the Polish ultimatum and ceded to Poland the whole contested area. According to the 1930 Census there were 227,000 inhabitants of which total only 35 per cent declared themselves as ethnic Poles. But within one year Poland as a state was destroyed and for the greater part annexed by Germany (the rest went to the USSR). After World War II the pre-1938 border has been re-established. At the time of writing there are about 70,000 ethnic Poles living in the area.

Chapter Seven

1. G. Rhode, 'The Protectorate of Bohemia and Moravia 1939–1945' in V.S. Mamatey and R. Luža, (eds.), *A History of the Czechoslovak Republic 1918–1948* (New Jersey: Princeton University Press, 1973), pp. 298–9.
2. A. Ritter, *Hitler's Tischgespräche*, 20 May 1942, p. 91; 2nd edition, p. 363. Quoted in V.S. Mamatey and R. Luža, p. 298.
3. V. Mastný, *The Czechs Under Nazi Rule. The Failure of National Resistance, 1939–1942* (New York and London: Columbia University Press, 1971) p. 198.
4. *ibid.*, pp. 207–25.

5. Estimates based on official Czechoslovak population statistics and on data collected by R. Luža in *The Transfer of the Sudeten Germans* (New York University Press, 1964) pp. 297–9, and by R. Hilberg in *The Destruction of the European Jews* (New York and London: Holmes & Meier, 1985, vol. 3) pp. 1048–153.

6. The story is told in more detail in C.J.C. Street, *President Masaryk* (London: Geoffrey Bles, 1930) pp. 120–7.

7. Hilberg, p. 1048.

8. E. Beneš, *Demokracie dnes a zítra* (*Democracy Today and Tomorrow*), Prague: Čin, 1946) pp. 247–73.

9. *ibid.*, pp. 314 and ff.

10. E. Táborský, *Communism in Czechoslovakia 1948–1960* (New Jersey: Princeton University Press, 1961) pp. 170–3.

11. J. Lettrich, *History of Modern Slovakia*, 2nd. issue (Toronto: Slovak Research and Studies Center, 1985) pp. 186–7.

12. See A. Josko, 'The Slovak resistance movement' in Mamatey and Luža, pp. 362–86.

13. See R. Luža, 'The Czech resistance movement' in Mamatey and Luža, pp. 343–61, and D. Brandes, *Die Tschechen unter deutschem Protektorat* (Munich and Vienna: R. Oldenbourg, 1975) vol. 2, pp. 61–106.

14. P. Reiman *et al.*, *Dějiny KSČ* (History of CPC; Prague: Svoboda, 1961) p. 476. A balanced view from the other end of the political spectrum is given by M. Hauner in 'Der Bürger gegenüber Staat und Gesellschaft' in J. Krejčí (ed.), *Sozialdemokratie und Systemwandel* (Berlin-Bonn: Dietz Verlag, 1978), pp. 105–20.

15. *Dějiny Československa v datech*, p. 372.

16. Apart from the trials of the leading Sudeten Germans held responsible for the Nazi atrocities, the politically most important trial was that of the Protectorate government and the Protectorate's President, Emil Hácha. The communists wanted two heads to roll. Hácha, however, was so old and fragile that he could not stand the trial and soon died in prison. The only genuinely pro-Nazi Protectorate minister, Emanuel Moravec, conveniently committed suicide. The specially constituted 'National Court' imposed only prison sentences of durations varying from three years to life. Only the

Finance Minister, whose support of the resistance movement was amply documented, was not punished, although he too was found guilty. The communists, however, launched a mass campaign of protest against the mild verdicts of the court.

Not only ministers and people connected with the Civil Service of the Protectorate administration were put on trial. Right-wing politicians active before 1938 were included. The communists tried to catch all those amongst their political opponents to whom their partners in the National Front, and President Beneš, were not keen to extend their protection. The most dramatic example was the Agrarian leader Rudolf Beran, Prime Minister from December 1938 to April 1939. Although during the Protectorate he spent most of his time in a German prison, he was sentenced by the retribution court to twenty years imprisonment. Confiscation of property was a part of all these sentences, but Beran's farm had been confiscated even before he was sentenced.

From the point of view of the relationship between Czechs and Slovaks, the most sensitive trial was that of Mgr. Josef Tiso, President of the Slovak state from 1939 to 1945. The retribution court in Bratislava (the capital of Slovakia) sentenced him to death in March 1947. An appeal for mercy to the head of state was first to be considered by the Council of Ministers. Only the Slovak Democrats Lettrich and Ursíny, and the ministers of the (Czech) People's Party interceded for clemency. All the others were against. Consequently President Beneš turned down the appeal for mercy and Tiso was executed.

For details on retribution in Czechoslovakia after World War II see especially: K. Kaplan, *Nekrvavá revoluce* (Bloodless Revolution; Toronto: Sixty-Eight Publishers, 1985) and V. Hejl and K. Kaplan, *Zpráva o organizovaném násilí* (Report on Organized Violence; Toronto: Sixty-Eight Publishers, 1986). The political aspect of Tiso's trial is discussed by R. Luža, 'Czechoslovakia between democracy and communism' in V.S. Mamatey and R. Luža, pp. 407–8. An unprejudiced account of individual cases in the retribution trials is also given in L. Feierabend, *Soumrak Československé demokracie* (The Twilight of Czechoslovak Democracy) vol. 2, (Surrey: Rozmluvy, 1988) pp. 366–72 and *passim*.

17. *Dějiny Československa v datech*, p. 369.

18. The other member parties of the National Front were to be satisfied with the deputy chairmanship of the Resettlement Office and with the chairmanship and vice-chairmanship of the Fund for National Renewal which was charged with the financial aspects of the project.
19. For details see J. Krejčí, *Social Change and Stratification in Postwar Czechoslovakia* (London: Macmillan, 1972) pp. 5–11.
20. The date 28 October was chosen with the intention of giving to a festive 'bourgeois' event a new 'socialist' content.
21. Taking price changes into account, at the beginning of 1946 the real wages of male blue-collar workers increased on average by about 20 per cent and those of women by 28 per cent in comparison with 1939; on the other hand, the salaries of male white-collar employees decreased in real terms by 30 per cent and those of women by 14 per cent.
22. For an evaluation of these elections and of their causes see J. Krejčí, 'Les événements imprévus de l'histoire tchécoslovaque moderne' in *Revue d'études comparative est-ouest*, September 1977, vol. 8, no. 3, pp. 25–36.
23. United Nations Relief and Rehabilitation Administration.
24. For details see J. Krejčí, *The Czechoslovak Economy During the Years of Systemic Transformation: 1945–1949* in *Yearbook of East-European Economics*, vol. 7, (Munich-Vienna: G. Olzog Verlag, 1977), pp. 311–14.
25. For details see E. Táborský, *Communism in Czechoslovakia 1948–1960*, pp. 19–20 and 100–2.
26. For details see J. Josten, *Oh My Country* (London: Latimer, 1949) pp. 75 ff and J. Korbel, *The Communist Subversion of Czechoslovakia 1938–1948* (New Jersey: Princeton University Press; and London: Oxford University Press, 1959).
27. A synoptic view of both plans, together with the economic programme of the National Socialist Party, was published in the Journal *Nové hospodářství* (New Economy), 1948, no. 1, pp. 1–12 (authors: D. Schejbal, J. Krejčí and J. Toman).
28. As the communists anticipated a loss of vote, they wanted to strengthen their position in the new parliament by allocating a number of seats to the communist-dominated mass organizations, such as the trade unions, associations of youth, of women, etc.
29. The dominant role of Beneš in the Czechoslovak democratic

camp and the consequent dependence of other leaders on his judgement and action had been amply demonstrated by all his collaborators. Of the scholarly books the most important is: E. Táborský, *President Eduard Beneš, Between East and West 1938-1948* (Stanford, California: Hoover Institution Press, 1981); of the memoires: L. Feierabend, *Soumrak Československé demokracie*; P. Drtina, *Československo můj osud* (Czechoslovakia My Destiny), 4 vols., (Toronto: Sixty-Eight Publishers, 1982).

30. For a poignant account of these events see esp. P. Zinner, *Communist Strategy and Tactics in Czechoslovakia 1918-1948* (New York and London: Columbia University Press, 1963).

31. The most detailed account of the relationship between the social democrats and the communists between 1944 and 1955 is given in K. Kaplan, *Das verhängnisvolle Bündnis* (Wuppertal: POL-Verlag, 1984).

32. *Dějiny Československa v datech*, p.469.

33. J. Krejčí, *Social Change*, pp. 44-5.

34. For a comprehensive account of the various statistical estimates of the 'Czechoslovak Gulag' see V. Hejl and K. Kaplan, *Zpráva*, pp. 229-36.

35. For regular reports on the position of Churches see Bohuslav and Olga Hrubý, (eds.), *Religion in Communist Dominated Areas* (New York: Quarterly).

36. J. Krejčí, *Social Change*, pp. 108-9.

37. For details see esp.: G. Golan, *The Czechoslovak Reform Movement* (Cambridge University Press, 1971) and *The Czechoslovak Reform Policy* (Cambridge University Press, 1973); V. Kusín, *The Intellectual Origins of the Prague Spring* (Cambridge University Press, 1917) and *Political Groupings in the Czechoslovak Reform Movement* (London: Macmillan, 1972).

38. The development reminds us of the discovery of the theorists of revolution, namely that one of its first advanced symptoms is the 'desertion' or 'transfer of the allegiance of the intellectuals'. See J. Krejčí, *Great Revolutions Compared: the Search for a Theory* (Brighton: Harvester Press, 1987, 2nd ed.) pp. 194-5.

39. For a review and evaluation of various periods of Czech-Slovak cohabitation see J. Krejčí and V. Velímský, *Ethnic and*

Political Nations in Europe (London: Croom Helm; and New York: St Martin's Press, 1981) pp. 147–51.

40. For a personal account of a person involved see Z. Mlynář, *The Nightfrost in Prague: the end of humane socialism* (New York: Karz, 1980).

41. Calculated from the population balance sheets in the Czecho-slovak Statistical Yearbooks 1968 and 1969.

42. Translated from *Studie* (1988), 118–19, IV–V, Rome, p. 364.

43. *ibid.*, p. 382.

44. 'The Truth prevails' was first used as an emblem motto by George of Poděbrady, the fifteenth-century king of Bohemia. Thomas Masaryk revived it in the struggle for independence. For Václav Havel's understanding of his motto see Havel, V. *et al.*, *The Power of the Powerless*, edited by J. Keane (London: Hutchinson, 1985).

Select Bibliography

Barton, P., 'La guerre sociale en Tchécoslovaquie' in *Preuves*, Paris, July 1953.

Bartoš, F.M., *The Hussite Revolution 1424–1437* (New York: Columbia University Press, 1986).

Beneš, E., *Problémy nové Evropy a zahraniční politika československá* (Prague: Melantrich, 1924).

— *Demokracie dnes a zítra* (Prague: Cin, 1946).

Beneš, V., 'Czechoslovak democracy and its problems' in V.S. Mamatey and R. Luža (eds), *A History of the Czechoslovak Republic 1918–1948* (New Jersey: Princeton University Press, 1973).

Bernard, V., 'The suppression of the Czechoslovak Social Democratic Party' in *Socialist World* (1948) Bd. 3, London.

Betts, R.R., *Essays in Czech History* (London: Athlone Press, 1969).

Bosl, K. (ed.), *Handbuch der Geschichte der böhmischen Länder*, 4 vols., (Munich: Collegium Carolinum, 1966–74).

Brandes, D., *Die Tschechen unter deutschem Protektorat*, 2 vols., (Munich and Vienna: R. Oldenbourg, 1969 and 1975).

Brock, P., *The Slovak National Awakening* (University of Toronto Press, 1976).

Bruegel, J.W., *Czechoslovakia Before Munich. The German Minority Problem and British Appeasement Policy* (Cambridge: Cambridge University Press, 1973).

Brügel, J.W., *Stalin und Hitler. Pakt gegen Europa* (Vienna: Nymphenburger, 1973).

— *Tschechen und Deutsche 1918–1938* (Munich: Nymphenburger, 1967).

— *Tschechen und Deutsche 1939–1946* (Munich: Nymphenburger, 1974).

Brügel, L., *Geschichte der österreichischen Sozialdemokratie*, 5 vols., (Vienna: Wiener Volksbuchhandlung, 1922–5).

Čapek, M. and Hrubý, K., (eds.), *T.G. Masaryk in Perspective, Comments and Criticism* (Ann Arbor: SVU Press, 1981).

Černý, V., *Pláč koruny české* (Toronto: Sixty-Eight Publishers, 1977).

Československá vlastivěda, vol. IV, History (Prague: Sfinx, 1932).

Dějiny Československa v datech (Prague: Svoboda, 1968).

Denis, E., *Fin de l'indépendence bohême* (Paris: Colin, 1890).

— *La Bohême depuis la Montagne Blanche* (Paris: Leroux, 1903).

— *La question d'Autriche, les slovaques* (Paris: Delagrave, 1917).

Dittrich, Z.R., *Christianity in Great Moravia* (Groningen: J.B. Wolters, 1962).

— 'K 1100-letému výročí smrti sv. Metoděje' in *Proměny* (1985) vol. 22, no. 2.

Drtina, P., *Československo můj osud*, 4 vols., (Toronto: Sixty-Eight Publishers, 1982).

Duff, S.G., *German Protectorate. The Czechs Under Nazi Rule* (London: Frank Cass, 1970).

Dvorník, F., *The Slavs in European History and Civilization* (New Jersey: Rutgers University Press, 1962).

Evans, R.J.W., *The Making of the Habsburg Monarchy 1550–1700* (Oxford: Clarendon Press, 1979).

Feierabend, L., *Soumrak Československé demokracie*, 2 vols., (Surrey: Rozmluvy, 1986 and 1988).

Fiala, Z. (ed.), *Pokračovatelé Kosmovi* (Prague: Svoboda, 1974).

Fic, V.M., *Revolutionary War for independence and the Russian Question. Czechoslovak Army in Russia 1914–1918* (New Delhi: Abhinav Publications, 1977).

— *The Bolsheviks and the Czechoslovak Legion* (New Delhi: Abhinav Publications, 1978).

Galandauer, J., *Bohumír Šmeral 1880–1914*, 2 vols., (Prague: Svoboda, 1981).

Golan, G., *The Czechoslovak Reform Movement* (Cambridge: Cambridge University Press, 1971).

— *The Czechoslovak Reform Policy* (Cambridge: Cambridge University Press, 1973).

Graus, F., *Dějiny venkovského lidu v Čecháchj v době předhusitské* (Prague: SNPL, 1953).

Graus, F., *Die Nationenbildung der Westslawen in Mittelalter* (Sigmaringen: Jan Thorbecke Verlag, 1980).

Hájek, J., *Setkání a střety* (Köln: Index, 1983).

Hauner, M., 'Der Bürger gegenüber Staat und Gesellschaft' in J. Krejčí (ed.), *Sozialdemokratie und Systemwandel. Hundert Jahre tschechoslowakische Erfahrung* (Berlin-Bonn: Dietz, 1978).

Haubelt, J., *České osvícenství* (Prague: Svoboda, 1986).

Havel, V. *et al.*, *The Power of the Powerless* , edited by J. Keane, (London: Hutchinson, 1985).

Havlík, L.E., *Velká Morava a středoevropští Slované* (Prague: ČSAV, 1964).

Hejl, V. and Kaplan K., *Zpráva o organizovaném násilí* (Toronto: Sixty-Eight Publishers, 1986).

Herben, J., *Huss and his Followers* (London: G. Bles, 1926).

Hermann, A. H., *A History of the Czechs* (London: Allen Lane, 1975).

Heymann, F.G., *George of Bohemia, King of Heretics* (New Jersey: Princeton University Press, 1965).

Hilberg, R., *The Destruction of the European Jews*, 3 vols., (New York and London: Holmes & Meier, 1985).

Hlaváček, I., *Ze zpráv a kronik doby husitské* (Prague: Svoboda, 1981).

Hoensch, J.K., *Geschichte Böhmens von der slavischen Landnahme bis ins 20. Jahrhundert* (Munich: C.H. Beck, 1987).

Hosák, L., *Nové československé dějiny* (Prague: Komenium, 1947).

Hrubý, K., 'Senior Communitas – Eine revolutionäre Institition der Prager Hussitischen Bürgerschaft in Bohemia' in *Jahrbuch des Collegium Carolinum*, Band 13 (Munich and Vienna: R. Oldenbourg, 1972).

— 'Kirche und Arbeiter' in F. Seibt (ed.), *Bohemia Sacre* (Düsseldorf, 1974).

Jaksch, W., *Sudeten Labour and the Sudeten Problem* (London: Gollancz, 1945).

Janáček, J., *Ženy české renesance* (Prague: Československý spisovatel, 1977).

— *Doba předbělohorská 1526–1547* (Prague: ČSAV, 1984).

— *Rudolf II. a jeho doba* (Prague: Svoboda, 1987).

Janát, B., 'Světlo a stín českých dějin' in *Proměny* (1989) vol. 26, no. 1.

Jelínek, Y.A., *Hlinka's Slovak People's Party 1939–1945* (Michigan: Ann Arbor, 1966).

Josko, A. 'The Slovak resistance movement' in V.S. Mamatey and R. Luža (eds.), *A History of the Czechoslovak Republic 1918–1948* (New Jersey: Princeton University Press, 1973).

Josten, J., *Oh My Country* (London: Latimer, 1949).

Kalista, Z., *Tvář baroka* (Surrey: Rozmluvy, 1983).

Kalivoda, R., *Husitská ideologie* (Prague: ČSAV, 1961).

Kalvoda, J., *The Genesis of Czechoslovakia* (Boulder, New York: Columbia University Press, 1986).

Kaminský, H., *A History of the Hussite Revolution* (Berkeley and Los Angeles University Press, 1967).

Kann, R.A., *The Multinational Empire*, 2 vols., (New York: Columbia University Press, 1950).

Kaplan, K., *Poválečné Československo* (Munich: Národní Politika, 1985).

Kaplan, K., *Das verhängnisvolle Bündnis* (Wuppertal: POL-Verlag, 1984).

— *Nekrvavá revoluce* (Toronto: Sixty-Eight Publishers, 1985).

— *The Short March. The Communist Take-over of Power in Czechoslovakia 1945–1948* (Oxford: Holdan Books, 1985).

Kárník, Z., *Socialisté na rozcestí: Habsburk, Masaryk či Šmeral* (Prague: Svoboda, 1968).

Kárníková, L., *Vývoj obyvatelstva v českých zemích 1754–1914* (Prague: ČSAV, 1965).

Kejř, J., *Husité* (Prague: Panorama, 1984).

Kimball, S.B., *Czech Nationalism: A Study of the National Theatre Movement 1845–83* (Urbana: University of Illinois Press, 1964).

Kirschbaum, S.J., *Slovaques et Tchèques, essai sur un nouvel aperçu de leur histoire politique* (Lusanne: L'Âge d'Homme, 1987).

Klassen, J.M., 'The nobility and the making of the Hussite revolution' in *East European Quarterly* (Boulder, New York: 1978).

Klofáč, J., *Sociální struktura ČSSR a její změny v letech 1945–1980* (Köln: Index, 1985).

Korbel, J., *The Communist Subversion of Czechoslovakia 1938–48* (New Jersey: Princeton University Press, 1959).

Koudelková, J., *Naše dějiny v datech* (Prague: Albatros, 1987).

Kovtun, J., *Masarykův triumf. Příběh konce velké války* (Toronto: Sixty-Eight Publishers, 1987).

Králík, O., *Labyrint dávných dějin českých* (Prague: Vyšehrad, 1970).

Krejčí, J., *Social Change and Stratification in Postwar Czechoslovakia* (London and Basingstoke: Macmillan; and New York: Columbia University Press, 1972).

— 'Les événements imprévus de l'histoire tchécoslovaque moderne' in *Revue d'études comparative est-ouest* (September 1977) vol. 8, no. 3.

— 'The Czechoslovak economy during the years of systemic transformation: 1945–1949' in *Yearbook of East European Economics*, vol. 7, (Munich-Vienna: G. Olzog Verlag, 1977).

— *Great Revolutions Compared: The Search for a Theory* (Wheatsheaf Books, Harvester UK, 2nd Ed., 1987).

— 'Ruptures and traumas in Central European consciousness: Czech history as a test case' in *History of European Ideas* (1989) vol. 10, no.11.

Krejčí, J., (ed.), *Sozialdemokratie und Systemwandel, Hundert Jahre tschechoslowakische Erfarhung* (Berlin-Bonn: Dietz Verlag, 1978).

Krejčí, J. and Velímský, V., *Ethnic and Political Nations in Europe* (London: Croom Helm; and New York: St Martin's Press, 1981).

Křen, J., Kural, V., Brandes, D. *Integration oder Ausgrenzung der Deutschen und Tschechen 1890–1945* (Bremen: Donat & Temmen Verlag, 1986).

Křen, J., 'Historické proměny češství' in *Proměny* (1988) vol. 25, no. 2.

Krofta, K., *Stará a nová střední Evropa* (Prague: Československá národní demokracie, 1929).

— *Duchovní odkaz husitství* (Prague: Svoboda, 1946).

— *Dějiny selského stavu* (Prague: Laichter, 1949).

Kryštůfek, Z., *The Soviet Regime in Czechoslovakia* (Boulder: East European Monographies, 1981).

Kunoši, A., *The Basis of Czechoslovak Unity* (London: A. Dakers, 1944).

Kusín, V., *The Intellectual Origins of the Prague Spring* (Cambridge: Cambridge University Press, 1971).

— *Political Groupings in the Czechoslovak Reform Movement*

(London: Macmillan, 1972).

— *From Dubček to Charter 77* (Edinburgh: Q Press; and New York: St Martin's Press, 1978).

Lettrich, J., *History of Modern Slovakia* (New York: Praeger, 1955; 2nd ed. Toronto: Slovak Research and Studies Center, 1985).

Luža, R., *The Transfer of the Sudeten Germans* (New York University Press, 1964).

— 'The Czech resistance movement' in V.S. Mamatey and R. Luža (eds.), *A History of the Czechoslovak Republic 1918–1948* (New Jersey: Princeton University Press, 1973).

— 'Czechoslovakia between democracy and communism' in V.S. Mamatey and R. Luža (eds.) *History of the Czechoslovak Republic 1918–1948* (New Jersey: Princeton University Press, 1973).

Macartney, C.A., *The Habsburg Empire 1790–1918* (London: Weidenfeld & Nicolson, 1969).

Macek, J., *The Hussite Movement in Bohemia* (London: Lawrence & Wishart; and Prague: Orbis, 1965).

Machonin, P., (ed.), *Československá společnost* (Bratislava: Akademia, 1969).

Machovec, M., *Husovo učení a význam v tradici českého národa* (Prague: ČSAV, 1953).

— *Tomáš G. Masaryk* (Prague: Melantrich, 1968).

Macura, V., *Znamení zrodu. České obrození jako kulturní typ* (Prague: Československý spisovatel, 1983).

Mamatey, V.S. and Luža, R., (eds.), *A History of the Czechoslovak Republic 1918–1948* (New Jersey: Princeton University Press, 1973).

Masaryk, T.G., *The Meaning of Czech History*, edited by R. Wellek (The University of North Carolina Press, 1974).

Masaryk, T.G., *Otázka sociální* (Prague: 1898). German edition *Die philosophischen und soziologischen Grundlagen des Marxismus. Studien zur sozialen Frage* (Vienna: 1899).

Mastný, V., *The Czechs under Nazi Rule* (New York and London: Columbia University Press, 1971).

— *Russia's Road to the Cold War* (New York: Columbia University Press, 1979).

Mezník, J., 'O české malosti (a také velikosti)' in *Proměny* (1989) vol. 26, no.1.

Míka, A., *Petr Chelčický* (Prague: Svobodné Slovo, 1963).

— *Stoletý zápas o charakter českéhó státu, 1526–1627* (Prague: SPN, 1974).

Minulost našeho státu v dokumentech (Prague: Svoboda, 1971).

Mlynář, Z., *Československý pokus o reformu 1968* (Köln-Rome: Index-Listy, 1975).

— *Nightfrost in Prague: the end of humane socialism* (New York: Karz, 1980).

Molnár, A., *Na rozhraní věků. Cesty reformace* (Prague: Vyšehrad, 1985).

— (ed.), *Husitské manifesty* (Prague: Odeon, 1986).

Moravec, F., *Špión, jemuž nevěřili* (Toronto: Sixty-Eight Publishers, 1977).

Müller, A., (ed.), *Systémové změny* (Köln: Index, 1972).

Myant, M., *Socialism and Democracy in Czechoslovakia, 1945–1948* (Cambridge: Cambridge University Press, 1981).

Nedvěd, J., *Cesta ke sloučení sociální demokracie s komunistickou stranou v roce 1948* (Prague: ČSAV, Academia, 1968).

Newman, E.P., *Masaryk* (London: Campion Press, 1960).

Odložiliík, O., *The Hussite King. Bohemia in European Affairs 1440–1471* (New Jersey; Rutgers University Press, 1965).

Olivová, V., *The Doomed Democracy, Czechoslovakia in a Disrupted Europe 1914–38* (London: Sidgwick & Jackson, 1972).

Ostrý, A., *Československý problém* (Köln: Index, 1972).

Painter, G. and Chrástek, D., *Printing in Czechoslovakia in the 15th Century* (British Museum, 1969).

Patočka, J., *Kacířské eseje o filosofii dějin* (Munich: Arkýr, 1980).

— *O smysl dneska* (Surrey: Rozmluvy, 1987).

Pech, S.Z., *The Czech Revolution of 1848* (Chapel Hill: University of North Carolina Press, 1969).

Pekař, J., *Wallenstein 1630–1634 Tragödie einer Verschwörung* (Berlin: Metzner, 1937).

— *O smyslu českých dějin* (Rotterdam: Stojanov, 1977).

— *Bílá Hora* (Surrey: Rozmluvy, 1986; first edition, Prague: Vesmír, 1922).

Pelikán, J., (ed.), *The Czechoslovak Political Trials 1950–54* (London: Macdonald, 1971).

Peroutka, F., *Budování státu, československá politika v létech popřevratových*, 4 vols., (Prague: F. Borový, 1933–6).

Petráň, J., *Poddaný lid v Čechách na prahu třicetileté války* (Prague: ČASV, 1964).

Pfaff, I., *Historické kořeny reformního hnutí v české společnosti* (Köln: Index, 1988).

Pirenne, H., *Economic and Social History of Medieval Europe* (London: Kegan, Trench, Trubner, 1947).

Polišenský, J.V., *The Thirty Years War* (London: B.T. Batsford, 1971).

Purš, J. and Kropilák, M. (eds.), *Přehled dějin Československá 1526-1848* (Prague: ČSAV, 1982).

Rádl, E., *O smysl našich dějin* (Prague: Čin, 1925).

Rechcígl, M. Jr., *Czechoslovakia, Past & Present*, 2 vols., (The Hague and Paris, Mouton & Co, 1968).

Reiman, P., *et al.*, *Dějiny Komunistické strany Československá* Prague: Svoboda, 1961).

Reinfeld, B.K., *Karel Havlíček 1821-1856* (New York: Columbia University Press, 1982).

Renner, H., *A History of Czechoslovakia Since 1945* (London and New York: Routledge, 1989).

Rhode, G., 'The Protectorate of Bohemia and Moravia' in V.S. Mamatey and R. Luža (eds.), *A History of the Czechoslovak Republic 1918-1948* (New Jersey: Princeton University Press, 1973).

Robert, R.J., (ed.), *The Czechoslovak Crisis 1968* (London: Weidenfeld & Nicolson, 1969).

Rupnik, J., *Histoire du Parti communiste tchécoslovaque* (Paris: Presses de la fondation nationale de sciences politques, 1981). 1981).

Rydlo, J.M., (ed.), *Slovensko v retrospektíve dějin* (Lausanne: Liber, 1976).

Schmidt-Hartmann, E., *Thomas G. Masaryk's Realism* (Munich: R. Oldenbourg, 1984).

Scruton, R., *et al.*, *Czechoslovakia – The Unofficial Culture* (London: The Claridge Press, 1988).

Seibt, F., *Hussitica. Zur Struktur einer Revolution* (Köln-Graz: Böhlau Verlag, 1965).

— *Deutschland und die Tschechen: Geschichte einer Nachbarschaft in der Mitte Europas* (Munich: List Verlag, 1974).

Seton-Watson, R.W., *Slovakia Then and Now; a political survey* (London: Faber, 1931).

— *A History of the Czechs & Slovaks* (London: Hutchinson, 1943).

Šimečka, M., *Kruhová obrana* (Köln: Index, 1985).

Skála Pavel ze Zhoře, *Historie česká od defenestrace k Bílé Hoře* (Prague: Svoboda, 1984).

Sked, A., *The Decline and Fall of the Habsburg Empire 1815–1918* (London and New York: Longman, 1989).

Skilling, G., *Czechoslovakia's Interrupted Revolution* (New Jersey: Princeton University Press, 1976).

Slavík, J., *Vznik českého národa*, 2 vols., (Prague: Pokrok, 1946 and 1948).

Šmahel, Fr., *Idea národa v husitských Čechách* (České Budějovice: Růže, 1971).

Smelser, R.M., *The Sudeten Problem 1933–1938* (Conn.: Dawson, Kent & Muddleton, 1975).

Sobota, E., *Co to byl Protektorát* (Prague: Kvasnička a Hampl, 1946).

Šolle, Z., 'Die Sozialdemokratie in der Habsburgermonarchie und die tschechische Frage' in *Archiv für Sozialgeschichte*, Bd. VI/VII, (Hanover: 1966–7).

Sousedík, S., *Valerián Magni 1586–1661* (Prague: Vyšehrad, 1983).

Spěváček, J., *Václav IV. 1361–1419* (Prague: Svoboda, 1986).

— *Rozmach české státnosti za vlády Lucemburků v souvislostech evropské politiky* (Prague: Academia, 1987).

Spinka, M., *John Hus at the Council of Constance* (New York: Columbia University Press, 1965).

— *John Hus and the Czech Reform* (Hamden: Archon Books, 1966).

— *John Hus: A Biography* (New Jersey: Princeton University Press, 1968).

Steiner, E., *The Slovak Dilemma* (London: Cambridge University Press, 1973).

Street, C.J.C., *President Masaryk* (London: Geoffrey Bles, 1930).

Strmiska, Z., *Sociální systém a strukturální rozpory společnosti sovětského typu* (Köln: Index, 1983).

Suda, Z., *Zealots and Rebels, A History of the Ruling Communist Party of Czechoslovakia* (Stanford: Hoover Institution Press, 1980).

Šusta, J., *Z dob dávných i blízkých*, (Prague: Vesmír, 1924).

— 'První Habsburkové a Lucemburkové' in *Dějiny lidstva*, díl 4, (Prague: Melantrich, 1942).

— *České Dějiny II. 4. - Karel IV.* (Prague: Laichter, 1948).

Sviták, I., *The Czechoslovak Experiment 1968-1969* (New York and London: Columbia University Press, 1971).

Szporluk, R., *Communism and Nationalism* (New York and Oxford: Oxford University Press, 1988).

Táborský, E., *Communism in Czechoslovakia 1948-1960* (New Jersey: Princeton University Press, 1961).

— *President Edvard Beneš Between East and West 1938-1948* (Stanford: Hoover Institution Press, 1981).

(La) Tchécoslovaquie in *Revue d'études comparatives est-ouest* (1988) vol. XIX, no. 3. Edited in cooperation with Jaroslav Krejčí, (Éditions du centre national de la recherche scientifique, Paris)

Tigrid, P., *Why Dubček fell* (London: Macdonald, 1971).

— *Kapesní průvodce inteligentní ženy po vlastním osudu* (Toronto: Sixty-Eight Publishers, 1988).

Tomášek, F., 'Velikonoční poselství' in *Studie* (1988) 118-119, IV-V, (Rome: Christian Academy, 1988).

Urban, O., *Česká společnost* 1848-1918 (Prague: Svoboda, 1982).

Všehrd Vičkotrin Kornel, *O právilech, o súdiech i o dskách země české knihy devatery* (1495-9; modern edition, Prague: 1874).

Wallace, W.V., *Czechoslovakia* (London and Tonbridge: E. Benn, 1977).

Werstadt, J., *Odkazy dějin a dějepisců* (Prague: Historický klub, 1948).

Wisekemann, E., *Czechs & Germans, A Study of the Struggle in the Historic Provinces of Bohemia and Moravia* (London: Macmillan, 1967).

Wižďálková, B., *Konkordance Koniášových klíčů, indexu, Jungmanna a knihopisu* (Prague: Statni knihovna ČSR, 1987).

Zeman, Z.A.B., *The Break-up of the Habsburg Empire 1914-1918* (London: Oxford University Press, 1961).

— *The Masaryks, The Making of Czechoslovakia* (London: Weidenfeld & Nicolson, 1976).

Žemlička, J., *Století posledních Přemyslovců* (Prague: Panorama, 1986).

Zessner, K., *J. Seliger und die nationale Frage in Böhmen* (Stuttgart: Seliger-Archiv, 1976).

Zinner, P.E., 'Marxism in action: seizure of power in Czechoslovakia',

Foreign Affairs, XXVIII (July 1950), pp. 644–58.
— *Communist Strategy and Tactics in Czechoslovakia 1918–1948*
(New York and London: Columbia University Press, 1963).

Subject
Index

absolutism, 98–9, 112
Academy of Sciences, Czech, 124
'action committees' (1948), 180
'alternative culture', 191–2, 200
Adalbert, Saint see Vojtěch
Adamites, 42
Agrarian Party, 125, 141, 168
agrarian reform, 141–2
Albrecht of Habsburg, 49
Alexander II, Tsar of Russia, 123
Ambrose, Hussite priest, 42
Anabaptists, 65, 221
Anarchists, 123
Andrew, Bishop of Prague, 18
Anna of Bohemia (Jagiellon), 66
Anna of Bohemia (Luxembourg), 31
Antichrist, 33, 37
Aquileia, 2
Augsburg Confession, 94, 98
Austria, 26, 49, 78–136, 139, 152 and passim
Austro-Hungarian Agreement, 114–7
Avars, 2–3
Avignon, 30, 32
'Away from Rome', 125, 145

Balbín, Bohuslav, 94
Balkan War, 131
barons, 20, 219, 222

Baroque, 84, 92
Bauer, Otto, 128, 136
Bavaria, Bavarians, 2–4, 24, 83–4, 97
Beghards, 32
Beguines, 32
Belcredi, Richard, Count, 135
Beneš, Eduard, 132, 147, 150–5, 160–1, 165–71, 232–4
Beran, Karel, Cardinal, 186, 193
Beran, Rudolf, 232
Beria, L.P., 187
Bernolák, Anton, 103
Bernstein, Eduard, 127
Bible, 4, 34, 35, 125
biblical Czech, language, 103
'Black death', 26
Bohemia, 8–14 and passim
Bohemian Confession, 76, 79, 98
Bohemian Repeal, 104
Boleslav I, the Cruel, 13
Boleslav II, the Pious, 13–4
Bolshevik Revolution, 134
Bolzano, Bernard, 101
bondage or serfdom, 19–22, 59, 91, 99, 111, 216, 220
Boniface VIII, Pope, 29
bookprint, first specimen, 62
Bořivoj, Duke of Bohemia, 11
Bosnia & Herzegovina, 129, 131
Breslau (present Wroclaw), 52, 55–6

Brest-Litowsk, Peace of, 134
Brezhnev, L.T., 196
Brno, 20, 127, 128, 130, 226
Budovec, Václav, 221
Bulgaria, 4, 7, 132
bureaucracy, 97
Byzantine Empire, Byzantines, 2–7

Calixtins, 38, 58
Calvin, Calvinists, 65, 69, 77–83, 98
Carolinum, 88
Carpathian German Party, 150
Čáslav, Hussite Assembly of, 218
Catholics, Catholic Church, 69–125, 183–194 and passim
Catholic political parties, 125, 130, 138–9, 145 ff.
Charles Albert, Elector of Bavaria, 97
Charles I, of Habsburg, 133–5
Charles IV, Emperor and King of Bohemia, 25–30
Charles V, of Habsburg, 66–8
Charles VI, of Habsburg, 96
Charter 77, 192, 200
Cheb (Eger), city in Bohemia, 47
Chelčický, Peter, 50
Chronicles of Troy, 62
Church policy of the Communist Party, 183–6
Cisleithania, 137, 225
Civic Forum, 201
Clement V, Pope, 29
Clement VI, Pope, 25
Clement VII, Pope, 67
Clementinum, 88
Cluny, 16
Cola di Rienzi, 27
collectivization of agriculture, 182
Comenius, Jan Amos, 89
Committee for the Defence of the Unjustly Prosecuted, 192

Communist Party of Czech-oslovakia, 143 and passim
Compacts of Basle, 48–9, 52, 58, 67, 75
concordat, 53, 116
Congress of Vienna, 100, 108
Constantine (Cyrillus), 4–8, 14
Constantinople, 2, 3, 10
Constituent Assembly, 111
consumerism, 191, 195
Copenhagen, Congress of Socialist International, 130
cordon sanitaire, 139
corvée, 18, 21, 59, 91, 99, 222
Council of Basle, 6, 47–8, 53, 75
Council of Constance, 38–9, 53
Council of Pisa, 34, 35
Council of Trent, 75
Council of Vatican, Second, 50, 186, 193
Counter-Reformation, 79, 90, 96 and passim
Crecy, battle of, 25
Croatia, Croats, 11, 130, 131, 225
Crusades, 46, 56,
crypto-communists, 173, 176, 179
Cuius regio eius religio, 80, 85
Curia, Holy See, 4, 25, 30, 50, 52–4, 80 and passim
curial system (elections), 113, 129
Cyrillus, see Constantine
Czech Brethren Evangelical Church, 145
Czech-German relationship, 24, 36, 40, 77, 93–4, 104–17, 122, 139–175
Czech National Council (1945), 168
Czechoslav Social Democratic Workers' Party, 121, 130, 137
Czechoslovak Church, 145, 185
Czecho-Slovakia, 156
Czechoslovak Army abroad (WWII), 160

Czechoslovak Legions (WWI), 132–3, 145, 227
Czechoslovak National Council (WWI), 132–4
Czechoslovak Social Democratic Party, 137 ff.
Czech-Slovak relationship, 141 ff.

Danish, Denmark, 84
Danube River, 1, 8
Defenestration of Prague, first, 39
Defenestration of Prague, second, 83
'defensors' (Protestant), 79
'desertion of intellectuals', 234
Devotio Moderna, 32
dissidents, 191–4
Dubček, Alexander, 189, 190, 201

Eastern Silesia, Czech-Polish strife for, 229–30
Ecloga, 6
Edict of Bondage, 99
Edward III, King of England, 25
Elbe River, 8, 59
economic planning, 176, 179, 186, 233
economic reform, 186
elections, 123, 124, 129, 130, 140, 143, 144, 150, 176, 181, 201
Eliáš, Alois, 159
emphyteusis, 21, 220
England, 31, 33, 51, 78 and passim
Enlightenment, 90, 95–101
Ernest of Pardubice, Archbishop, 26, 29
Eucharist, 34, 37, 40–2, 48, 52–4, 69, 75, 85
Execrabilis, Papal Bull, 54
expulsion of Germans, 174–5

faked manuscripts, 123, 226

Fantino de Valle, 220
February Agreement of 1927, 229
February Constitution (1861), 113
February *coup d'état* (1948), 112, 180–1
February Revolution (Paris), 104–5, 107
feudal, feudalism, 19–22, 215–6
Ferdinand d'Este, Franz, Crown Prince, 131
Ferdinand I, of Habsburg, 66–75
Ferdinand II, of Habsburg, 81, 84, 87
Fierlinger, Zdeněk, 176
filioque, 6
Four Articles of Prague, 40, 43–4, 47
France, 23, 153, 162 and passim
Francis II, of Habsburg, 100
Frankfurt, Parliament of, 108
Frankish Empire, Franks, 1–7
Franz Joseph I, of Habsburg, 112–7
Fredegar, Frankish annalist, 213
Frederic I, Barbarosa, 18
Frederic II, Emperor, 18
Free Spirit, heresy of, 42
French Revolution, 100
Friedrich of Palatinate, 83
Fuggers, Augsburg financiers, 67, 83
'Fundamental Articles', 117

gentry, 20, 45
George of Poděbrady, King of Bohemia, 50–7, 235
German Confederation, 100, 108
German political parties in Czechoslovakia, 140–153 and passim
German *Reich*, 117
German speakers in the Bohemian Lands see Czech-German

relationship
Glagolitsa, prototype of Cyrillic, 4
glasnost, 198
Gloria in Exclesis Deo, Papal Bull, 4
Golden Bull (Charles IV), 28
Golden Bull of Sicily, 18, 20
gold standard, 148
Gorbachev, Mikhail, 196–9
Gothic, 25–6, 62
Gottwald, Klement, 144, 168, 174
Great Moravia, 3, 203
Gregory XI, Pope, 30

Hácha, Emil, 159–60, 231
Hadrian II, Pope, 4
Hainfeld, Congress at, 124, 127
Havel, Václav, 200–2
Havlíček, Karel, 103, 224
Hay, John Leopold, Bishop, 98
Helsinki Agreement, 192
Henlein, Konrad, 152, 229
Henry IV, 18
Henry VII, of Luxembourg, Emperor, 24
Herder, Johann Gottfried, 102, 224
'Hereditary German Lands', 98, 108
Heydrich, Reinhard, 159, 161
Hitler, Adolf, 149, 151–4, 156
Hlinka, Andrej, 138
Hlinka's guards, 169
Hodža, Milan, 151–2
Holy Communion see Eucharist
Horáková, Milada, 183
Horeb, Horebites, 40, 47, 219
Hradec Králové, city in Bohemia, 40, 43, 89
Hromádka, Josef, 185
Huguenots, 78
Hungary, Hungarians, 8, 22, 29, 55–7, 78, 94, 98, 103–4, 110, 131, 152–6, 175, 195, 199
Hus, John, 33–8, 53, 64, 125, 146
Húska, Martin, 42
Hussite, Hussites, see also Calixtins or Utraquists, 38–62, 102, 125–6, 185

Industriae Tuae, Papal Bull, 5
Innocent III, Pope, 18
Iro-Scottish missionaries, 3
Italy, 23–30, 110, 156

Jacobellus de Misa see Jakoubek of Stříbro
Jagiellon Dynasty, 44, 57–66
Jakoubek of Stříbro, 34, 218
James I, King of England, 83
Jan Milič of Kroměříž, 32
Jan of Nepomuk, 90, 217
Jerome of Prague, 39, 53
Jesuits 74–92 and passim, 222
Jews, 86, 99, 125, 149, 161–5
Jihlava, city in Moravia, 48
Jobst, Margave of Moravia, 29
John VIII, Pope, 5
John Friedrich of Saxony, 71
John George of Saxony, 83
John of Jenstein, Archbishop, 29, 217
John of Luxembourg, King of Bohemia, 24–5
John Paul I, Pope, 10
Joseph II, of Habsburg, 98–9

Kafka, Franz, 163
Kaunits, V.A., Prince, 99
Kautsky, Karl, 127
Kazimir, Jagiellon, 48
Kinsky, B.K., Count, 91
knights, 73, 219
Kocel, ruler of Panonia, 4

Konias, A., 89, 222
Košice Programme, 171, 177
Kralice Bible, 77, 94
Kramář, Karel, 129, 132, 150
Kroměříž, city in Moravia, 111
Kulturkampf, 186
Kutná Hora, Agreement of, 58
Kutná Hora, Decree of, 36
Kutná Hora, royal borough, 24, 59, 62

Ladislas, the Posthumus, 50
Landfrieden, 49
Lasalle, Ferdinand, 121
Lateran Council, 18
League, Catholic, 71
Leipzig, disputation in, 64
Lenin, V.I., 150, 197
Leo X, Pope, 67
Leopold II, of Habsburg, 100
Leopold of Passau, Bishop, 80
Leszno, in Poland, 89
Ležáky, 161
liberalism, liberals, 108 and ff.
Lidice, 161
Lipany, battle of, 47
Lithuania, 44
Little Entente, 152
'Living within the Truth', 202
Louis, King of Bohemia, 65, 67
Ludmila, Saint, 13-4
Lusatia, Lusatians, 28, 84, 87, 214
Luther, Martin, 64, 93
Lutheranism, Lutherans, 64-85, 98, 169

Machar, J.S., 163
Magni, Valerian, 222
Magyars, 7, 16, 65, 103-4, 137, 154
Mair, Martin, 220
Maria Theresa, 96
Marini, Antonio, 220

Marshall Plan, 177
Marx, Karl, Marxist, 121, 127, 143
Marxism/Leninism, 184, 196, 199, 226
Masaryk, Thomas Garrigue, 126, 130, 132, 134-5, 143, 145-7, 150-1, 163, 166, 172, 202, 226
Matthew of Janov, 32
Matthias Corvinus, King of Hungary, 56-7
Matthias of Habsburg, 78-82
Maximilian I, of Habsburg, 62
Maximilian II, of Habsburg, 75-6
Maximilian of Bavaria, 84
Methodius, Saint, 4-7, 14
Metternich, C.L.W., Prince, 107
Michael III, Byzantine Emperor, 3-4
'millionaires' levy, 178
Mohacs, battle of, 65
Mojmír of Moravia, 3, 213
monetary reform, 186, 233
Moravia, Moravians, 1-14, 29, 44, 48, 56, 68, 105, 130, 146
Moravian Pact, 128
Movement for Civil Liberties, 193, 200
Munich, Agreement (Dictate) of, 153, 160
Münzer, Thomas, 65
Mussolini, Benito, 153

Napoleon I, Bonaparte, 100
National Committee of 1848, 104
National Councils (1945 and after), 168, 174
National Democratic Party, 145, 150, 168
National Fascist Community, 150
National Front, 171, 181, 232
nationalism, 105 and ff.
nationalization see socialization

National Socialists (Czech), 141 and ff.
National Socialists (German), 149 and ff.
National Social Party, 127, 134
National Theatre (Czech), 122
National Unity Party, 150
Netherlands, 78, 80
Neudörfl, 120
Nicholas of Dresden, 217, 218, 220
Nicholas of Pelhřimov, 42
Nitra, city in Slovakia, 6
nominalists, 35
'normalization', 189
Novotný, Antonín, 187

Ockham, William, 30
Odra River, 9
Old-Czechs, 123 and ff.
Olomouc, city in Moravia, 11, 20, 52
Otto I, Emperor, 13
Ottoman Empire, Ottomans, 56, 65, 114
Oxford, 31, 35

Pacem in terris, 184
paganism, 12-4
Palach, Jan, 191
Palacký, František, 102, 108-9, 114, 135
Palatinate, 80
Pannonia, 2, 4, 7
'parallel polis', 191
Paris, 35
partisans, 161, 169, 170
party apparat, 180 and ff.
Passau, 2, 5, 80, 213
patrimonium, 19, 97
patriotism, patriots, 95, 102 and ff.
'Peace Committee of Catholic Clergy', 184

Peace of Prague, 87
Peace of Westphalia, 88
Peace Treaty of St. Germain, 137
Peace Treaty of Trianon, 137
peasants, see also bondage, corvée, 21, 38, 219
people's democracy, 176
People's Party (Czech), 130 and ff.
People's Party (Slovak), 138-9, 145 and ff.
perestroika, 198
Petrarch, Francesco, 27, 217
Pika, Heliodor, General, 183
Pikharts, 42
Pius II, Pope, 54
Phillip VI, King of France, 25
Photius, Byzantine Patriarch, 3
Pittsburgh Agreement, 138
Placetum regium (royal assent) 99, 112
Plzeň, city in Bohemia, 62
Polabic Slavs, 12
Poland, Poles, Polish, 9, 25, 35, 65, 123, 166-7, 196, 199
Popovici, Aurel, 136
Potsdam, Conference at 175
Pragmatic Sanction, 97
Prague, 11, 18, 24, 26, 34, 41-9, 59, 72-4, 77, 92, 105 and ff., 127, 171
Prague Party, 41, 48
'Prague Spring', 189-190
Přemysl Otakar I, King of Bohemia, 18
Přemysl Otakar II, King of Bohemia, 22
Přemyslids, 11-23
Pribina, Duke of Nitra, 213
Protectorate Bohemia-Moravia, 156-172
Protestant, Protestants, 44, 71-6, 89, 98, 185, 194
Prussia, 9, 97-117

Pruz, 12, 14
'The Public Against Violence', 201
purgatory, 41

'reactionary plots', 178
realists, 35
Red Army, 180
Reformation, 66 and passim
refugees, 149
Regensburg, 2, 213
Reginhar, Bishop of Passau, 213
Regnum Teutonicorum, 216
Reichsrat, 123 and ff., 225
Renaissance, 28, 54, 70
Renner, Karl, 128, 136
Resettlement Office, 175
retribution (after WWII), 174, 183,
    231–2
Richard II, King of England, 31
Richelieu, A.J., Cardinal, 87
Risorgimento, 101
Rokycana, John, Hussite leader,
    48–9, 54
Romanticism, 95–6
Rome, 2, 25, 27, 30
Rostislav, ruler of Moravia, 3
royal boroughs, 20, 219
Rudolph's Charter, 79–81
Rudolph I, of Habsburg, Emperor,
    22
Rudolph II, of Habsburg,
    Emperor, 77–8
Russia, Russians, 103, 116, 123,
    139, 197–9
rustical, 59, 99
Ruthenia, 137, 150, 156, 171

Salzburg, 2
samizdat literature, 192, 194
Samo, Frankish merchant-ruler, 213
Sarajevo, 131
Saxony, Saxons, 25, 71–2, 84

Savoy, 80–2
Schmalkalden, Union of 71
Seipel, Ignaz, Catholic ideologist,
    136
self-immolations as manifestations
    of protest, 191
Serbia, Serbs, 131
serfdom see bondage
Sigismund Korybut, 44
Sigismund of Luxembourg, 29, 38,
    44
Sikorski, Wladyslaw, 166
Silesia, 9, 22, 28, 34, 79, 105, 122,
    130
Silvester Patents (1851), 112
Slavic Congresses, 109, 129
Slavnikids, 13–4
Slovakia, Slovaks, 8–10, 66, 93–6,
    103, 115, 119, 135, 137–9, 185,
    189, 201
Slovak Republic, 157 and ff.
Slovak Uprising, 169
Slovenes, 10, 129
Šmeral, Bohumír, 134
Social Democratic Workers' Party.
    120
social insurance, 124, 141
socialization, 141, 175–6
Sokol (Falcon), Czech gymnastic
    organization, 114, 132, 160
Spain, 66
Spiritual Renewal, Ten Year Pro-
    gramme, 193
Šrámek, Jan, Monsignor, 146–7
Stalin, J.V., 144, 177, 197
Stalin-Hitler Pact, 162
Staufen Dynasty, 17
Štefánik, Milan Rostislav, 132
Stephen VI, Pope, 7
Stockholm, Congress of Socialist
    International, 134
Strakonice, League of , 50

Stránský, Pavel, 89
student demonstrations, 159, 188, 201
Štúr, Ľudovít, 103
St. Wenceslas Bath, 107
St. Wenceslas Treaty, 61
sub una (the Romanists), 38–62
Sudetendeutche Heimatsfront (Sudeten German Fatherland Front), 149
Sudenten German Party, 150
Sudeten Germans, 108
Sudetenland, 157
suffrage, universal, 123, 129, 181
Svárov, strike at, 120
Svatopluk, ruler of Moravia, 5–7
Švehla, Antonin, 142
Svoboda, Ludvík, 190
Sweden, Swedish, 84, 87
Syrmium, 4

Taaffe, Eduard, Count, 122
Tabor, Taborites, 40–50, 219
Thirty Years War, 84–8
Thomas of Štítné, 33
Thun, Leo, 110
Thurn, Heinrich Matthias, 221
Tiso, Jozef, Monsignor, 169, 232
Toleration Edict, 98
Tomášek, František, Cardinal, 193
Trade Unions, 130, 144
Transleithania, 137, 225
Transylvania, 65–6
Trotskyites, 182
'The Truth Prevails', 202
Tschernembl, Georg Erasmus, 222
Tuka, Béla, 148
Turks see Ottoman Empire
Turnverein, German gymnastic organization, 114, 149

Ukraine, Ukrainians, 1, 10, 130, 149, 167

Unam Sanctam, Papal Bull, 29
Unitas Fratrum (Unity of Brethren), 50. 61, 65, 73–9, 87, 89
United Kingdom, 153, 160
United States, 160
University of Prague, 25, 36, 39, 51, 79, 88, 122
USSR, 160, 165–71, 196
Utraquists, 37–62, 64–70, 85

Vatican, 146, 169, 183–4
'Velvet Revolution', 195, 200
Vienna, 68, 71, 77, 81, 91, 106
Vienna, Arbitration of, 156
Virgin Mary, 90
Vladislav II, Duke of Bohemia, 18
Vladislav Jagiellon, King of Bohemia, 57
Vlasov, Andrei, 170
Vojtěch, Saint, 13–4
Völkerwanderung, 1, 20
Vratislav II, Duke of Bohemia, 18
Všehrd, Viktorin Kornel of, 220

Waldensians, 218
Waldhauser, Conrad, 26, 32
Wallenstein, Albrecht, 85–6, 222
Warsaw Pact, 189
Wenceslas, Saint, 13–14, 147
Wenceslas I, King of Bohemia, 22
Wenceslas II, King of Bohemia, 23
Wenceslas III, King of Bohemia, 22
Wenceslas IV, King of Bohemia, 28–31, 217
White Mountain, battle of, 84
Whitsun Uprising in Prague (1848), 110
Wiching, Bishop, 6–7
Wilson, Woodrow, 132
Windischgrätz, Alfred, Prince, 110
Worms, Concordat of, 17
Wycliff, John, 31, 33, 42, 51

Young-Czechs, 124

Zajíc, Jan, 191
Želivský, Jan, 39, 218

Žerotín, Karel of, 221
Žižka, Jan, 44–5
Zwingli, Ulrich, 69.